THE POLITICS
OF
URBAN LIBERATION

THE POLITICS
OF
URBAN LIBERATION

by
Stephen Schecter

BLACK ROSE BOOKS   Montréal

BLACK ROSE BOOKS NO. H 42

Paperback — ISBN: 0-919618-78-2
Hardcover — ISBN: 0-919618-79-0

Canadian Cataloguing in Publication Data

Schecter, Stephen, 1946-
  The Politics of urban liberation

ISBN 0-919618-79-0 bd.   ISBN 0-919618-78-2 pa.

1. Municipal government. 2.   Metropolitan government.
3. Political participation. I.   Title.

JS78.S33   320.9'173'2   C78-000046-3

Cover Design: Michael Carter

BLACK ROSE BOOKS LTD.
3934 rue St. Urbain
Montréal H2W 1T7, Québec
Printed and bound in Québec, Canada.

Contents

Preface 9

Chapter One: The Political Economy of the Urban
          Question 17

    Monopoly capital and the transformation of social
        life 19

    The fiscal crisis of the state 36

Chapter Two: Urban Politics and the Redefinition
          of the Revolutionary Project 55

    The strategic implications of urban struggles and
        their contradictions 57

    Libertarian socialism: the material and political pos-
        sibilities 71

Chapter Three: Revolution From Below: The His-
          torical Experience.................. 81

    Leninism vs. Social-Democracy: Russia and
        Germany 83

    Italy, 1920 95

    Spain: the anarchist tradition 99

    Hungary, 1956 106

    Portugal, 1974-75 113

    Revolutionary politics: the libertarian
        alternative 120

Chapter Four: Revolution From Below: Contem-
          porary Urban Struggles 129

    Chile 131

    France 137

    Italy 138

Chapter Five: Elements of a Socialist Strategy on the Urban Question 151

   The dialectic of revolution and reform 153

   Revolutionary politics: theory, organisation and the new praxis 163

Chapter Six: The Experience of the Montréal Citizens' Movement (MCM) 171

   A short history of the MCM: strategic difficulties and class contradictions 173

   The Québec left, the current political context and the MCM 185

   The future of the MCM 189

Chapter Seven: The Impossible Revolution and its Historical Necessity 193

   Urban politics as metaphor and practice 195

   Revolutionary politics in the here and now 200

Bibliography 203

Preface

THIS BOOK IS in part the product of a specific political experience and the questions it has raised. For the past five years I, together with others, have been active in urban politics in Montréal as members of the Montréal Citizens' Movement. That experience has been enriching, conflictual and frustrating, but the contradictions that experience has brought to the surface have ultimately proved to be a source of growth as some of us have searched for ways to resolve them. It has become clear, in the course of our political struggles, that the answers to many of our questions could only emerge if placed in a theoretical perspective that went beyond our daily practice. What we needed to develop was a distinctive praxis, a process whereby theory and practice both contributed to improving our understanding of society and our efforts to change it. This book was written as a contribution to that process; as such, it discusses not only the development of Montréal as a city and recent aspects of its urban politics, but also the larger questions which such a discussion raises about the nature of urban space, the transformation of cities, the significance of urban politics.

It will soon become apparent to the reader that this book presumes a radical stance towards the world, radical in the sense of a willingness to go to the root of the problem. Such a stance ultimately opens onto a revolutionary perspective, for a truly radical look at the way we currently order our social lives must sooner or later lead us to understand the need to change our ways of living and to confront the forces of class and power that stand in the way of that change. That is what Marx meant when he wrote that the task of philosphers is no longer only to understand the world, but also to change it. Much of this book, therefore, deals with questions of strategy, with ways of bringing about fundamental change, and with the issues and problems that make it difficult to conceive of and practise revolutionary politics. The book opens with a discussion of the political economy of the urban question, but then goes on to deal with the strategic implications that flow out of the political economy analysis. These implications, it will be argued, point to a redefinition of the revolutionary project, whose full import can only be grasped by rereading the experience of insurrectionary movements since the Russian Revolution of 1917. The lessons to be learned from both the successes and failures of some of the major working-class movements of the twentieth century teach us that there is an alternative to traditional conceptions of the revolution in terms of the Party and the State. They also suggest a number of strategic principles that can help us elaborate a praxis appropriate to the conduct of urban struggles redefined as the politics of everyday life, or the politics of the reproduction of social life. It is for this reason that a book whose subject matter is urban politics also contains a section devoted to the analysis of the Spanish anarchist movement and the Hungarian revolution of 1956.

However disparate such themes may seem, there is an underlying design of unity to this book which focuses on questions of praxis. This concern with praxis reflects in part the concrete experience out of which this book emerged, in part the author's feeling that contemporary Marxist writing is already heavily weighted towards political economy, towards analyses of what capital is up to rather than towards an understanding of working class action and considerations of questions of revolutionary strategy. This focus on praxis also governs the political economy section of the book and explains the extensive use made of Braverman's analysis of the changes in the production process in order to understand the transformations of cities. It is not that the work of others such as Lefebvre, Castells, Lojkine, Bookchin, Mumford, to name but a few, is not important. It is more that the themes of Braverman's work, and the direction in which they seem to point, are particularly useful to the issues at the heart of the urban question as I perceive it; and the same considerations apply to the work of O'Connor and others around the fiscal crisis of the of the state.[1] Once again, it is the strategic implications of this work that have preoccupied me.

The importance of Braverman's work is that it looks at the growth of monopoly capital from the viewpoint of its effect on the labour process, showing how the increases in productivity have been accomplished at the expense of the workers' relationship to the work process.

The degradation of work characteristic of capitalist industrialisation has continued apace, while everywhere the new techniques of production have called forth the need for more elaborate mechanisms of social control to deal with the dissatisfaction and opposition workers have displayed, and continue to display, in the face of these changes. Central to Braverman's analysis is the insight that changes in the work process have not remained confined to the factory gates, but have called forth equally severe transformations in the everyday lives of people outside the workplace. It is here that Braverman's analysis of the transformation of work meets the analysis advanced in this book regarding the transformation of social life in the contemporary city. The concept of social control which keeps cropping up in Braverman's description of the capitalist organisation of work is equally important in understanding the capitalist organisation of urban life.

The prominence accorded to social control as a key organising principle of social life in the workplace and the community is not incidental to the argument outlined in this book. The dominant class' ongoing concern with social control is testimony to the very active presence of the working class, for without people's daily resistance in so many different forms to a repressive social order, the ruling forces' need to keep exerting such control would hardly be so great. An approach to the political economy of cities which accords such salience to the question of social control thus leads, as befits a book whose major focus is on questions of praxis, to a consideration of those social struggles, urban and other, which have made and continue to make such control necessary. It is also an approach which places not capital, but the proletariat at the heart of the analysis, thereby reminding us that capital does not have it all its own way, that our present social arrangements are not simply the result of the dictates of capital but the outcome of a protracted and ongoing struggle between working people and capital. Such an approach also reminds us that the ultimate value of political economy lies in the insights and help it can provide to people engaged in the struggle for social liberation.

A similar concern permeates the discussion in this book of the fiscal crisis of the state and its ramifications. The work of O'Connor has generated considerable debate on the role of the state and the nature of state expenditures, especially in relation to the process of capital accumulation in the private sector. This debate has now amplified into a discussion of the nature of the contemporary crisis. It is beyond the scope of this book to deal with all the arguments of this debate; it is also beyond its concern. Again, this is not to assert that the debate over whether the current economic crisis can best be understood in terms of underconsumption theory or the laws of motion of capitalist accumulation, most notably the falling rate of profit, is not important.[2] Rather, it is to assert that ultimately the present crisis cannot be understood without reference to the working class as an historical actor, and not simply as a passive subject in the dynamics of capital accumulation. There are many ways in which this latter assertion is important for clarifying some of the issues in this debate, not all of which are dealt with in the ensuing pages. Some, however, are; for example, it is a central thesis of this book that if capital is in crisis today, both in the private and state sectors, it is because of the pressure of working class demands in both those areas. The resulting profits squeeze on private capitalists and the fiscal claims on the state have provoked much of the present crisis at a time when the present productive capacity makes the age-old dream of releasing human beings from the threat of scarcity a material possibility. The implications of this seeming paradox are elaborated in the book, but two points are worth mentioning if only to explain once again the focus of the political economy section and its relation to the general argument of the book.

The first is that capitalism, being inherently an exploitative and repressive social order, cannot realise the promise of liberation its own productive capacity has raised and therefore requires the reimposition of scarcity through new forms of social control. The second is that the state has assumed a key role in carrying out this project, such that whatever the differing assessments of the current relationship between the state and the private sector, there is considerable agreement that the drift of the future is towards increasing coordination between the state and monopoly capital. The growth of the state sector was itself originally a result of the transformations wrought by monopoly capital in all areas of social life. Drastic social change is not the exclusive hallmark of monopoly capital. The rise of industrial capitalism brought many changes in family relations, the shape of cities, people's attitudes to time, sex, and love, the nature of schooling, and many other aspects of social life. Nonetheless, the economic concentration which accompanied the rise of monopoly capital entailed a drastic overhaul of the labour process which, in turn, brought about many changes in social life even as it intensified earlier ones. One of the most distinctive features of these changes was the ever-growing dependency of people on the state for the satisfaction of their most elementary needs. Today the state, along with monopoly capital, represent the key sectors of an economy in which the once all-pervasive competitive sector retains an important, but junior, role. For purposes of the analysis developed in this book, it is the central role of the two former sectors and their relationship which is important. The convergence of these two sectors, it will be argued, is bound up with capital's response to the current crisis, which amounts to the reassertion of its command over labour on a global scale. Command over labour is but another side of the social control which governs so much of the social relations of everyday urban life. In that sense the relationships I have tried to explore in the following pages between the changes in urban life, the rise of monopoly capital and the growth of the state have a conceptual consistency that reflects the reality of contemporary social life.

That reality is not one-side, however, but dialectical, and full of contradictions; and if social control lies at the heart of the capitalist project, it announces that the struggle for social liberation cannot be very far away. What is significant about the current crisis is that it has emerged out of a period of class conflict and popular struggle that has opened up new vistas for the project of social liberation. Moreover, it has occurred against a background of expanding productive wealth that has made the revolutionary project of liberation from toil, the abolition of the state and the democratic ordering of social life a realistic alternative. Contemporary urban struggles are important precisely because they raise this possibility and draw our attention to a consideration of the obstacles which stand in its way and the means to overcome them. Most of this book deals with issues related to this question. The introductory chapter on political economy was written not to provide an exhaustive analysis of the urban question but to show that the concern with these issues is a result of social changes that have placed these issues squarely on the historical agenda.

Writing this book has raised a number of questions for me, just as reading it will probably raise a host of questions for the reader. One such question is the whole nature of the relation between cities and capitalism. Cities have predated the rise of capitalism and will probably outlast it; and despite the specific features cities have assumed under capitalism, a true political economy of cities remains to be fashioned. A consideration of this issue, however, rapidly leads one to pose a certain number of questions about the nature and origins of capitalism itself, the utility of the concept 'mode of production', and so on. Such questions are clearly important, and if they are not directly addressed in this book, it is in large part because the central focus of this book lies elsewhere. In some way, however, I have tried to address myself to the older and larger questions about cities and social life. This became clear to me when a friend to whom I had read the last chapter remarked that I had posed very well the issue of what it means to be a good citizen in today's metropolis. Given the nature of this preface so far, perhaps it is worth reminding the reader that the main concern of this book is with such issues, although the question might best be framed in terms not only of how to live in the city, but how to live so as to change the city, what kind of change are we working for and what kind of politics do we need to bring that change about.

It will become clear to the reader, if it is not already, that I do not consider such questions can be answered without addressing oneself to the wider questions of class and power in our society. That is why extensive reference is made in the text to the working class, even though the thrust of the argument makes clear that I consider traditional approaches, which tend to reduce individual workers to the category of working class, part of the obstacle to revolutionary change. Workers are citizens, as the traditions of the French Revolution of 1789 and the Paris Commune of 1871 keep reminding us. Capitalism separated the two, obliterating the concept of citizen and reinforcing that dimension of the term worker which refers to a passive and subordinate role in the hierarchy of work. Much of orthodox Marxist practice has maintained this dichotomy, which has crept into the use of language itself. If greater use has been made in this text of the terms worker or working class when the reader might feel the terms citizen or people would equally apply, it is not to suggest that the terms are mutually exclusive, but rather to remind one that the questions of urban politics are also the questions of class politics, that we are all people and citizens, but that we live in a society which assigns to different groups of people and citizens different class interests, which affect how they react to some very basic issues.

In a similar vein, I use the term working class in the large sense, in much the way the term proletariat used to be used, to refer to all oppressed people in society, to all the strata of the working class who suffer the consequences of living in capitalist society, whatever their specific position in the work world. The expansion of monopoly capital, as Braverman has made amply clear, has led to the integration of increasing numbers of people into the wage/labour relationship, such that today the working class is composed of a wide range of groups or strata active in different sectors of the economy. The bourgeoisie has also undergone considerable expansion with the emergence of a whole new stratum that exercises management and control functions on behalf of capital. Considerable debate has emerged around the economic identification of this social group, a debate which is beyond the scope of this book just as is the detailing of the internal composition of the working class. It is nonetheless assumed that a working class does exist, despite its internal differences, whose class position places it in antagonistic relation to the technocracy, as this new management stratum is referred to in the text, despite the ambiguities and strains to which this stratum is subjected. This stratum too is rather heterogeneous, with its senior management members clearly on the side of capital while its subordinate groups verge on the point of proletarianisation. It is the ambiguity in the latter groups' position that is explored in this book, especially as regards their impact on the conduct of urban struggles.

There are probably other caveats that ought to be made, but the above will have to suffice. Ultimately this book is conceived as part of a debate of practical as much as theoretical significance. For that reason I have tried to draw upon examples from the Montréal experience whenever possible. For that reason too the chapter on the MCM focuses on only specific aspects of that party's history, those which appear to me more relevant to the themes and questions raised in this book. Hopefully the questions it addresses will prove to be among the important ones with which other people are grappling. Hopefully too, the ideas it advances and the criticism it elicits will help get us a little closer to that libertarian society of which I write in these pages. If these ideas at times seem only to raise contradictions, they reflect nonetheless the extent to which their resolution is a matter of future praxis and collective effort. They also reflect, to some extent, the contradictions of living under capital, as the contrast between some of the ideas elaborated in these pages and my conduct in everyday, personal interactions became all that more obvious to me in the course of writing this book. Yet that dichotomy too reflects the extent to which liberation is truly a social process, a matter of friendship in the profoundly political and, as this book tries to argue, personal senses of that word. Different friends, in different ways, have contributed to the making of this book; for that, and to each of them, I am deeply grateful.

NOTES

(1.) J. O'Connor, *The Fiscal Crisis of the State*, N.Y., 1973; H. Braverman, *Labor and Monopoly Capital*, N.Y., 1974; see also, for example, M. Castells, *La question urbaine*, Paris, François Maspéro, 1972; H. Lefebvre, *La révolution urbaine*, Paris, 1970; M. Bookchin, *The Limits of the City*, N.Y., 1974; L. Mumford, *The City in History*, London, 1966; J.'Lojkine, *La politique urbaine dans la région Parisienne 1945-72*, Mouton, Paris, 1972.
(2.) A. Gamble, P. Walton, *Capitalism in Crisis*, London, 1976, for an account of this debate.

CHAPTER ONE

THE POLITICAL ECONOMY OF THE URBAN QUESTION

Monopoly capital and the transformation of social life

"But the industrialization of food and other elementary home provisions is only the first step in a process which eventually leads to the dependence of all social life, and indeed of all the interrelatedness of humankind, upon the marketplace. The population of cities, more or less completely cut off from a natural environment by the division between town and country, becomes totally dependent upon social artifice for its every need. But social artifice has been destroyed in all but its marketable forms. Thus the population no longer relies upon social organization in the form of family, friends, neighbours, community, elders, children, but with few exceptions must go to market and only to market, not only for food, clothing, and shelter, but also for recreation, amusement, security, for the care of the young, the old, the sick, the handicapped. In time not only the material and service needs but even the emotional patterns of life are channeled through the market.

It thereby comes to pass that while population is packed ever more closely together in the urban environment, the atomization of social life proceeds apace."[1]

IN 1871, 271, 851 people, or 22.1% of the Québec population, lived in cities. By 1961 3,906, 404 people, or 74.3%, did so.[2] Most of this growth has occurred in the Montréal region, which by 1971 contained 2,757,000 people.[3] 'Contained' is a rather apt word, for it expresses that feeling of bewilderment we have all felt at one moment or another when contemplating contemporary cities. How did we arrive at this situation where so many people are living in such close quarters? The tone of the question implies not only a feeling that there is something basically wrong with our living arrangements but also a sense that they have somehow happened to us. Surely no people could have consciously decided upon the urban habitat we have today, and yet there is a logic to the process, even if it appears highly irrational.

It has often been alleged that concentrated urban space is the logic, and price, of industrialism, but the questions we share about contemporary industrial society are no less and no different than those we have about our cities. Industrialism was much more a process that happened to people than a process that they controlled. The industrialisation of Montréal from 1871 to 1931 led to a rapid growth in population based mainly on the urban migration of rural French-Canadians. This migration was a highly uprooting process which shattered previous patterns of family life, removed the little control people had over their economic activity and brought misery to the vast majority. By 1930 average family incomes for 47% of the Montréal labour force still fell below official poverty lines, while another 25% hovered on the edge.[4] If we reject the idea that people choose misery, then we must look elsewhere for an explananation of the nature of our urban and industrial growth.

Part of the explanation is usually formulated in technical terms. The growth of Montréal, for example, has often been attributed to its location as a centre of maritime and railway transportation; yet that in itself does not explain why Montréal has continued to dominate Québec economically and demographically.[5] More important was the fact that the people who owned the railroads and steamships and related industries that grew up around them needed workers to produce and ship the goods whose sale ultimately provided the owners with their profits. The goods were produced in factories, in which large numbers of workers were assembled under one roof and required to carry out specific tasks. Lacking both capital and machines, they were forced to sell their labour to those who did own the means of production, the capitalists, while the goods they produced with their labour helped the capitalists to realise greater profits, and thereby accumulate even more capital and greater control of the means of production. The rise of the factory system thus led to the emergence of the proletariat, and the housing of this proletariat led in turn to the rise of cities which rapidly grew in size and density.

The economic concentration which has characterised this process of capital accumulation has continued unabated and has drawn in its wake a pattern of geographic concentration of people and resources of all kinds. Today it is argued that the concentration of people in contemporary cities makes it possible to provide them with services that the dispersal of population would render prohibitive in terms of cost and efficiency. The inference is that such considerations explain the rise of cities as we know them. However, as anyone who has had to deal with today's schools, hospitals or city governments must know, the benefits of large-scale concentration are far from apparent; and the same could be said of the modern corporation. It is not the economies of scale but the advantages of power which explain latter-day corporate concentration, just as they explain much of contemporary city life:

> "The reasons for the continued existence of large economic organisations are that the large organisations are more powerful than the small. The large organisations are able to pursue strategies that work to their advantage against the small organisations. Furthermore the very structure of the market economy is such that once inequalities of size are established, the tendency will be for the share of economic activity in the hands of the large to get larger. The gigantic organisations of the present-day are not in any absolute sense economically more efficient or technologically necessary. All we can say is that in the circumstances of the commodity exchange economy the pressures of competition, translated into pressures to increase productivity as a means of increasing profits, led to new techniques of mass production symbolised by Fordism and Taylorism."[6]

The commodity market economy which dominated industrial growth in the nineteenth century also dominated the growth of cities. Goods were produced for exchange in the market, and the profits realized on their exchange were appropriated by capitalists who controlled the production process, and ploughed back into further capital accumulation. Human needs were met to the extent that they were compatible with the logic of capital accumulation; most of the time they were subordinated to it. Not much has changed in this respect, although capitalism itself has, most notably in the shift from a predominantly competitive economy to a highly concentrated one dominated by huge multinational corporations.

The continuously changing nature of capitalism points to the difficulty of identifying those characteristics which mark it out as a mode of production distinct from pre-industrial social structures and from other forms of industrial societies such as those of eastern Europe. Capitalism bears certain similarities to both as much as it presents marked differences from each; and the same may be said of the different stages of capitalism itself. These questions have become more acute as the reexamination of the origins of capitalism has reversed earlier interpretations about the relationship between cities and capitalism which placed towns at the center of capitalist progress. Recent studies locate the origins of capitalist accumulation in the countryside, outside and often against the towns. The world market that developed remained weak until machine production paved the way for the integration of all sectors into capitalist production relations, the rise of factory cities and a truly global market economy. Town and country, in this newer interpretation, still remained in opposition, but progress is no longer viewed as the monopoly of cities.[7] In a similar vein, the contradictions of capitalism have not lost their force, even if our understanding of its evolution, such as the transition from a laissez-faire economy to monopoly capital, has undergone, and continues to undergo, considerable revision.

Bearing this in mind, it would not be inaccurate to assert that the transformation of urban life cannot be understood apart from the transformations of capitalism in the past century and a half. Capitalism as it exists in liberal democracies must therefore be seen as an historical process rooted in commodity production and a class structure based on the private ownership of the means of production, powered by unceasing accumulation and rent by the contradictions of its own accumulation process as well as the class struggle it unleashed. The attempt to grasp the relationship between capitalism and urban life will bring out different features of capitalism, as well as different contradictions, as we examine the various links in this relationship.

The first such link has to do with the physical structure of the city itself. Montréal's first major spurt of population growth in the latter part of the nineteenth and early twentieth centuries centred around Sainte-Anne in the south-west and spread eastwards to Hochelaga-Maisonneuve. New industries grew up linked to the development of the railways which British capitalists used to plunder the economy with the aid of the Canadian state.[8] Based on an increasing division of labour, these factories assembled large numbers of workers who then settled down in the immediate vicinity; low salaries and inadequate transport ruled out any alternative. As is the case today, land and housing were treated as commodities for capitalist speculation and investment. As a result capitalism stamped its imprimatur on the built structure of cities in a variety of ways: appalling housing conditions for the working class, continuous encroachment on valuable farmland and open spaces, vivid changes in architecture, and the geographical separation of social classes. Summary as this list is, it indicates that transformations in the physical and social structures of cities went hand in hand.

Because the provision of housing was subject to what workers' salaries could purchase and to the criteria of capitalist profits, new tenements were thrown up using every available space. The city government exercised no control. Overcrowding, lack of sunlight, poor sanitation, multi-storied row housing became the norm in working class districts.[9] Older, single-dwelling houses were subdivided or replaced;

gardens disappeared; green spaces shrunk. It happened on a grand scale, as in the area known today as Plateau Mont-Royal, where industrial capital's need to lodge as many workers as possible as cheaply as possible led to the subdivision of rural lands into standardised housing lots. It happened on a small scale as exterior staircases were implanted in the courtyards and gardens of traditional dwellings.[10]. At the same time the bourgeoise retreated to suburbs like Hampstead, held up as a model, in 1912, of a "new'garden suburb' in which the infant mortality rate was only one-third of the city average."[11] The withdrawal of the bourgeoisie from the old center city reflected the latter's transformation into the heart of a commercial metropolis, a transformation mirrored in the new architecture where "the factory chimneys point henceforth as high as the church spires, and the immense grain elevators built along the harbour now look from on high at the two towers of O'Donnell's Notre Dame Church."[12] For the vast majority this new architecture symbolized the imposition of a new form of social control on top of another, older one.

These new forms of social control were intimately linked to the growth of capitalism, but their impact was not limited to the factory gates. They emerged out of a process of economic concentration, which in a later period came to be known as monopoly capital, whereby a few firms came to dominate entire sectors of economic activity. This process had equally severe consequences for labour, as the reorganisation of work it entailed led to the destruction of skills, the replacement of craft workers by machines, the division of tasks into ever smaller and repetitive steps, and the increasing separation of planning from the execution of work. As a result production was vastly expanded, new workers were integrated into the labour force, but to perform relatively unskilled tasks, under greater stress and surveillance, at relatively reduced wage rates. Rural migrants and women usually formed two distinct groups among these new workers, whose integration into the labour market involved profound changes in family and community life.[13]

Food processing industries in Montréal provide an excellent example. Much of Montréal's industrial growth in the first part of the twentieth century centred around the transformation of agricultural products. By the 1930s concentration in this sector had reached the point where two companies controlled 95% of the beer industry in Canada; five companies, 73% of the flour mills; five companies, 100% of the sugar industry; two companies, 83% of the canning of fruits and vegetables; one company, 75% of the tobacco industry.[14] Among these companies were St. Lawrence Flour, Imperial Tobacco, and St. Lawrence Sugar, whose factories and mills dominated the Montréal landscape. Women provided much of the unskilled labour in these industries, as they did in related ones such as textiles and shoes. Over a period of time less and less consumer goods were produced by the family. Instead of baking bread at home, women went to work in flour mills and bought the bread which they themselves had helped to produce, package and sell. So it went too with fruits and vegetables, such that the disappearance of gardens from the cities went hand in hand with the transformation of family life.

This process was indissociable from the proletarianisation of the general population, the penetration of the market into the countryside and the urbanisation of rural life physically and socially. It is a process, however, that has extended over a long period of time, in very uneven fashion. The urban population of Québec remained fairly stable during the thirties, only to surge ahead during and after World War Two as industrial expansion underwent a new boom with the extension of mechanisation into both the agricultural and manufacturing sectors and the incorporation of the service sector into the ambit of monopoly capital.[15] From 1941 to 1971 the farm population of Québec has dropped both absolutely and percentage-wise, from 25.2% to 5.6% of the total population. At the same time capitalist production relations now characterise the agricultural sector as agribusiness expands. The number of farms in Québec has dropped in the same period by 60%, the number of high capital-intensive farms has increased, and the agricultural salariat has grown.[16]

Far from leading to any general amelioration in social life, this process has only fueled the global food crisis, driving food prices up and creating world famine through monopoly capital's use of food to discipline the working class in both the metropoles and the underdeveloped hinterlands.[17] Central to this process has been the denaturing of our food through the use of inorganic fertilizers at the production end and preservatives at the consumption end. The ironic denouement to this process, which began with the penetration of the countryside by urban capitalism, has been the recent transformation of much of contemporary urban space by the proliferation of plastic food chains.

During the same period the city has encroached on the countryside. In 1941 two thirds of the Montréal area's population lived within a four mile radius of the city centre. By 1961 it was an eight mile radius. Between 1951 and 1976, the population of the region grew by 79.5%, of the island of Montréal by 42%. The biggest population increase was registered in the suburban belt: 400%.[18] The story these figures tell is the growth of the suburbs, but that process itself was tied to the expansion of the economy after the war and to the transformation, once again, of both physical space and social structure.

In the first place it means that more of the best soil in Québec has been withdrawn from agricultural production. Not only has suburban growth been of a relatively light density, thereby increasing the total amount of built-up land, but the interstices in urban development due to land lying fallow or subject to speculation now amount to 140% of the urbanised area.[19]

In the second place, the growth of the suburbs, despite its uneven internal distribution in the period 1951-75, was intimately linked to the growth of the network of autoroutes and bridges surrounding Montréal. From 1964 to 1975 the number of miles of autoroute jumped from 31 to 157.[20] The expansion of autoroutes in turn was linked to the central role automobile production played in the growth of monopoly capital. Today General Motors has a gross national product that exceeds those of most of the countries in the world. By controlling the production of the means of transport, the large corporations have been able to determine the ways in which people move about, thereby generating a whole set of individual needs for cars and a whole set of social needs for autoroutes. From 1951 to 1971 the percentage of households owning an automobile in the Montréal metropolitan region jumped from 27.8% to 68.1%.[21] Yet the consequences of automobile transport are there for all to see and suffer daily—pollution, noise, congestion, and an ever-growing commitment of funds and space to service the needs of car transport. Since 1962 there has been a 57% increase in parking lots in the downtown section of Montréal. More than 100,000 automobiles descended daily on the city in 1974. Whole areas of the city have been uprooted in order to make way for these highways. Thousands of families were evicted and thousands of houses were demolished to build the expressways encircling Montréal; in the process entire communities were destroyed.[22]

The transformation of physical and social space has a distinct class component. The central city tends to be populated by lower-income working-class people; the suburbs by the bourgeoisie, especially those who perform control functions for capital. 10% of Montréal's population is composed of administrators and professionals. The figures for parts of Laval are 17% and 19%; for Longueuil, 12%; for St. Lambert 25%; for Brossard 20%; for Dorval 22%. In Montréal only 32% of families had revenues over $10,000 in 1971; in the other municipalities cited the percentage was over 50% except for Longueuil and parts of

Laval.[23] Obviously cities are not homogeneous class enclaves, although there are distinct class enclaves within them.

It is clear, nonetheless, that suburbanization also represents a process of class segmentation. From 1951 to 1961 the suburbs grew wealthier relative to the central part of the island. From 1961 to 1971 the central city did not become any more impoverished, while in the eastern end of the island, in Longueuil and in Pierrefonds, the population became relatively poorer after the upswing of the 1950s. What these indices mean, however, is that the process of urban renewal which followed the first wave of suburbanization had an equally strong class component. The working class families displaced by the autoroutes moved to the eastern section of the island, while parts of the bourgeoisie reappropriated the downtown core.

Nothing much changed for the working class core of Montréal, who continue to defray the costs of suburbanization. Their taxes help pay for the amenities suburban dwellers enjoy, including access to the big city, while the workers themselves have to cope with the stress of living in an environment of diminishing services. Those who live in this working class core tend for the most part to work in this sector or in the downtown area. The suburb of Ville Saint-Laurent, where many manufacturing industries in the monopoly sector of the economy provide high-paying jobs, constitutes the third main area of secondary employment. Much of its inaccessibility to the Montréal working class resides in the fact that there is no adequate and rapid public transport to this area, while the portion of the population owning cars is lowest in the low-income core of Montréal. Public transport is on the whole slower than private transport, but the deficit per user is twice as high for the latter mode compared to the former.[24]

If the process of suburbanization reflects the growth in the number of those occupied in managing capital in one form or another, that growth in turn is linked to changes in the organisation of production. The intensification of work in giant concerns that accompanied the introduction of machinery has called forth a need for greater control of the labour force. This need expands as monopoly capital gathers more and more activity under its control and subjects it to the same principles. Hence office work is now organised on the same basis as factory production: a tremendous increase in clerical staff who perform routine tasks, the mechanisation of many operations through the introduction of computers which at the same time reduces most workers' autonomy and intensifies the rhythm of their work, the increasing separation of the work force into those who plan and those who execute the designs.

Finally, as more and more people are drawn into capitalist production relations, they are less and less able to provide for individual and social needs, now defined as services, transformed into commodities and delivered by monopoly capital and the state. This is the reality behind the service economy which Braverman has so brilliantly and lucidly explained;[25] and it underlies the physical and social transformation of Montréal since 1941.

As economic activity in Québec continues to be concentrated in the Montréal region, there has been a marked shift in favour of the tertiary sector. Two-thirds of the labour force in the Montréal region work in this sector. The downtown core is the major pole of attraction. Two-thirds of the influx onto the island of Montréal work in the tertiary sector and 37% concentrate in the downtown area. The latter is also the major employment basin for tertiary workers coming from low-income working-class areas of Montréal. The nature of the economic activity concentrated in the downtown core is reflected in the transformation of its physical space. Since 1941 there has been a tremendous increase in the total floor space occupied in the central business district by office buildings, corporate headquarters, government services, hotels, department stores and recreational facilities. Between 1949 and 1962 the increase for office buildings alone was 77%.[26]

Contemporary cities have become, in a very essential respect, the control center of capital's international empire. 25% of the head-quarters of large Canadian companies are located in Montréal, the majority in the downtown area. At the same time less and less indus-trial activity goes on in these urban areas as capital shifts its sites of production to new regions within advanced industrial countries or to the underdeveloped world outside them. Within the metropolitan re-gions this pattern is repeated as the technologically advanced man-ufacturing industries at the core of the monopoly sector are located in the suburbs. Montréal's share of industrial jobs in the region has dropped from 65.7% in 1961 to 47.6% in 1976; that of the eastern and western parts of the island, Laval, Longueuil and satellite cities like Ste-Thérèse, St-Jean and Sorel, grew.[27]

The dynamics of space, the dynamics of class and the dynamics of capital accumulation are all of a piece. The ever-increasing introduc-tion of machinery into manufacturing industry requires plant expansion in a horizontal direction, which the spiralling costs of downtown land translate into suburban relocation. The process is facilitated by developments in communications technology which make possible the physical separation of planning, investment and control from the production of goods and by the growth of autoroutes necessary for the transport of goods. Yet the expansion of autoroutes has also made possible the growth of suburbs as residential quarters for the new technocracy responsible for managing the organization of work on the production sites and for taking the decisions regarding planning and investment in the control centers located in the downtown core. The transformations in the residential patterns, life styles and consumption activities of this class, however, emerge directly from their position in the production process, a position untenable but for the transformation of work under monopoly capital. Braverman's description of what went on in the car industry is typical of this process:

> "The quickening rate of production in this case depended not only upon the change in the organization of labor, but upon the control which management, at a single stroke, attained over the pace of assembly, so that it could now double and triple the rate at which operations had to be performed and thus subject its workers to an extraordinary intensity of labor."[28]

The transformation of work did not occur without opposition. Workers slowed down production deliberately to prove that the new methods could not work. The introduction of machinery and the destruction of the skilled workers' control over production led, as in the U.S. steel industry at the turn of the century, to violent strikes. Others often walked off their jobs when newer and more exploitative methods were introduced. The subsequent developments in the reorganisation of the work process have led to equally strong ripostes on the part of the workers—wildcat strikes, sabotage, slowdown, absenteeism, high turnover rates, etc. The automation of the Canadian post office is a notorious contemporary example.[29]

The worker resistance that the transformation of the labour process provoked and the disciplining of the labour force it required increased the control functions which capital had to assume. This was true of its early stages, witness the rapid increase in lower-level supervisory personnel such as foremen, but it is no less true today. It is not insignificant, in this respect, that throughout the 1951-1971 period in Québec there has been an absolute increase in the number of occupations involving managerial and control functions, with the greatest increase registered in those subaltern, white-collar positions requiring the performance of surveillance tasks. They predominate in the Montréal region. Greater Montréal, with 45% of the Québec labour force, contains 63% of supervisory personnel in manufacturing industries and 70% of engineers in all of Québec.[30]

At the same time, the degradation of work experienced by the working class at the point of production parallels the degradation of social life. The relatively greater salaries that workers in monopoly industry receive is paid for with stepped-up work requirements and increased regimentation on the job. If their salaries permit them to move to the suburbs, they pay for it by spending much of their time in traffic jams trying to get to and from work. Only 59.3% of those who work in Montréal live in Montréal; 24.8% of those who work in Laval come from Laval, as do 17.5% of those who work in Longueuil. Even outside of the workplace workers are still doing time for capital.

The impact of the changes in the labour process is not limited to monopoly sector workers. The mechanization of work also leads to the ejection of workers from this sector, who then either swell the welfare rolls or find low-paying jobs in the competitive manufacturing sector and the new clerical, sales and cleaning occupations. Thus the expansion of wealth made possible by the increased productivity in the monopoly sector is accompanied by a relative immiseration of the working-class as a whole. This is exactly what happened from 1951-71 in the working class core of Montréal, running right down the centre of the island and then east-west along the St. Lawrence from Verdun to Montréal-Est. The process has been vividly described for St. Henri:

> "Between 1900 and World War Two, many important companies such as RCA Victor, Stelco, Johnson Wire and Imperial Tobacco build plants in St. Henri and provided the local population with better than average incomes and working conditions. After the war, a large number of key companies left the district and were replaced by smaller companies paying lower wages. After 1960, important layoffs by many companies further contributed to its economic decline. It is estimated that since 1966, a total of 30 companies either left St. Henri or transferred important parts of their operations. Throughout this process, the government was a passive observer, contenting itself with providing unemployment insurance or social welfare to an increasingly large proportion of the population."[31]

From July 1958 to December 1962 the amount the Québec government spent on unemployment assistance increased form $1.1 million to $5.7 million and the major part of this increase went to those able to work, whose numbers increased by 500% in 1960-1 alone.[32]

This relative surplus population thrown up by capitalism's expansion has increased "the numbers of those cheaply available for dancing attendance upon capital in all of its least mechanized functional forms".[33] Under periods of rapid accumulation their numbers are augmented by new groups like immigrants and women who are used as sources of cheap labour in those areas to which the surplus capital, generated by the expansion of production, is attracted. Much of the activity in these areas is itself linked to the expansion of monopoly capital—the clerical work of the modern corporation; the sales and service jobs in the large department stores, food chains, hotels, restaurants, etc; and the cleaning required by the expansion of floor space devoted to these activities and performed by "women who, in accord with the precepts of the division of labor, perform one of the functions they formerly exercised in the home, but now in the service of capital which profits from each day's labor."[34] This situation is very much the fate of the Montréal working class, whose jobs in the manufacturing sector are located within the city in low-paying, competitive industries; and in the service sector, in those low-paying occupations within the downtown core. Their living conditions also parallel their position in the occupational structure. Trapped in the city core, they have to endure pollution, congestion, poor and inadequate housing that is nonetheless overpriced as the demolition of working-class districts leads to such vacancy rates for family dwellings as 0.4% in 1977. Less motorised than the rest of the population, they depend on a public transport system whose workings are subordinated to the private automobile and have less access to green spaces and recreational areas that exist, for a large part, outside the city.[35]

On the one side, therefore, we have the degradation of work and social life, "the accumulation of misery"; on the other a vast expansion of productive wealth, "the accumulation of capital", which powers the whole process and seeks new areas of investment in its unrelenting drive to expand. As such, the surplus capital created moves into areas previously untouched by the market, either by creating new needs or by taking over services which were formerly provided outside the market and drawing them into commodity production; hospitality, amusement, etc. Expo '67 and the 1976 Olympics are not simply accidents, quirks of eccentric administrations, but part and parcel of the very process whereby eventually we must go to market, and only to market, to satisfy our needs. Like all the other processes described so far, its effect on social life is multiple and interlinked. The building of the Autostade, for example, involved the total demolition of houses in the area and the relocation of 305 families from the inner city to Verdun and the South Shore, a relocation which also reduced them to tenants.[36]

The city has become, under the driving force of capitalism, at once a vast area of investment for the surplus capital released and the site for the organization of consumption so necessary to its continued circulation and expansion. The whole process of suburbanisation provided an immense outlet for the construction industry in the form of highways and houses. From 1946 to 1970, of the $6,602.1 million handed out by the Central Mortgage and Housing Corporation (CMHC), $4,411.8 million went to the private sector for owner-occupied and rental housing.[37] The redefinition of needs in terms of the consumption of goods and services, fostered by advertising, is necessary to maintain consumer demand at levels high enough to stimulate accumulation; but the goods and services produced do not entail any significant amelioration of social life:

> "The 'average American,' now consumes, each year, about as many calories, protein, and other foods (although somewhat less of vitamins); uses about the same amount of clothes and cleaners; occupies about the same amount of newly constructed housing; requires about as much freight; and drinks about the same amount of beer (twenty-six gallons per capita!) as he did in 1946. However, his food is now grown on less land with much more fertilizer and pesticides than before; his clothes are more likely to be made of synthetic fibers than of cotton or wool; he launders with synthetic detergents rather than soap; he lives and works in buildings that depend more heavily on aluminum, concrete, and plastic than on steel and lumber; the goods he uses are increasingly shipped by truck rather than rail; he drinks beer out of nonreturnable bottles or cans rather than out of returnable bottles or at the tavern bar. He is more likely to live and work in air-conditioned surroundings than before. He also drives about twice as far as he did in 1946, in a heavier car, on synthetic rather than natural rubber tires, using more gasoline per mile, containing more tetraethyl lead, fed into an engine of increased horsepower and compression ratio."[38]

The technical processes required to produce these goods have considerably increased environmental pollution, accounting, except in the case of passenger travel, for 95% of the total output of pollutants since 1946. The use of these new, polluting technologies has also yielded considerably higher profits, much as have the new and related forms of the organization of work. Once again, the degradation of work and the degradation of the environment go hand in hand. In the process the city has become, in one sense, one vast shopping center, organizing the flow patterns of people around the purchase of those goods and services so necessary to the accumulation of capital. It is estimated that in the Place Ville-Marie complex alone, 15,000 people work and 60-100,000 pass through daily.[39]

The growth of the service sector has resulted not only from capitalist penetration into new areas of social life but also from the increasing role the state has had to assume. The integration of women into the labour force, for example, led in the early part of the century to demands for school reform that would take into account the new role of women. The expansion of the education system in general is linked to the new socialization requirements of our society—a vast army of workers properly trained to accept their subordinate positions in dead-end jobs, and a more select group of workers to manage the rest. Much of state expansion is a result of the state's underwriting the costs of capital accumulation; but much of it also is a result of the need to provide some care for all those unable to fend for themselves under the "pressures of capitalist urbanism":

> "Thus understood, the massive growth of institutions stretching all the way from schools and hospitals on the one side to prisons and madhouses on the other represents not just the progress of medicine, education, or crime prevention, but the clearing of the marketplace of all but the 'economically active' and 'functioning' members of society, generally at public expense and at a handsome profit to the manufacturing and service corporations who sometimes own and invariably supply these institutions."[40]

The factors governing the growth and organization of the public sector have been no different from those governing the private corporation, such that the physical and social transformation of the city linked to the growth of the public component of the tertiary sector has been much the same as that already described. The amount of floor space devoted to public sector activities increased between 1949 and 1962 by 31% in Montréal. Clerical work in government offices is just as low-paying and routinized, as is the cleaning of schools, hospitals and government buildings. Furthermore, both public and private services are located predominantly in the central city, thus requiring of their clients considerable personal mobility in order to obtain the desired services.[41]

The new downtown core, dominated by the office buildings of the modern corporation and the state, is a fitting architectural representative of the domination of monopoly capital. Not for nothing does it house those social organs of the bourgeoisie, like the Conseil du Patronat du Québec, the Montréal Board of Trade and the General Council of Industry, whose task it is to influence state policy in the interests of the large corporations.[42] Many of these state policies are devoted to the social control of the working class; and indeed, much of the pattern of contemporary urban life has to be understood in terms of the social control functions it exercises.

The growth of suburbs meant the separation of work and residence, thus making it more difficult to develop community solidarity around working class issues at the workplace. The post-war shift of manufacturing industries to the suburbs in the United States was motivated in part by the vulnerability to which their location in working-class neighbourhoods exposed them. Early social policies around housing in France also emerged in part from the difficulties employers faced in disciplining their labour force. As long as job opportunities were highly irregular, workers had only one aim: to get a lodging as close as possible to the sources of work. When the cost of such lodging became prohibitive, they either moved secretly, defaulting on the rent, or doubled up, thereby contributing to overcrowding. Under such conditions the local café played an important role, both as the place where the worker and his family came to eat and the site where the workers organised resistance against the bosses. There was thus a unity to life at work and outside work which the rise of large scale industry in the twentieth century burst apart. The new working-class living quarters separated workers from their place of work, isolated families and changed their patterns of consumption. The disappearance of older communal forms thus gave rise to a new framework of social discipline.[43]

In Canada the first planned budgetary deficit in 1938 was based on a $60 million plan to stimulate residential construction with federal loans. The plan was both an attempt to help the economy recover from the depression and a response to growing working class mobilisation. City councillors in Montréal who expressed concern about the deteriorating housing situation in the thirties were also motivated by a fear that it would prove to be terrain for communist penetration. 1942 and 1943 were both years of working class militancy in Canada and Québec. In 1944-5 the CMHC was set up to facilitate housing construction. Over the next thirty years it was to prove a key agent in the development of suburbs and the housing of higher-income groups. Yet the growth of suburbs and the other urban processes to which suburbanization was intimately linked have led to the atomization of social life. As the market spreads to every nook and cranny of social life, the model of social interaction developed in the workplace is applied to all features of daily life. The "atrophy of competence" at work is followed by the total dependence of the population on the market, while "the care of human beings for each other becomes increasingly institutionalized."[44]

Furthermore, as Cottereau has pointed in his study of early urban reform movements in France around the Paris metro, the discipine imposed by the mechanisation of factory life was reproduced in the urban planning of daily life. Housing, transport and other services were planned so as to reinforce the discipline of the household and the structure of the family. The obligations of family life bound one to regular attendance in the workplace while the patterns of family interaction, in conjunction with those of other social institutions like schools, led to the inculcation of 'proper' values compatible with the reproduction of the entire system. Time outside work and outside the family was viewed as time lost; and the whole interlocking network was represented in condensed form in the French expression 'metro-boulot-dodo'.[45]

Suburbanization is very much part of this control network, giving workers a stake in the system of private property and isolating people within the nuclear family, physically and socially. At the same time families become important units of consumption, reinforcing the process whereby most activity outside work becomes the consumption of goods and services in the universal market. 'Free' time is now time also spent in the service of capital; as such, the orgnization of consumption provided by today's city is but one more means of social control. For people trapped in the urban core, shopping, television viewing and spectator sports become the substitutes for active and self-initiated activity as well as compensation for crummy jobs and run-down communities.

Social control is thus at the very heart of the many-sided process to which the term monopoly capital refers. The intensification of work and the growth of suburbs, the rise of the technocracy and the pollution of the environment, the expansion of autoroutes and downtown urban renewal, the relocation of industry and the growth of the state are all interlinked and mutually reinforcing processes, propelled by the accumulation dynamic. Yet the process is highly contradictory. The increase in productive forces only serves to further the exploitation of workers in the factories and offices, while the resulting transformations in urban life diminish its quality. Instead of producing a more harmonious environment, more amicable and enriching social relations, cities in which people feel at home and whose development they can control, this process seems only to have produced crises—a housing crisis, an environmental crisis, an urban crisis and, lastly, a fiscal crisis. People feel overcrowded, harassed, hemmed in on all sides; when the social wraps are removed, as occurred when the police went on strike in Montréal in 1969, the pent-up frustration is released in attacks on the sources of social misery. Not for nothing did people begin to loot the downtown stores; nor was it the first time. As far back as December, 1918, similar events took place when the police went on strike and the Montréal populace responded with extensive looting.[46] Such heralded forms of working-class opposition to daily life under capitalism are only a sign of the less-documented, but nonetheless omnipresent forms of resistance that go on daily in both the industrial and social factories, the workplace and the city. Many of the contradictions of contemporary life are as much the result of capital's responses to working-class resistance as the consequence of the transformations brought about by the process of capital accumulation.

In that sense social control lies at the heart of the current organization of urban life, and at the heart of the urban crisis. That crisis takes many forms, but its most salient expression has been the fiscal crisis of the city, and beyond the city, of the state. As social life becomes more, rather than less, oppressive, more demands are voiced, from many directions, and usually directed at the state, to deal with these problems. The state, and particularly the city, has encountered increasing financial difficulties in meeting these demands, with the result that its most recent response has taken the form of new measures of social control, and thereby unleashed new forms of workers' struggles. This whole process is itself part of the wider contradictory dialectic of capitalist growth as a whole, on a world-wide level, just as the urban fiscal crisis is indissociable from the fiscal crisis of the state and the more general crisis of stagflation which the capitalist world is currently experiencing.

The process seems complex, as indeed it is, but not so complex that we can make no attempt to understand it. To ignore the relationship between the contemporary city and the fiscal crisis would be tantamount to trying to solve a jigsaw puzzle with a few of the pieces missing. Like the other questions we have addressed, this question too is many-sided. Many of its features are bound up with the transformations we have already examined. Looking at the city from the perspective of the fiscal crisis, however, gives to these transformations a new dimension which opens onto the question of urban struggles and the possibilities of radically altering urban life.

The fiscal crisis of the state

THE FISCAL ROLE of the capitalist state has traditionally been twofold: on the one hand it makes investments to help directly the process of accumulation, on the other it spends money to help palliate the social consequences of capitalist growth, soak up discontent and thereby legitimate and reproduce the wider social order. In the era of laissez-faire capitalism the state spent most of its largesse on accumulation functions, or what we would today call welfare capitalism. The history of Canadian confederation is in part the history of the Montréal financial plutocracy's use of the state to bail itself out of railway speculation and shore up its credit position on the London money markets. The CNR was financed by the Canadian state from boom to bust.

Over the years this role of the state has only increased. It played an important part in the growth of monopoly capital and has continued to assume those economic activities necessary to the growth of the corporate sector. The Canadian state formed the airline today known as Air Canada "because the necessary capital couldn't be mobilized in the private sector for this risky adventure," although the airline overwhelmingly serves the corporate sector. The provincial states have been essential in developing hydro-electric power, of which 70% is consumed by industry.[47]

Many of the crown corporations and industrial development projects emerged in the fifties and sixties as the economy underwent a new wave of expansion in Canada. Much of the Quiet Revolution in Québec had to do with the growth of such state aid to the corporate sector. The Industrial Funds Act of 1961 gave municipalities government money to set up industrial parks, which amounted to providing cheap loans to companies. The Ministry of Industry and Commerce greatly expanded its services to business. The Québec Industrial Development Corporation set up in 1971 gave $53 million to 201 companies in its first two years, the bulk of it going to the technologically advanced sector. ITT-Rayonnier got $17.5 million worth of access roads and $19 million worth of wood-harvesting machinery as well as exclusive cutting rights to over 51,000 square miles of domanial forest, at cheaper than usual royalty fees. The examples abound, dominated by the multi-billion dollar investment in the hydro-electric development of James Bay.[48]

Much of municipal spending is likewise directed to further capital accumulation. As early as 1926, the Montréal City Improvement League was demanding the construction of roads that would facilitate the transport of freight and people between Montréal and parts beyond. Many of the public works projects undertaken by the city during the thirties provided an infrastructure favourable to industrial growth. Between 1944 and 1956, 52.3% of the suggested improvements to the road system were situated in the downtown core, while from 1960 on the policies of the Drapeau administration which has ruled Montréal have clearly favoured the needs of corporate capital. The growth of autoroutes, the construction of the metro subway and the redevelopment of the downtown core have all been fostered by the Drapeau administration. The metro system of subways itself has been laid out to bring tourists to the prestigious sites of the Olympic Games and Man and His World, and to bring workers and consumers to the downtown commercial and financial core. Many of the metro stations are located directly beneath the large department stores. The result is that "the community is in fact paying for a service which the corporation should be providing through higher salaries to their employees or through higher taxes. The lower salaries paid to their employees, and the increase in their number of clients and profits which followed the introduction of rapid subsidised Métro service, have consolidated the economic position of these institutions and enterprises." The expansion of the Montréal metro has continued along these lines, the latest example being the location of the Namur station. Originally designed to be built in a low-income residential neighbourhood and close to a large number of plants, it was shifted to a site much closer to a development project on the existing Blue Bonnets racetrack, proposed by one of Canada's leading developers, Campeau Corporation. Furthermore, "the station was to be linked to the Blue

Bonnets project by an underground shopping centre built by public funds alloted to Métro construction, which was to be leased to Campeau Corporation on a long-term basis at very favourable conditions." The cost of the planning services provided by the various municipal bodies involved came to somewhere between $2.4 and $3.2 million, while the projected expenditure of all state levels related to this project ranged from $63.4 to $64.2 million.[49] The city, like other levels of the state, absorbs the cost of private capital accumulation.

Much of state expenditure, however, is also directed to its legitimation functions, that ensemble of activities designed to maintain social peace through the distribution of state goodies and the inculcation of proper values. Behind these programmes stands a vast repressive apparatus, ready to step into the breach when the state's efforts at legitimation falter. Together the state's coercive and legitimating activities make up its contribution to the reproduction of the workers' subordinate position in the class structure, and of the capitalist system as a whole. Although the effectiveness of the state's legitimating activities depends on its latent coercive powers, in the long run legitimacy rather than violence is the more effective and stable means of social control. Both state functions have tended to expand over the years, but the state's legitimating activities have assumed increasing importance.

Rural migration to the cities in the early part of the century created new forms of dependency. Families were now totally dependent on the salary of the wage earner. Older and younger members of the family tended no longer to contribute to the economic activity of the family; instead they were a drain on it. Downward business cycles resulting in unemployment made the entire family more vulnerable. People would be evicted for failure to pay their rent. There were no garden plots on which to depend for food, as was the case on the farm. Provision for the destitute and the infirm in urban centres had hitherto been made by private charities, but by the 1920s they found themselves overburdened. In 1919 the Québec government had to cover a deficit of $250,000. The result was the Public Assistance Act of 1921 which made the state increasingly responsible financially for the care of the needy and increasingly involved in the supervision of the subsidised private institutions.[50]

This initial and very limited involvement of the state in the care of the needy has grown and the category of those officially defined as poor has come to embrace both the unemployed and active members of the work force. Unemployment insurance was established in 1940; unemployment assistance for those working in 1956. By 1969-70 those workers receiving unemployment assistance represented 53% of all those receiving benefits under either programme. These figures reflect the process whereby increasing use of technology ejects workers from the monopoly sector of the economy and contributes to the relative immiseration of the working class as a whole.

Welfare is not the only area in which the state's role in the reproduction of the class structure has expanded. As child labour was phased out, the school system was expanded to keep children in there longer. Vocational and technical education streams were introduced into the schools in order to provide those workers, destined to hold the positions of foremen in the new revamped factories, with the proper attitudes. School reforms in the sixties had much to do with turning out the new supervisory personnel to fill the expanded control functions of post-war capitalism and preparing the vast majority for positions in the workplace that required less and less skill. Every step in the process of school reform, however, increased the fiscal burden on the state and the power of the central bureaucracy. Québec government expenditures increased from $91.1 million in 1945 to $3,148.3 million in 1970. As a percentage of gross national product it represented an increase from 3.7% in 1946 to 14.6% in 1970. The biggest increase came in the legitimation areas of health, welfare and education, which jumped from 34.7% of government expenses in 1945 to 67.6% of government expenses in 1970.[51]

The state's increased involvement in the areas of capital accumulation and the reproduction of labour has produced a fiscal crisis as expenditures outstrip revenues. The net total accumulative deficit for all levels of government in Canada in the period 1950-1970 was $2.3 billion. Only the federal government registered an increase of revenues over expenditures in this period, while municipal governments have experienced the greatest gap between income and expenses. All three levels of government, however, have had recourse to deficit financing, though again the burden of the debt is greatest at the provincial and municipal levels. "Between 1950 and 1968 the Federal government increased its debt (direct and indirect) by 136%, the Provincial and Municipal governments by 505% and 511% respectively." The distribution of taxes between corporations and individuals has only exacerbated the problem. At all levels of government the corporate share of taxes fell while the individual share of taxes rose.

From 1961 to 1970, Québec corporation taxes increased by 47%, individual taxes by 905%. In Montréal too the burden of the fiscal crisis has fallen on the working class. From 1968 to 1977 the net direct bonded debt of Montréal has grown from $686,091,485 to $1,013,744,117. Debt per capita has grown from $477 to $938; yet the debt as a percentage of equivalent taxable evaluation has shrunk from 11.72% to 11.05%. Part of this debt has therefore been financed by continuously revaluating assessed property, which increased by more than 50% in that period, and by increasing the general assessment on real estate, which more than doubled. Nonetheless, cities have become increasingly dependent on superior levels of government.[52]

The fiscal crisis of the city, like that of other levels of government, has been fueled not only by the increasing demands which capital has placed on it, but also by the contradictory nature of these demands and their consequences. Much of the city budget goes towards transport, but within this item the majority of funds are still directed to road transport. In 1977/8 7.2% of the budget was allocated to roads and only 3% to mass transit. The continuing subsidies given to road transport contradict the efforts made to improve rapid transit and make less funds available for it. The construction of autoroutes and the allocation of CMHC funds to single-family housing encouraged the growth of suburbs, whose relatively light density increases the costs of providing the necessary services in terms of sewers, lighting, fuel, transport, etc. The growth of the suburbs in turn shifts much of the wealth out of the city, thus undermining its fiscal base, while the higher-income groups of the suburbs enjoy the amenities of the central city paid for by the working class. This process made itself felt in Montréal as early as the 1920s and severely limited the efforts of reform groups. Even the construction of the Montréal metro has contributed to the growth of the suburbs as the profits realised by the big corporations in the downtown core have been "channelled through the financial institutions to develop the huge regional shopping centres in the suburbs such as Carrefour Laval and Les Galeries d'Anjou." The role of the city as the site for the circulation of surplus capital, now on an international level, has also exacerbated its fiscal crisis. The sale of much of Montréal real estate to European capitalists did not increase the wealth of Montréal, as the profits realised on these sales were reinvested "in the high growth areas like the U.S. and Western Canada."[53]

Although much of municipal expenditure is related to the process of capital accumulation, the pattern of urban life which city funds do so much to sustain is predicated on the social control of the working class. Municipal government is very much the controlling of people: in 1977/8, $112 million was earmarked for general administration and $64 million for the police in the Montréal budget, while total expenditures on programmes only came to about $492 million.[54] Similarly at other levels of the state, much of the expenditure on legitimation functions which has so fueled the fiscal crisis was designed to contain anticipated working class resistance or to respond to open discontent and working class demands. Although these demands may have been generated by the process of capital accumulation, they express the very real opposition workers have put up to that process. As such, the fiscal crisis of the state is not simply the outcome of monopoly capital's accumulation needs but also of the class struggle which arose in opposition to them.

The urban reform movement in Montréal at the turn of the century was motivated in part by a concern lest the deterioration in living conditions threaten the fabric of society as a whole. In the words of one of its leaders, Herbert Brown Ames, "those who study city life arc each day more fully persuaded that ordinary urban conditions are demoralizing and that no portion of the community can be allowed to deteriorate without danger to the whole". The first decade witnessed considerable working-class militancy in Montréal, both in the form of strikes and in the activity of the Parti Ouvrier, whose socialist wing was gaining considerable influence. On May 1, 1906, 500 to 600 workers paraded through Montréal with red flags to assemble at the Champs de Mars to hear Albert St-Martin tell them that the workers did not want to increase salaries or reduce their working hours but to get rid of the bourgeois ('ne pas avoir de bourgeois'). In 1910 a reform slate of businessmen and professionals captured City Hall. Although they accomplished little, they did help to mask fundamental social conflicts by framing city problems in terms of inefficient administration. In so doing they helped to defuse some of the radical thrust in the socialist critique of urban life at the time and they channelled workers' energies into attempts at resolving the issues of class conflict through the representative institutions of municipal government. In April, 1914, for example, St-Martin's socialist party had mobilised 12,000 unemployed to march on City Hall, since Martin, the mayor, had promised to find jobs for all the unemployed. Of course he could not make good on his promise and economic depression disciplined the working class instead.[55]

In countries where the working class was stronger, the dominant class had to yield more tangible concessions. In Paris, for example, the petite-bourgeoisie and small capitalists who dominated city government at the turn of the century succeeded in imposing a plan for the metro which favoured the Paris populace against big capital. What the latter lost in economic concessions, however, it more than made up in political advantages, reflecting how the dominant elites can use the local level of the state as a shock absorber for working class opposition. In the first place, in mobilising working class support for their project, local elites helped drive a wedge into the workers' movement, for while one wing developed a whole praxis around municipal politics, another attacked it as reformist. In the second place, the success of the local elites helped foster the illusion that class had nothing to do with urban struggles, which were much more a question of institutional conflict between local and national levels of the state.[56]

In Montréal, as elsewhere in Canada, the workers' movement was weaker and the dominant class responded much more with repression than with integration. Nonetheless, part of the state's response to working-class militancy following World War One lay in certain measures of social reform. In December, 1918 the federal government set up a $24 million loan fund to aid in the construction of low-cost homes and by 1923 Québec had accepted $4.1 million. The Québec state's initial involvement in welfare policy was also a response to worker militancy. The Parti Ouvrier had advocated many of the measures, while the progressive elements of the petite-bourgeoisie embraced some of them in order to maintain their hold over the working class, just as they were to elaborate a programme of social reform during the thirties.[57]

The Public Assistance Act of 1921 required the fiscal participation of the municipalities in the care of the indigent sick, but it was the cities' provision of relief during the Depression that drove many of them into bankruptcy leading to their first fiscal crisis. Much of the state aid provided to the unemployed in the form of direct payments or public works was initially undertaken to disarm the growing working-class discontent, directed especially at the federal government and led by communist organisations. In Québec most of those who received aid were urban workers concentrated in Montréal, where 30% of the population lived off state aid in 1933/34. Although the two major unions were politically weak, the Communist Party was active and the workers did protest. In spite of considerable repression, 15,000 people attended the funeral of a worker killed by the police in 1933 when trying to stop a bailiff's seizure. In the same year 60,000 unemployed marched on the St.Joseph's Oratory to pray for work.

The programmes put forward by the government required joint provincial and municipal participation. From 1930 to 1940 the province and the municipalities in Québec together accounted for 72.4% of all assistance extended to the unemployed. Montréal alone spent over $27 million between 1930 and 1937, of which $3.8 million was in interest on the loans contracted to provide this aid. The amounts allocated to the workers always remained below the minimum subsistence level, such that the disciplining force of the incentive to work never lost its effect.

The social control functions behind the disbursement of aid were never forgotten. The first act of the Industrial Commission on Unemployment set up in Montréal, dominated by businessmen with token labour representation, was to make it compulsory for all unemployed workers to register with the police and the private charitable institutions. In response to working-class pressure, the city also got involved in helping the unemployed with their medical expenses, rents and supplies of gas and electricity. In light of the city's rising costs, a Commission of Inquiry was set up in 1937 which ultimately recommended that superior levels of government intervene to relieve the city of its impossible fiscal burden. The growing indebtedness of the cities, combined with the recognition by the progressive wing of the bourgeoisie that more long-term measures were needed to help stabilize the economy during future cycles, led to Prime Minister Bennett's New Deal and the subsequent rise of the welfare state in Canada in the post-war period.[58]

Not all the laws passed in the post-war period involved fiscal transfers to the workers, but they reveal the basic political aim behind the entire programme: the political integration of the working class into post-war capitalism. The 1944 federal Order-in-Council recognizing the union's right to organize and bargain collectively also introduced binding arbitration. In strengthening the hands of the union leadership the government hoped to defuse the militancy expressed at the base in the previous years. To some extent this policy succeeded as the major unions returned to an overall policy of collaboration with the state in the post-war period. On the other hand, the reforms which were introduced as the price of this collaboration strengthened the workers' bargaining power and drove up state expenses. By 1963-4, for example, there was less than $1 million left in the unemployment insurance fund as unemployment rose after 1957. The state's commitment to full employment for both political and economic reasons led to an increase in the state's share of total investment and consumption. By 1970 the public sector accounted for nearly 20% of total investment in Canada, while "government spending for all purposes in 1970 amounted to close to one third of Gross National Product."[59]

The process has been pretty much the same in all of the major capitalist countries. The post-war European settlement involved the political defeat of the working-class but also the growth of state expenditures. This development was not in itself antagonistic to private capital accumulation. Much of state expenditure, even in legitimation areas, contributed to it. State borrowing to finance much of its activity did not prove to be a drain on its resources until economic growth started to slow down in the 1970s. At that point deficit financing contributed appreciably to the overall inflation. In Britain the borrowing requirement as a percentage of state expenditure rose from 1.7% to 5.9% from 1971 to 1973. Inflation in the private sector also increased throughout the western world, as monopoly sector industries introduced price increases in order to counter working class success in driving up wages during the 1960s, thereby creating a profits squeeze. Ironically, it was the growth of the welfare state that created the conditions which made this working class advance possible. The working class advance not only pushed up the share of individual wages in national production, but also that of the social wage. The establishment of medicare in Québec was ultimately a response to working class pressure, yet the reform has substantially driven up health costs and thereby exacerbated the state's fiscal crisis.[60]

Clearly this fiscal crisis is not merely fiscal, but fundamentally political. The integration of women into the labour force has further sundered the nuclear family, radically changed the role of women and led to demands on the state for free day-care centres. The urban renewal of the sixties has not halted the deterioration of much of urban life. Many of the promises raised by earlier reforms have been dashed. The construction of comprehensive high schools and the creation of community colleges known as CEGEPs were justified on the grounds that they would provide increased economic opportunity for all. The nature and needs of monopoly capital, such as the deskilling of work, undermined these claims. The legitimation programmes which have fueled the state's fiscal crisis have resulted in their own legitimation crisis, as the state's ability to deliver on its promises diminishes. New struggles form around these contradictions, as people demand better housing, cheaper public transport, state-funded child-care.

Yet the state's resources are already being severely stretched, and at the back door the capitalist class is knocking too, asking the state to bail it out of its profits squeeze. The Conseil du Patronat du Québec recommended to the Québec government prior to its preparation of the 1972/3 budget that it limit the increase in government spending to 5% but increase its investment in capital accumulation sectors. In fact, the government responded by limiting its increase to 8.1%, down from more than 15% three years ago. The increase in education fell from 15% to

5.5%, in social affairs from 12.5% to 8%, but rose for para-public investments by 23%.

The fiscal crisis of the state marks a new stage in the class struggle which has taken an acute form at the urban level. The first step in the bourgeoisie's counter-attack has been to introduce cutbacks in the public sector, by reducing the salaries of public employees and cutting back on social services. The Québec state throughout the seventies has confronted public and parapublic workers head on in two Common Front Strikes in attempts to reduce their salaries or increase their workload. Municipal employees in Montréal have encountered stiff resistance to their wage demands and all sectors have gone out on strike at one point or another—policemen, firemen, transport workers, blue and white-collar employees. At the same time the federal government has imposed wage controls and tightened up the eligibility criteria for unemployment insurance. This counter-attack has not been confined to Canada. The state in both Britain and Italy has imposed drastic cutbacks on the social wage, while in New York the most severe form of austerity yet encountered is being practised. It is not insignificant that this austerity is being imposed on the weakest countries in the capitalist chain and on the weakest level of government within the national economies. The growth in municipal expenditures which so served the interests of the establishment during the sixties was encouraged by the banks who often funded their deficits. With the collapse of the international monetary system the cities have become exceedingly vulnerable to the banks, who have not hesitated to impose a drastic form of austerity, much as the International Monetary Fund (IMF) has not hesitated to make it the condition of its loans to Britain and Italy. The situation is no different for Montréal. The decline in the Canadian dollar has considerably increased the city's debts, since many of its loans are raised on foreign money markets.

Once again the city has been called upon in a period of crisis to carry out the political task of defusing working-class militancy. It does so by imposing an austerity programme of a definite class character in the name of a fiscal crisis that is blamed on improper management and whose international dimension severely limits any government's room for manoeuvre. In New York this process has gone so far that municipal union pension funds have been used to help bail out New York, but their use in this way has severely curtailed the bargaining power of municipal workers. By early 1977 New York had cut 50,000 workers from its 1974 workforce, reduced salaries and underfunded the five major pension plans by $6 billion, according to a state commission report. The situation is highly reminiscent of Montréal in the 1930s when the city's spiralling debt occasioned by its provision of relief made it very dependent on the banks. The city's position was then blamed on poor management, while the banks succeeded in imposing drastic cuts on the municipal administration. In the thirties the Montréal administration fired 30% of its workforce while it was forced to tolerate the dismissal of thousands of employees in the private sector whose employers benefited from municipal tax concessions. Attempts to increase the salaries of those on the municipal payroll met stiff opposition from business interests.[62]

Such drastic austerity measures seem part of the general crisis facing capitalism on a world wide level. As with earlier periods of crisis, it marks one step in the restructuring of the economy which today seems to be taking the form of strengthening the capital-intensive sector dominated by the multinational corporations, especially in the areas of food and energy. The rise of the muiltinationals marks the truly global reach of contemporary capitalism, as Fiat and Pepsi Cola have penetrated even the Soviet Union. In this contemporary world system, the multinationals are using their monopoly position in key commodity areas to reimpose discipline on the working class from Warsaw to New York. Using every opportunity to drive up the prices of these commodities, they hope to wrest from the working class the gains they have made in these and other areas during the post-war period. By pushing up the costs of these basic commodities, capital effectively reduces the real living standards of workers and makes more money available for capital investment. Money itself has become an important weapon in this process, as floating exchange rates and periodic devaluations further weaken the position of the working class which is nowhere near as mobile as capital. Inflation has shifted from being an element of government policy in stabilising the economy to being an element in the global restructuring of capital. So has unemployment, as capital seeks to reduce the wage demands of the working class and replace labour with machinery in as many sectors as possible, thereby laying the basis for a new wave of capital expansion.

There are both political and economic obstacles to this process. A savage attack on working class demands runs the risk of returning to a pre-Keynesian situation where the lack of working class purchasing power would bring the production process to a halt. Such an attack would also undermine even further the letigimacy of the state, and involve continuous confrontations. Already the Québec government's retrenchment policies have provoked one general strike and two Common Fronts, while the federal wage freeze stimulated the Canadian Labour Congress to its first national general strike, although it only lasted one day. At the same time, as the state attempts to cushion some of the blows in this restructuring process at a global level through various transfer payments to the working class, it lengthens the time it takes capital to convert money into badly needed investments. It is likely, therefore, that we are moving into a period of managed crisis, where instability in commodity supplies and money circulation become part of capital's new global strategy of planned crisis in which the state, once restructured, will play an increasingly important role.[63]

The state will have to manage tensions both by imposing discipline and ameliorating living conditions, yet the state consumption required will have to be more closely tailored to investment needs. In this situation of fiscal crisis, the state will have to centralize at one level all major decisions relating to investments in both legitimation and accumulation areas, so that it can reorder priorities in a much more planned fashion than occurs at present. This is one of the contradictions underlying federal-provincial tensions in Canada at the present time, exacerbated by the provinces' responsibility for both resources and welfare and the federal government's command over fiscal revenues. One of the architects of Québec planning in the sixties, in a review of the experience of a decade, mentioned how difficult planning was in a confederal system precisely because such planning requires both fiscal and decisional centralisation. The chief loser in this process is the city. Already a creature of the provincial government, there is no way that the latter can permit the former to continue its projects of capital expansion, or even of social control, without jeopardising this whole strategy. The establishment of the Québec Housing Corporation has meant that the Montréal planning department must now submit every proposed renewal or housing project to it. Bill 82, which extends Québec's fiscal control over Montréal's capital expenditures, is a very important step in this direction. Already the extension of the Montréal metro has been blocked in the name of the fiscal crisis.[64] From the economic viewpoint it is totally understandable, when already at the provincial level the Parti Québécois is unable to deliver on its promise of free day-care centres, given its commitment to capital accumulation projects like the James Bay development.

Eventually the problems of day-care and urban transport will be tackled, although the model of social control which has accompanied other reforms like medicare will persist. Health care is still delivered through large, bureaucratic institutions and oriented towards cure rather than prevention, given that so many of contemporary diseases have their origins in the social conditions of work and urban life. Health insurance schemes and health reform have therefore led to a greater dependency on experts, technology and drugs, with little attention being paid to those social and economic changes which could do so much to change our state of health. The paradigm of health reform presages what the state has in store for us in other areas.[65]

These reforms will generate more consumption and investment, but their timing will depend on the planning process as a whole, the needs of the corporate economy and the needs of specific sectors within it. People will therefore have to wait for these reforms, and the state will play a key role in adjusting people's expectations to this new framework. The dominant ideology will have to be revamped, which is precisely what Trudeau announced in 1977 as the end of the free enterprise system: ". . .a large part of my message as a politician is to say: we have to put an end to rising expectations. We have to explain to people that we may even have to put an end to our love for our parents or old people in society, even our desire to give more for education and medical research." The recent proposed changes in the education system in Québec, like elsewhere, have much to do with this process: the reimposition of discipline within the schools under the guise of the back-to-basics movement; the abandonment of the need for upward mobility, for children to do better than their parents, as economic reality shattered the illusions of earlier reforms; cutbacks and tightened fiscal control in the administration of programmes. 'Decentralization' of educational and medical systems has been advanced only in order to enlist citizen participation in this policy of fiscal retrenchment and centralisation.[66]

The emphasis on planning in this entire process has legitimized the rise of the new technocracy, who carry out the same control functions here as they do within the modern corporation. The shift in the Montréal City Planning department in 1964 from administration to conceptualisation in the planning process led to the hiring of many new professionals. Yet the planners have traditionally hailed urban renewal as a progressive measure and backed many of the transformations Montréal has undergone. The rise of the planner has been linked to the restructuring of the state, as control of more and more decisions are taken out of the hands of elected bodies at lower levels, which are subject to all kinds of special-group pressures, and placed in regional or higher levels of governments and commissions that are more removed from this modicum of democratic control. The creation of regional governments in Québec was seen in part as an attempt to meet the fiscal needs of the cities by centralising certain administrative and fiscal powers. In the Québec government's original proposal, these new bodies would have been responsible for seven areas of municipal government, including land planning and development, housing and environmental control. Little was left for the cities, while many of these functions would have been exercised by bodies like the Public Security Council and Transport Commission which are immune from control even by the regional government called the Montreal Urban Community. The Parti Québécois criticised the proposal for not going far enough and providing mechanisms that would make regionalization obligatory.[67]

This criticism by the PQ reflects very well the technocratic elements which are its leading force. Its programme, often labelled social democratic, reflects very much the needs of dominant capital and its technocratic strata: progressive measures taken by the state for a dependent population within a planned process of ordered priorities. The priorities remain those of capital, the population is turned into clients of the state, and austerity is imposed on the working class in the name of progressive measures whose articulation robs politics of its class content. Each social measure increases the state's power and intervention in social life, and consequently the importance of that technocracy. The use of the state to push through these reforms and the progressive allure associated with them lend this strategy its social democratic character.

When unions and labour parties, the very organisations of the working class, undertake to impose social discipline, the combative capacity of the working class is further undermined. Not for nothing has it been the British Labour Party and the Italian Communist Party who have ultimately been called upon by capital to do its dirty work. The recent British Labour government has imposed drastic cuts on the social wage while the Communist Party of Italy has played a crucial role in stopping workers' struggles against transport, electricity and telephone rate increases. In Poland it was the Communist Party government that tried to impose food price increases in 1970 in order to make city workers pay for its programme of capital accumulation. The workers responded with a series of strikes and rebellions that spread all over the country forcing the government to roll back the price increases. An attempt by the Polish government to repeat this manoeuvre six years later met with an equally resounding defeat.

This riposte of the Polish working class was not unique. Despite the stances of their official leadership, the British and Italian working classes have not rolled over and played dead. The success of New York's ruling class has not been duplicated everywhere. Workers' struggles among Montréal's municipal employees have gone on, provoking new forms of militancy and new responses by the municipal administrations.

While the counter-attack to the fiscal crisis has begun to emerge on a global level, it has also unleashed a class struggle that has acquired new dimensions. Urban and factory struggles, worker and farmer struggles have linked up to forge new means of working class resistance. In Poland in 1970, for example, the turning point in the workers' victory over the government came when 10,000 textile workers in Lodz struck for a 16% wage increase to offset the price rises; the majority were women. In 1976 workers burned down Communist Party headquarters in Radom and looted food stores. In Italy community and factory-based groups linked up to organize payment of transport and electricity at the old rates. Again many of the militants were women, who had to bear the brunt of electricity rate increases in the form of household drudgery, as the increases forced them to cut back on the use of electricial appliances. In the United States in 1975 consumer groups and the International Longshoremen's Union protested against the U.S.-Russian grain deal, forcing the suspension of further sales so as to prevent grain sales from being used to drive up food prices. This working class resistance reflects a basic contradiction in the present crisis, a contradiction which was already manifest in the working class advance during the 1960s. The riots in American cities were "acts of direct appropriation of social wealth, the wealth that was denied ghetto residents most acutely because of their wagelessness." The welfare state makes it possible for many people to receive income without working. In the factories workers insisted on driving up wages but refused to accept discipline. Turnover, absenteeism, sabotage were familiar complaints of management. At the heart of this struggle was the working class' refusal to work and their demand to separate work from income. Although not articulated in this way, in effect this is what the different working class demands came to, made possible by the advances wrested in a previous era of struggle:

> "The political strategy of the working class in the last cycle of struggles upset the Keynesian plan for development. It is in this cycle that the struggle for income *through* work changes to a struggle for income *independent* of work. The working class strategy for *full employment* that had provoked the Keynesian solution of the Thirties became in the last cycle of struggle a general strategy of the *refusal of work*."[68]

The bourgeoisie has realized this quite clearly. Programmes for a guaranteed income that are now being developed have placed the incentive to work at the heart of their operation, such that a subsistence level can be maintained only if one works. The distinction between those fit to work and those unable to work, as well as the insistence upon work as the basis of income, remained at the heart of Quebec's Castonguay Report. The right to work is really "an obligation to work." The irony of the situation is that the evolution of technology has made it possible for perhaps the first time in history to conceive of the possibility of the separation between work and income. The organization of science and technology has become the driving force behind the production of wealth. The substitution of machines for living labour has been a key factor in the expansion of productive capacity. Labour becomes a less important component in the process of production, yet this system is inconceivable without the exploitation of labour and the extraction of surplus value. Capital needs labour even as it makes it possible to do away with it. Instead of ushering in an era of relative abundance, the ruling class has to use the wealth produced in order to impose a new division of scarcity, this time on an international level, which shows up in the metropolitan heartlands in the form of social control: the enforcement of work and the imposition of austerity, such that "the very moment capital does away with labor *in production*, it attempts to impose labor again as *a form of control of the working class.*" The very heart of this system shows up in the present crisis for what it is: command over labour; and becomes the focal point of the current crisis.[69]

Our story seems to have come full circle. The city fashioned in the image of capital is the city organized on the basis of social control, yet the question of social control and therefore of social liberation lies at the very centre of today's crisis, whether it takes the form of slumpflation, the fiscal crisis of the state, a crisis of legitimacy, or the urban crisis. Within this perspective, the urban question takes on new significance, rich in strategic implications for both the conduct of urban struggles and the revolutionary project.

NOTES:

(1.) H. Braverman, *Labor and Monopoly Capital*, N.Y., 1974, p. 276-7.
(2.) J. Meynaud, J. Léveillée, *La régionalisation municipale au Québec*, Montréal, Nouvelle Frontière, 1972, p. 18.
(3.) J.-C. Marsan, *Montréal en évolution*, Montréal, Fides, 1974, p. 309.
(4.) T. Copp, *The Anatomy of Poverty*, Toronto, 1974, p. 39-43; Marsan, op. cit., p. 188-94; M. Pelletier, Y. Vaillancourt, *Les politiques sociales et les travailleurs*, Cahier 1, Montréal, 1974; and for England, E.-P. Thompson, *The Making of the English Working Class*, Hammondsworth, 1968.
(5.) Office de planification et de développement du Québec (OPDQ), sous la direction de B. McDonough, *Esquisse de la région de Montréal*, Montréal, September, 1977, p. 30-1; M. Saint-Germain, *Une économie à libérer*, Montréal, Les presses de l'Université de Montréal, 1973, p. 48.
(6.) S. Bodington, *Computers and Socialism*, Nottingham, 1973, p. 143.
(7.) J. Merrington, "Town and Country in the Transition to Capitalism", in *New Left Review*, 93, Sept.-Oct., 1975.
(8.) T. Naylor, *The History of Canadian Business*, Toronto, 1975, 2 vols.
(9.) Copp, *op. cit.*, ch. 5.
(10.) Marsan, *op. cit.*, p. 270-5 and more extensively, p. 188-204, 267-303.
(11.) Copp, *op. cit.*, p. 86.
(12.) Marsan, *op. cit.*, p. 203-4. (My translation-S.S.)
(13.) Braverman, *op. cit.*, ch. 13.
(14.) C. Larivière, *Crise économique et contrôle social : le cas de Montréal (1929-1937)*, Montréal, Coopératives Albert St-Martin, 1977, p. 61.
(15.) M. Pelletier, Y. Vaillancourt, *op. cit.*, cahier II, p. 260-3 and cahier III, p. 5-9: H. Quinn, *The Union Nationale*, Toronto. 1963, p. 80-1; D. Lessard, *L'agriculture et le capitalisme au Québec*, Montréal, l'étincelle, 1976, p. 33.
(16). Lessard, *op. cit.*, p. 28-9; 48-53; 62-5.
(17.) H. cleaver, "Food, Famine and the International Crisis" in *Zerowork, Political Materials 2*, N.Y., fall, 1977, p. 7-69; D. Mitchell, *The Politics of Food*, Toronto, C. Gonick, F. Gudmundson, *Food, Glorious Food*, Winnipeg.
(18.) OPDQ, *Esquisse...*, *op. cit.*, p. 61.
(19.) Ibid., p. 70-3.
(20.) F. Dumont, P. Labonté, "Urbanisation et réseau de transport de la région montréalaise (1945-1975)" in *Esquisse. . .*, *op. cit.*, Annexe complémentaire I, OPDQ, Montréal, January, 1977, p. 79-86; M. Camus, L. Roy-Renaud, *Impact social du REM sur les populations*, Montréal, OPDQ, May, 1977, p. 6.
(21.) H. Braverman, *op. cit.*, p. 146-51; Marsan, *op. cit.*, p. 323.
(22.) M. Camus, L. Roy-Renaud, *op. cit.*, p. 1; OPDQ, *Esquisse. . .*, *op. cit.*, p. 51, 80; P. Hamel, J.-F. Léonard, *Dossier sur les luttes urbaines à Montréal : six mobilisations populaires sur le logement*, Montréal, L'Association canadienne d'urbanisme, division du Québec, Conseil canadien de recherches urbaines et régionales, April, 1976, p. 33-4.
(23.) M. Camus, L. Roy-Renaud, *op. cit.*, p. 139-40; 135-6.
(24.) A. Markusen, "Class and Urban Social Expenditures: A Local Theory of the State", in *Kapitalistate*, 4-5/1976, p. 50-65; M. Camus, L. Roy-Renaud, *op. cit.*, p. 52-5,72-6,122-3; OPDQ, *Esquisse. . .*, *op. cit.*, p. 51-2.
(25.) H. Braverman, *op. cit.*, especially chs. 12-16.
(26.) OPDQ, *Esquisse. . .*, *op. cit.*, p. 30-1,99-101,131; J.-C. Marsan, *op. cit.*, p. 320.
(27.) M. Saint-Germain, *op. cit.*, p. 61; J. Mollenkopf, "The Fragile Giant: The Crisis of the Public Sector in American Cities" in *Socialist Revolution*, number 29, vol. 6, no. 3, July-Sept., 1976, p. 16-17; OPDQ, *Esquisse. . .*, *op. cit.*, p. 65-70.
(28.) H. Braverman, *op. cit.*, p. 147-8.
(29.) K. Stone, "The Origins of Job Structures in the Steel Industry" in Root and Branch (ed.), *Root and Branch: The Rise of the Workers' Movements*, Greenwich, Conn., 1975, p. 123-57; M. Glaberman, "Work and Working Class Consciousness" in *Our Generation*, Vol. 11, 2, winter, 1976, p. 24-32; S. Faber, "Working Class Organisation" in *Our Generation*, vol. 11, 3, summer 1976, p. 13-26; J. Rinehart, "Wage Controls, Unions and Class Conflict in Canada", *ibid.*, p. 27-34; M. Glaberman, "A Review of Braverman's Labor and Monopoly Capital", *ibid.*, p. 49-52; H. Braverman, op. cit., ch. 6.

(30.) D. Brunelle, "La structure occupationnelle de la main-d'oeuvre québécoise 1951-1971" in *Sociologie et Sociétés*. VII, 2, Nov., 1975, p. 77-8; M. Saint-Germain, *op. cit.*, p. 61.

(31.) *Les Gens du Québec: St. Henri*, Montréal, 1972, cited in P. Fournier *The Quebec Establishment*, Montréal, 1976, p. 167; see also H. Braverman, *op. cit.*, ch. 17; M. Camus, L. Roy-Renaud, *op., cit.*, p. 9, 67-71; F. Des Rosiers, O. Grundberg, "Répartition de l'emploi et de la main d'oeuvre dans les principales agglomérations urbaines, région administrative de Montréal: lieu de travail et lieu de résidence"; statistical table, Montréal, OPDQ, 1976.

(32.) M. Pelletier, Y. Vaillancourt, op. cit., cahier IV, p. 233.

(33.) H. Braverman, *op. cit.*, p. 384, also chs. 11-14 and 17 for the discussion that follows.

(34.) *Ibid.*, p. 281.

(35.) OPDQ, *Esquisse...*, *op. cit.*, p. 37, 56; M. Camus, L. Roy-Renaud, *op. cit.*, p. 78-80, 86-7.

(36.) H. Braverman, *op. cit.*, p. 389, citing Marx, *Capital*, vol. 1, Moscow, n.d., p. 604; J.-F. Léonard, "L'évolution du rôle du service d'urbanisme de la Ville de Montréal dans l'orientation de la politique d'aménagement de la Ville de Montréal (1941-1971)", master's thesis, political science, Université du Québec à Montréal, Sept. 1973, p. 106-7.

(37.) D. Harvey, *Social Justice and the City*, London, 1973, ch. 6; L. Robert, P. Racicot, *La politique de rénovation urbaine; le cas québécois*, EZOP, *Une Ville à Vendre*, cahier 3, Québec, 1972, p. 36.

(38.) B. Commoner, *The Closing Circle*, N.Y., 1971, p. 145, ch. 9.

(39.) *Ibid.*, p. 176, 259-68; J.-C. Marsan, *op. cit.*, p. 344-5.

(40.) H. Braverman, *op. cit.*, p. 280; S. Schecter, "Capitalism, class and educational reform in Canada" in L. Panitch (ed.), *The Canadian State*, Toronto, 1977, p. 373-416, especially p. 386.

(41.) J.-C. Marsan, *op. cit.*, p. 320; OPDQ, *Esquisse...*, *op. cit.*, p. 131.

(42.) P. Fournier, *op. cit.*

(43.) J. Mollenkopf, "The Post-War Politics of Urban Development" in *Politics and Society* 5, winter 1976, p. 268-9; S. Magri, "Politique du logement de l'état : exigences du capital et lutte des classes" in *International Journal of Urban and Regional Research*, vol. 1, no. 2, 1977, p. 218-20.

(44.) M. Pelletier, Y. Vaillancourt, *op. cit.* cahier II, p. 322-3, cahier III, p. 50; C. Larrivière, *op.cit.*, p. 170; P. Racicot, L. Robert, *op. cit.*, p. 38; H. Braverman, *op. cit.*, p. 279-81.

(45.) A. Cottereau, "Les origines de la planification urbaine en France, le Métro et les mouvements sociaux" in *Politiques urbaines et planifications des villes*, Colloque de Dieppe, 8, 9, 10 avril, 1974, p. 789-90.

(46.) T. Copp, *op. cit.*, p. 133.

(47.) R. Deaton, "The Fiscal Crisis of the State in Canada" in D. Roussopoulos (ed.), *The Political Economy of the State*, Montréal, 1973, p. 23-4; Naylor, *op. cit.*; Larrivière, *op. cit.*, p. 73-5.

(48.) Deaton, *op. cit.*, p. 30-1; Fournier, *op. cit.*, p. 170-94.

(49.) A. Limonchik, "The Colonization of the Urban Economy" in *Our Generation*, vol. 12, no. 2, fall, 1977, p. 10-14; Léonard, *op. cit.*, p. 40-3; 79-81; Larrivière, *op. cit.*, p. 252-3.

(50.) Pelletier, Vaillancourt, *op. cit.*, cahier I, p. 31-4, 98-104.

(51.) Pelletier, Vaillancourt, *op. cit.*, cahier III, p. 56; cahier IV, p. 57; Schecter, *op. cit.*; D. Latouche, "La vraie nature de... La Révolution tranquille", in *Canadian Journal of Political Science*, VII, no. 3, p. 529-35.

(52.) Deaton, *op. cit.*, p. 38-40; B. R. Lemoine, "The Growth of the State in Québec" in Roussopoulos (ed.), *op. cit.*, p. 69; City of Montréal, *Report of the Director of Finance, 1977*, Montréal, 1977, p. 46, 51-3; Meynaud, Léveillée, *op. cit.*, p. 30-4.

(53.) Limonchik, *op. cit.*, p. 9, 19; Harvey, *op. cit.*, ch. 6; City of Montréal, *Budget 1977-8*, Montréal, p. 168-75; Racicot, Robert, *op. cit.*, p. 38; Markusen, *op. cit.*, p. 56-61; Copp, *op. cit.*, p. 147.

(54.) City of Montréal, *Budget 1977-8*, p. 168-9.

(55.) Copp, *op. cit.*, p. 15, 132, 146-7; Pelletier, Vaillancourt, *op. cit.*, cahier I, p. 61, 120 (f 62).

(56.) Cottereau, *op. cit.*, p. 785-790.

(57.) Copp, *op. cit.*, p. 82-3; Pelletier, Vaillancourt, *op. cit.*, cahier I, p. 64-6, cahier II, p. 139.

(58.) Pelletier, Vaillancourt, *op. cit.*, cahier I, p. 99, cahier II, p. 119-20, 131, 179, 197, 215-6; A. Finkel, "Origins of the Welfare State in Canada" in Panitch (ed.), *op. cit.*, p. 348-51; Larrivière, *op. cit.*, p. 149-50, 163-75, 192-3, 221, 225-7, 232-5.

(59.) Deaton, *op. cit.*, p. 32-4; Pelletier, Vaillancourt, *op. cit.*, cahier III, p. 42-3, 60-1, f 92.

(60.) I. Gough, "State Expenditure in Advanced Capitalism" in *New Left Review*, 92, July-August 1975, p. 53-92; Pelletier, Vaillancourt, op. cit., cahier IV, p. 160; M. Renaud, "Réforme ou illusion ? Une analyse des interventions de l'Etat québécois dans le domaine de la santé" in *Sociologie et Sociétés*, vol. 9, no. 1, April, 1977, p. 131, 151; D. Swartz, "The politics of reform; conflict and accommodation in Canadian health policy" in Panitch (ed.), *op. cit.*, p. 311-43.

(61.) Fournier, *op. cit.*, p. 278; Schecter, *op. cit.*
(62.) Pelletier, Vaillancourt, *op. cit.*, cahier IV, p. 195: Y. Collonges, P.G. Randal, *Les Autoréductions: grèves d'usagers et luttes de classes en France et en Italie (1972-1976)*, Paris, Christian Bourgois, 1976, p. 7-51; C. Marazzi, "Money in the World Crisis" in *Zerowork, Political Materials 2*, op. cit., p. 107-10; D. Demac, P. Mattera, "Developing and Underdeveloping New York", *ibid.*, p. 125-31; Mollenkopf, "The Fragile Giant. . .", *op. cit.*, p. 16-20; Larrivière, *op. cit.*, p. 124-5, 234-7.
(63.) M. Montano, "Notes on the International Crisis" in *Zerowork, Political materials 1*, p. 39-47; Cleaver, *op. cit.*; Marazzi, *op. cit.*, p. 98-102. I am indebeted to these writers for my rethinking of the importance of the fiscal crisis of the state first elaborated by J. O'Connor, *The Fiscal Crisis of the State*, N.Y., 1973 and developed by Gough, *op. cit.*
(64.) R. Parenteau, "L'expérience de la planification au Québec (1960-1969)" in *L'Actualité économique*, vol. 45, no. 4, 1970, p. 690, 695; Léonard, *op. cit.*, p. 117-9.
(65.) Renaud, *op. cit.*, p. 149-50; Swartz, *op. cit.*, p. 334-6.
(66.) Finkel, *op. cit.*, p. 364; Schecter, *op. cit.*
(67.) Meynaud, Léveillée, *op. cit.*, p. 105-7, 128-40; Léonard, *op. cit.*, p. 81-2, 98-107; Mollenkopf, "The Fragile Giant. . .", *op. cit.*, p. 25-9.
(68.) Editorial Collective, "Introduction" in *Zerowork, Political materials 1*, p. 2; also P. Carpignano, "U.S. Class Composition in the Sixties", *ibid.*; Montano, *op. cit.*; P. Taylor, "The Sons of Bitches Just Won't Work: Postal Workers Against the State", *ibid.*, p. 108-9; B. Ramirez, "The Working Class Struggle Against the Crisis: Self-reduction of Prices in Italy", *ibid.*, p. 143-50; Collonges, Randal, *op. cit.* p. 75-121; E. Cherki, M. Wieviorka, "Luttes sociales en Italie: les mouvements d'autoréduction à Turin" in *Les Temps Modernes*, June 1975, p. 1793-1831; Cleaver, *op. cit.*, p. 31, 37, 58-9; Demac, Mattera, *op. cit.*, p. 115.
(69.) Montano, *op. cit.*, p. 39, 53-8; Carpignano, *op. cit.*, p. 25; Pelletier, Vaillancourt, *op. cit.*, cahier iv, p. 256-7.

CHAPTER TWO

URBAN POLITICS AND THE REDEFINITION OF THE REVOLUTIONARY PROJECT

The strategic implications of urban struggles and their contradictions

IF THE PATTERN of contemporary urban life is modelled on the social control needs of capitalism, then attempts to change this pattern must ultimately link up with a long-term strategy to abolish and surpass capitalism itself. Reforms that would significantly improve the quality of urban life for the vast majority immediately raise issues of class power. More efficient and cheaper, if not free, public transport that would not be paid for by the workers would have to be financed through corporate taxes. So would environmental cleanup, pollution control, free day-care centres. Caught in a profits squeeze, corporate capital would be sure to resist measures that would lay any further burden on investment, just as they would resist any attempt to take leisure activities or land allocation out of the domain of exploitation and control. Reforms that would be conceded by the system would also be subverted to its purposes. Demands for the municipalisation of urban land, for example, though voiced by urban reform groups, have also been supported by the big urban developers who have integrated finance, design, planning, construction, sale and rental aspects of development projects. Unlike small-time speculators, these large companies, like Campeau and Trizec Corporations, represent the monopoly wing of the real-estate industry, making their profits from technological advances like systems building. Land speculation has come to be more and more a drain on their resources, since the time it takes them to purchase all the plots of land necessary for a development project ties up badly needed capital, thus putting the entire financing of the project at risk. The difficulties experienced by the Cité Concordia project in

Montréal were very much of this type, as the word got out among the small landlords in the area that Concordia needed the land. These small speculators then held out for as long as possible for as much as they could get. Under such circumstances, the monied interests would very much like to see the city municipalise urban land and set up land banks which would be put at the disposal of the developers, when needed. In their scheme, of course, the small proprietors would be recompensed for their land at the expense of the working class, through municipal revenues, thus keeping the principle of private property inviolate, while the entire project would be justified on the grounds of more rational land use. Only if land were taken out of private hands and put under the control of citizens, organised in some form of neighbourhood councils autonomous from the local state, would the municipalisation of urban land open up the possibility of qualitatively improving city life. Government regulation of agriculture land in Québec has only encouraged the growth of large farms or permitted expropriation when capital needed new infrastructures like the airport at Ste Scholastique.[1]

Urban struggles are therefore a moment in the larger class struggle. As such they go beyond the narrow limits imposed by the definition of urban politics in terms of the current powers of municipal government, a definition which dooms these struggles to failure from the very outset. Rather they extend to the entire range of social life concerned with the reproduction of the class structure and the circulation of capital. By opening up new fronts in workers' historic battles, urban struggles raise new and important issues for the revolutionary project, not least of which is the demystification of the notion of the principal, or exclusive contradiction.

Adherents of this particular notion advocate that the basic contradiction of capitalism lies between capital and labour around the organisation of production, to which all revolutionary forces and struggles should be directed. Contradictions emerging from the reproduction of social life under capitalism are secondary, and struggles focusing on these contradictions should, in consequence, be subordinated to workers' struggles in the factory and office. Yet the political economy of the contemporary city has indicated that the contradictions in the sphere of reproduction have assumed a central importance. The fiscal crisis has become more acute because of the increased role of the state in legitimation activities, itself a response to growing working class strength. The social and physical focus of these contradictions is the modern city, where the working class, concentrated in a relatively dense urban space, threatens the very basis of daily life that is organized around the needs of corporate capital. As urban struggles, redefined as the politics of everyday life, come to occupy an important place in the class struggle, notions like that of the principal contradiction become revealed for the strategic fetishes that they are. As the Italian and French situations have clearly shown, there is a much needed dialectic between the workplace and the neighbourhood which allows both to set the stage for fundamental transformation.

It is no longer possible, for example, to ignore the importance of women's struggles or, even while recognizing them, relegate them to minor importance strategically on the grounds that only the overthrow of capitalism can abolish sexism. Adherents of such an approach usually wind up asking women to put aside their preoccupations as women until after the revolution and in the meantime to distribute leaflets outside factories where the labour force is nearly 100% male. The practice of existing "socialist" societies should in itself make one wonder about the wisdom of such an approach and underscore the importance and legitimacy of organising around these multiple contradictions. Such struggle can only proceed based on the mutual respect and support for the *independent* value of each area of struggle for the different social groups involved. Such an approach is to be valued in itself, for it signifies a refusal to work towards the liberation of some on the backs of others. At the same time, the impact of the demands raised by these diverse groups are explosive for the present organisation of social life. The demands of women for free day-care centres or wages for housework place claims on a state already in the throes of a fiscal crisis. Unsatisfied, these claims unmask its neutrality; accorded, they exacerbate the fiscal crisis and open up the space in which autonomous working class power can grow. At a more profound level, women's struggles raise the whole question of the sexist division of labour and the way in which the system reinforces its domination by distorting the most intimate aspects of our social relations. Sexism, and the nature of sexual relations on which it rests, feeds those psychic and emotional dispositions upon which capitalism thrives: fear, inadequacy, jealousy, guilt, sacrifice, betrayal. These very fierce emotional forces which tear families apart, sunder lovers, divide schoolchildren, also alienate workers one from another, turning objective social conditions into badges of ability and contests of dignity that keep workers at each others' throats instead of directing their energies against the social system that oppresses them. By raising these issues publicly the women's movement has directed our attention to very basic levels of social control that must be confronted for the revolutionary movement to advance.[2]

The plurality of urban struggles nonetheless raises the question of their coordination, as well as their integration with struggles at the workplace. In the same way that community control of land is incomplete without community control of schools, the thorough democratisation of the city is unthinkable without workers' assuming control of the production process itself. The traditional model of revolutionary organisation has been the political party, directing and coordinating the energies of the masses in line with the most recent identification of the principal contradiction. Indeed, it could well be argued that the same thinking that produces theories of principal contradictions also produces models in terms of the party. While it is clear that both theory and coordination are necessary elements to working class struggle, it is by no means clear that this model implies a centralised and directive party. On the contrary, the very multiplicity of fronts, and the principles of mutual respect and support which they require, point to more autonomous forms of working-class organisation which are capable of integrating those principles into their modes of operation. Community organisations, street committees, workers' councils and similar forms of autonomous working class organisation that have appeared on the scene of history each time the working class has dared seize power are much more the kind of forces in which the struggles on various fronts can coalesce without fear of having to submit to a line laid down elsewhere.

Autonomous working class organisation emerges from and in opposition to the nature of the present crisis and is intimately linked to the critique which urban struggles direct at contemporary society. The contemporary crisis has resulted in part from the increase in state power, while its resolution on behalf of capital would only intensify this process. Working class attempts to work through the state or through a political party committed to capturing state power which would then be exercised on its behalf would only play ultimately into capital's hands.

This has been the fate of both social-democratic parties in the West and Bolshevik or Marxist-Leninist governments in the East. Indeed, it has been the social-democratic parties and trade unions of the Western working class who have been the best defenders, even if defenders of the last resort, of capital. It is to them that the ruling class has turned to impose discipline on the working class as the present crisis intensifies; and it is they who have set in motion the transformations in the state apparatus so necessary to the restructuring of capital. In response the working class has rediscovered forms of direct action which pit its own autonomous power against that of the state, forms to which the Italian urban, or self-reduction struggles have given the clearest expression.

These struggles are significant not only because in them workers appropriate directly control of social life, but also because they announce that only such direct control is compatible with the socialist project. Fifty years of Stalinism, together with the growth of the positive state in the post-war boom, has buried the original Marxist project of the withering away of the state. Today, under the impact of the present crisis, that project is being revived in both theory and practice. As the state becomes an ever greater agency of social control it becomes clearer that the state must be dismantled and replaced with direct control by human beings over their social life. As long as the debate over the nature of capitalism was posed in terms of its productive capacity, however, it was easy to sidestep this question, and define and defend the revolutionary project in terms of its greater economic efficiency. Yet the kernel of the revolutionary critique of capitalism, as the present crisis is making clear, lies in the domination which capitalism builds into every social relation. Urban struggles, precisely because they focus on the terrain of everyday life, have to confront this issue unmediated by exclusive wage claims or other material demands.

The separation of work from income which underlay many working class demands in the sixties is indicative of this process. The demand for more welfare independent of work, which fueled the fiscal crisis, is revolutionary precisely because it refuses the present redistribution of scarcity and insists on freedom from toil now. Such a demand also reminds us that at the heart of the socialist project is not a more effective distribution of toil but the liberation from toil, the abolition of wage-labour and the introduction of play into all human activity. Toil, like the state, belongs to capitalism and its logic of domination. So too does commodity fetishisms, fostered by the current organisation of urban life and against which the need for self-initiated expression and activity assumes revolutionary force. Surely at one level the attempts to set up food cooperatives, free schools, housing communes, cooperative day care centres, street committees represent attempts on the part of people to reassert control over their lives free from the domination of the market place.

The appropriation of control over social life and the assertion of self-initiated activity which mark contemporary urban struggles stand in direct negation to the city organised around the functions of social control and to capitalism defined as command over labour. Thus urban struggles point to a redefinition of the revolutionary project in terms of the transformation of social relations in all their forms and to a rethinking of revolutionary strategy in organisational terms that attempt to put this redefinition into practice. The significance of urban struggles lies precisely in the fact that the critique of capitalism they raise makes it impossible to return to traditional modes of revolutionary organisation, which reproduces, despite its critical claims, the social relations of capitalist life. Whatever form the new autonomous working-class organisations take, it is clear that every attempt must be made to practice those demands that these organisations raise: thorough democratisation of political life, control from below, the sharing of manual and intellectual tasks, the struggle against sexism, respect and support for the multiple points of people's struggle against oppression, belief in the creative capacity of human beings. Such principles are indissociable from practice, just as revolutionary organisation is inseparable from its critique. The emphasis on autonomous working class organisation current in urban struggles is a direct reflection of the critique they are raising: against toil, against scarcity, against command as the principle on which social life is organised.

Other projects have their own coherence. The Leninist model of the vanguard elitist party is bound up with the preoccupation with the seizure of state power and the nationalisation of the means of production. The denouement to this project, as the Soviet Union has clearly shown, is the erection of a new dictatorship and the dispossession, once again, of the working class from real control over social life. Capital also has its project, as the multiple transformations in social life that it brought converge in an elaborate process of social control. Against it the working class has waged a new offensive which everywhere has been "productive of self-organisation"; and this new, autonomous form of working class organisation emerged from the extension of the struggle beyond the workplace:

> "It is crucial to see that in this cycle of struggles capital's political problems do not stem only from what was *traditionally* considered as the wage front. Surely the relation between capital and the working class is not measured only on Fridays, since the struggle is over more than the paycheck. It takes on many forms; absenteeism, lower productivity, uses and abuses of the union structure (e.g., 'cheating' on health benefits), pilfering and cargo theft, and the infinite degrees of sabotage ('counterplanning on the shop fllor'). But even more important the struggle is not limited to the assembly line, the dock or the highway; it is equally expressed in the community. From welfare struggles to rent strikes, from criminal activities such as shoplifting and robbery to direct appropriation attacks on supermarkets, from squatters to food price

boycotts, we see the opening of a whole spectrum of working class struggles for wealth.''[3]

Yet the opening up, important as it is, is insufficient. For urban struggles to succeed links must be made with struggles in the workplace. It is to the system's advantage to cordon off areas of legitimate political activity and so keep working class struggles within reformist bounds. This is especially true in the state sector where cutbacks on services are blamed on lazy workers and attacks on wages are launched in the public interest.

Since 1970 the federal government has been locked in battle with the postal workers, trying first to cut their wages and then introducing automation to increase productivity. As both attempts to discipline the postal workers met with resistance, the state tried to isolate them by describing them as slackers at the public's expense and blaming them for the increases in the price of stamps. The Québec government's run-in with the teachers has taken on much the same aspect, as has the running battle between the Montréal Urban Community's Transport Commission and its maintenance employees. If the fiscal crisis implies for capital the restructuring of the state at the expense of public employees and the clients of state services, for workers it means that the claims of each group must be posed in a way that leads them to a joint attack on capital. Better wages and working conditions for transport workers must be linked to demands for reduced fares, or the victory of one will lead to the defeat of the other.

Developing these links is not an easy process. Although urban struggles open up the possibilities of new alliances, much of the present ordering of urban life stands in their way. Urban renewal gives construction workers a stake in capitalism's transformation of the built structure. In 1975 municipal administrations in San Francisco and the Bay area withstood strikes by policemen, firemen and bus drivers, capitalizing on their inability to mobilise public support. In New York the state used the fiscal crisis to play off transit workers' demands against those of users, warning that any wage increase would lead to higher fares while claiming that the use of slugs by transit users instead of proper tokens made it impossible to grant any wage increase. Part of the problem in forging alliances between public sector workers and clients is the ambiguous nature of many of those services. Many of these services fulfil important functions of social control. The police help break strikes and defend private property. Teachers socialize children into their future slots in the work hierarchy. Public transport brings people to work and to market. Social workers have to tidy up the mess that capitalism produces. The discrepancy between the nominal and real functions of their jobs makes for considerable tension among public sector workers, a tension that opens them up to possible radical action. For teachers to be able to really teach they would need to abolish the existing school system and replace it with a community controlled learning environment geared towards the full expression of each child. Such a project would require a teacher-parent alliance across a broad range of issues from school closings to reduced staff/student ratios to class and sex biased textbooks. The tension propelling teachers towards such an alliance are, however, counter-balanced by their own training, which has armed them with the ideological justification of their role, and their relatively higher salaries, compared to those of most workers. At the same time, the social control functions which these public sector employees exercise alienate the very clients with whom the alliances must be made.[4]

The growth of these social control functions has emerged in direct proportion to the growth of monopoly capital, and with it the increase in the technocracy required to carry out these functions. This technocracy, to a considerable extent bearers of university diplomas, tends to monopolise political discourse in our society, and through that discourse convey the ambiguity of their class position. Their progressive leanings stem from the ambiguous nature of the tasks they are asked to perform, while the technocratic cast they give to all projects of social reform reflect the material and ideological constraints of their class position. As many of them work in the areas of social reproduction they become aware of the system's inadequacies and the need for change. Yet their fortunes are linked to the state, and consequently their prescriptions for change take the form of better planning, which only increases state functions. This dynamic has been especially prominent at the level of city politics where urban planning has dominated municipal reform movements.

The tendency for the technocracy to dominate or coopt urban struggles is facilitated by the nature of the urban terrain, where the contradictions of capital pose themselves as problems of distribution and circulation rather than as problems of production. For the technocracy, the problems posed by cars are not the organisation of work but pollution and traffic control; and their responses to these problems do not touch the production process upon which their class position rests, but the role of the state. To rectify the imbalances in capitalism the state must intervene at the level of distribution by making automobile users pay more for the costs of car transportation or by underwriting public transport. Land speculation must be replaced with land banks, assembled by the state and resold in line with master plans for urban development. Such responses clearly avoid the question of class power, as does much of the critique of contemporary urban life.

Analyses that identify today's urban ills with the disappearance of the corner store mask as much as they reveal. On the one hand they lament the loss of diversity and community which formerly gave urban life much of its charm. On the other hand they ignore the fact that the era of the small merchant was also an era of harsh proletarianisation and the historical predecessor of our present society. The nostalgia for this bygone era flies in the face of its harsh reality and reflects the technocratic bias of this critique, which would dearly like to do away with the unpleasant consequences of capitalism without doing away with capitalism itself. A similar ambiguity informs many of the alternative experiments in the areas of social reproduction which are dominated by the professional class. Ventures from natural food cooperatives to community gardens reflect the discontent with the anomie of present-day urban life, but their restriction to a search for time past gives them a limited and class-bound impact.

This ambiguity is reinforced by the process of suburbanisation, itself underpinned by the separation of work and residence. Although suburbs tend to be somewhat distinguished by their occupational and ethnic composition, they are not pure class suburbs. Professionals mix with monopoly sector blue-collar workers, and as the urban crisis intensifies, urban struggles around housing, transport and the environment come to assume a multi-class character, in which the professional, technocratic elements tend to dominate and give the struggles their particular class hue. This process is reinforced to the extent that migration to the suburbs represented for all occupational groups

> "an inward-looking response to dehumanizing capitalism; in this respect it represents a movement to circumvent the loss of control and human dignity under capitalism and is not merely a determined manipulation of political structure by the capitalist class. At the same time, it reinforces current forms of class domination and intra-class antagonism."[5]

The class configuration of suburbs also introduces a contradictory note into the opposition against the state's efforts at regionalisation or centralisation. Although the creation of metropolitan governments reflects the planning needs of the state and capital, it is not only the left that has put up resistance. Decentralisation has been taken up by local elites, anxious to preserve the suburbs' position of marginal privilege which attracted its residents in the first place. Both the Toronto Metropolitan government and the Montréal Urban Community were imposed from above by the provincial governments; and both engendered resistance from local suburbs. Although much of the debate is framed in terms of local sovereignty, much of the suburbs' dissatisfaction stems from the increased contributions suburban dwellers are called on to make for the provision of municipal services that are now integrated on a metropolitan basis. Skyrocketing police and transit costs and severe increases in property evaluation have fueled suburban mayors' anger within the Montréal Urban Community, as they are forced to underwrite the costs of economic expansion without any real say over the process. The budget of the Montréal Urban Community is not subject to any effective control by its members. The upshot of the whole process is a blurring of political claims that raise the issues of decentralisation and equality. The present set-up allows the advocates of centralisation to justify it on the grounds of equalising the burden of municipal expenses, while many of its opponents legitimate their stance under the banner of local control. The question of class power is skirted in both cases, reflecting the ambiguity in the call for local control which runs the risk of solidifying the dominant position which traditional elites and the new technocracy now enjoy in local urban politics.[6]

These contradictions in urban struggles are very real; they are not insurmountable. The position of public sector employees is ambiguous, but the forces operating on them have also a radicalising effect. Many of the technocracy's occupations have come to assume the features of increasing subordination and regimentation, a process reinforced by state actions to deal with the fiscal crisis. The Québec Teachers' Union, in spite of all its shortcomings, has injected a class analysis into its political actions as its confrontations with the government have become more conflictual. It was the public sector's conflict with the Québec government that sparked the general strike in 1972, while it was the construction workers who led the walkout in the private sector. Although the ruling class may have succeded in imposing austerity in New York for the time being, they have not succeded in doing so everywhere. Strikes in the public sector have continued, and have been forming links however tentative between struggles in the workplace and struggles in the community. Transport workers in Montréal have consistently received the support of the Montréal Citizens' Movement, which tried to organise a direct action campaign against the announced fare hike in 1975, with the support of the maintenance employees and bus drivers who had just been on strike, and whose victories were used to justify the fare increase. Support for the teachers in the 1976 negotiations with the government was more widespread among parents than it had been four years ago.

Today is not the only period in which links were attempted and made between struggles on various fronts. Municipal strikes in Montréal in 1943 were an important part of the working class offensive in the early 1940s that led to the welfare state. As far back as the 1890s the Knights of Labour had set up district assemblies open to skilled and unskilled labourers, the unemployed and the wives of working men. In their programme they advanced measures that dealt not only with working conditions but with the whole gamut of social life: the establishment of a progressive income tax, night schools, better libraries and other recreational services, accident insurance, the abolition of child labour, etc. The decline of the Knights of Labour parallelled the rise of the American Federation of Labour and its penetration into Montréal. Although the AFL served well the interests of the skilled craft workers whom it organised, it undercut the attempts of the Knights of Labour to effect a unity among all sections of the working class. This reformist thrust of the AFL was repeated in the 1930s as it resisted attempts by the CIO to organise industrial workers.

The history of union struggles is no more nor less reformist than that of urban struggles, and reflects the ambiguity which workers' struggles have shared in part with the claims of today's technocracy. Each wave of working class struggles has historically occurred in reaction to capital as it destroyed previous forms of social life integrating new masses of people into capitalist social relations. Although the struggles emerged around the new and brutal conditions of each successive stage, the harshness of each era was measured against what must have appeared as the relatively easier life of its predecessor. Urban life in Montréal during the first part of the twentieth century was a very violent and uprooting experience for the rural migrants that formed its working class, much as the experience of industrialisation was violent and uprooting for the British working class a century earlier. In each case voices were raised denouncing the existing order and offering some vision that went beyond it, but the dominant response remained confined within a critique in terms of the past, finding its counterpart in practice in the defense of certain privileged sections of the working class, a process which capital played on to keep the workers divided. Prime Minister King was a master at this process, advocating as early as 1903 a policy of buying off the conservative union leadership while repressing its more militant wing. Ultimately such working class reformism rested on capital's ability to integrate new groups of workers into the wage market, who could then be played off against each other. As monopoly capital succeeds in creating a universal market this process is reaching its limits. In the sixties it was the reformist demands of the working class that emerged in both the workplace and the community which produced the current crisis and gave it its particular twist. Ironically, the very combination of factors that produced the fiscal crisis has made it difficult for the establishment to find a way out through traditional reformist tactics. This is not to deny that part of the conservative counterattack has been to play off different sections of the working class against each other: monopoly sector workers against those in the competitive sector, public employees against state clients. Nonetheless, this policy no longer rests on the same material basis, which is reflected in the longer term strategy capital is being forced to adopt: managed crisis, the restructuring of the state, a reimposition of austerity and the reduction of aspirations, planned growth according to the priorities of capital.

These same changed material circumstances have also made it possible for the working class to forge more durable alliances between its different sections than it has in the past, developing a strategy that would go beyond traditional reformist practice. The history of recent urban struggles indicates that the victory or defeat of the working class will depend on its ability to do so. The significance of its new situation and internal composition is that the demands of the revolutionary option are so clearly posed. The links between struggles in the industrial and social factory must be made, and in a way that presents a united working class front against capital. Opposition to the restructuring of the state must be raised in a way that joins the themes of equality and popular control. The working class must face its own internal contradictions; and by doing so it engages itself in the revolutionary dialectic. The occupation of factories in Portugal in 1975 forced the workers' committees to come to grips with their own contradictions, not least of which was the machoist attitudes toward women workers. That dynamic is revolutionary. Men forced to confront their own sexism and understand its origins would be more likely to challenge domination in other areas. The significance of urban struggles is that they raise these questions in spite of the possibility of class cooptation, yet they raise them in large part because the transformations in social life have placed them on the agenda. The question, as Cottereau has posed it, is whether the undermining of the nuclear family will lead to a more fundamental transformation, or more generally, whether "the questioning of current urban planning will join up with movements of a generalised refusal directed against the programming of all activities?"[7]

Urban struggles have therefore opened up a new and important moment in the class struggle. For capital, success in restructuring the city will mark an important step in its attempt to manage the fiscal crisis on its own behalf, coopting the ecological critique which forms an important part of current urban movements. The state capitalist city, as it has been called, will involve regionalised political structures, more centralised fiscal control, tighter social discipline, increased taxes, greater urban planning and ordered growth in order to harmonize the circulation of capital with the need for social control. Ecology is a handy metaphor for this purpose, since it can be used to legitimate the reimposition of austerity in the name of unavoidable limits to growth. The truth in the assertion hides the fact that austerity is no longer a social necessity, while the limits are the parameters of capital's priorities. Against this project stands the revolutionary conception of the socialist city, which heralds nothing more or less than a new project of civilisation: the democratic control of all social life, an end to commodity fetishism, the subordination of technology to people's needs and control, common ownership of the wealth of the community, the abolition of the state, a vast increase in work-free time, support for self-initiated activity. In this project the city holds out the promise of finally reconciling humanity with its habitat that is contained in the same ecological image which capital tries to subvert to its ends. The city will no longer be one pole of a dichotomy—to the country, for example, a source alternately of degradation and liberation—just as the social relations between the men and women who live in it will no longer be marked by a repressive antagonism.[8]

The socialist urban project represents, therefore, a refusal to choose within the constraints of capitalism, opening up the possibility of new forms of social relations based on the democratic organisation of social life. Cities can be placed both of dwellings and gardens, of mystery and security, of community and individuality, just as schools can be places of freedom and learning, just as each sex can recognize the other which cohabits within. To reach that point all citizens must control the organisation of space, the provision of housing, the ordering of transport, the learning process in the schools, and the social definition of our sexuality. Once again, although this time in the guise of the urban question, the choice posed ever since the First World War presents itself as one between socialism and barbarism. Yet the socialist project raised by urban struggles not only poses an alternative to capital; it also poses one to traditional working class practices of the social-democratic or communist stripe. Raised in the form of a new revolutionary strategy which finds expression in autonomous and democratic working class organisations, its realisation is indispensable to the socialist transformation of urban life. There is, of course, no guarantee that these practices will be realised. Capital's options are far from exhausted. Yet the material transformations in society have introduced these practices into the realm of the possible and the practicable just as they have done for the demands of the socialist project itself. The irony is that the historical possibility may never become reality, but subverted instead into a new project of domination. Whether the revolutionary project does become reality is ultimately a question of praxis, of the capacity of human beings through struggle with their oppression to change the world, politics in its most fundamental sense. Within this realm of praxis theoretical reflection has some role, for it can inform our strategic choices and so help us arrive at the point where the future is no longer a reproduction of the past. Indeed, part of past failures to carry through the revolutionary project had to do with the very conception of that project itself; while much of our current dilemma stems from our failure to come to grips with that tradition, which now acts as a brake on our capacity to conceive of an alternative social order. It would be useful, therefore, before exploring some of the strategic options of socialist urban politics to analyse more fully the nature of the socialist project which urban struggles have raised.

Libertarian socialism: the material and political possibilities

THE REVOLUTIONARY PROJECT to which contemporary urban struggles point bears little resemblance to current socialist practice. To many it would appear utopian, for this project implies a society where no state exists, where people interact freely to determine how they live, where people's basic needs are satisfied independently of money, where goods and services are freely exchanged between people, where human energy is directed to exploring our creative potential in an atmosphere of mutual aid. This is the original communist project, articulated by many long before Marx sharpened its focus by placing it at the heart of the material contradictions of capitalism. Bohemian rebels of the fifteenth century spoke of the future society for which they fought as that time where

> "no king shall reign nor any lord rule on earth, there shall be no serfdom, all interests and taxes shall cease, nor shall any man force another to do anything, because all shall be equal, brothers and sisters."[9]

More than five hundred years later Spanish anarchists were developing similar themes. At the national congress of the million-strong CNT (National Confederation of Labour) in 1936 they "opened the most important discussion on the nature of a libertarian communist society to ever occupy a major working-class organisation." The vision they elaborated contained much that they had already put into practice in the Asturian miners' insurrection of 1934 and, faithful to their tradition, embraced the totality of human experience. The revolutionary society would be based on communal organisations that would retain political and economic sovereignty. Resources would be allocated based on people's needs. Money would be abolished, as would the state and all punitive institutions. New forms of social living would be encouraged: free love, nudism, vegetarian diets, libertarian forms of education and child-rearing.[10]

Such visions are quickly dismissed as unrealistic, yet compared to the prevailing realtiy, then or now, what could be more realistic and life-enhancing? Is it not absurd that people should starve because they lack money to buy food? Is it not ridiculous that some people should own the land on this planet? Is it not outrageous that women should be regarded as the possessions of men? Is it not unrealistic that some should command while others toil? In our moments of lucidity, have we not all experienced the realisation that happiness has very little to do with owning and possessing; and yet so much of our daily lives is organised around this principle. In a society based on production for exchange, money does mediate social relations to the point where living without it seems inconceivable. Under capitalism, indeed it is; and yet how much more logical it would be to organise production according to the needs and uses which human beings would together decide as the most appropriate. How much more useful would it be to distribute the necessities of life freely so as to enable us to get on with the really important matters of loving and growing, playing and creating. How much easier that process would be were we able to govern our social relationships, from earliest childhood, on solidarity and autonomy.

Social life under capitalism proceeds, as we have seen, according to a very different logic, a logic of domination that is the antithesis of the social order contained in the vision of libertarian socialism. Because that social order can only emerge out of the struggles of men and women for their own liberation, it cannot be described in the manner in which an engineer would draw up a blueprint for the construction of a factory. Nonetheless, there are certain features of that alternative society that can be envisaged. Human beings would group themselves in small units at their places of work and residence. These units would take those decisions governing the organisation of work and community life that would not require the intervention of other groups. For decisions that would require wider participation and discussion, these basic groups would elect delegates to local councils, who in turn would elect delegates to regional councils, each delegate being subject to recall by the body that elected then. These bodies would then take decisions that affect the wider community. For example, regional or even international federations of these basic community groupings would take decisions concerning investment in future energy resources, yet the organisation of work required to deliver this energy could easily be subject to the decisions of the workers involved. General principles might be elaborated regionally for the location of schools, yet their actual running would be left to local community groups. Obviously, in such a society the wealth produced, like the means of production of this wealth, would belong to everybody. The market would cease to determine what goods are produced and how they are distributed. Instead the production and consumption of goods would be planned by human beings acting and debating together through sovereign political units that they would effectively control. Arbitrary authority and hierarchy would cease to be the organising principles of social life in the work place and the community, as responsibility for all facets of social life would be equally shared by those involved in different activities. As exchange value no longer determined the social relations of production, social relations in other areas of human life would be freed from the constraints to which capitalism has subjected them. People could stop regarding each other as rivals, stop judging each other in terms of performance, and begin to accept and support each other as potential friends in a global community based on freely exchanged solidarity.

By any rational standard, such a society appears immeasurably preferable to the social order we must endure today. It is not surprising, therefore, that the dominant class has developed an extensive coercive and ideological apparatus, in the workplace, the state and throughout civil society, to maintain the existing order. The very weight of contemporary social life, and the thrust of capital's legitimating activities, are designed to ensure the prevailing order by ruling out in people's hearts and minds the possibility of an alternative one; and the success of capital's efforts can be measured by the extent to which people dismiss such alternative visions as impractical. In this capital has been helped by the experience of Soviet Russia and subsequent socialist experiments, where attempts at creating alternative social orders have only resulted in the extension of some of the worst features of capitalism; the reinforcement of the power of the state, increased social control and regimentation of the working class, the development of bureaucracy and hierarchy in even greater proportions, dull uniformity and the atomisation of social life. Much of Soviet social life, as we shall see, had to do with the Leninist conception of the revolution that the majority of bolsheviks shared, a conception that was linked to the organisational model of the Bolshevik Party. In this conception, it was the vanguard party of professional revolutionaries which represented the true interests of the proletariat, such that every time the Bolsheviks were faced with policy options of centralising or decentralising state power they opted for the former. The Supreme Council of National Economy set up in December 1917 to plan economic life was seen as a replacement for workers' control. At the first All-Russian Congress of Trade Unions held in January, 1918, the factory committees which had played such an important role in the Russian revolution were transformed by the Bolsheviks into union organs, which themselves were regarded eventually as organs of the socialist state, responsible for organising production. In practice this meant that the trade unions were called upon to discipline the working class. Lenin himself, fascinated with the techniques of Taylorism, asserted in April, 1918 that "today, the Revolution demands, in the interests of socialism, that the masses *unquestioningly obey the single will* of the leaders of the labour process." Although the centralising features of the Bolshevik Revolution have often been justified as a response to the Civil War and the failure of revolution in Germany, it ought to be remembered that these practices were implemented before those events had occurred.[11]

Today the Bolshevik tradition weighs heavily upon the working class, equating socialism with centralised planning and bureaucratic monopoly and making the conception of a revolutionary alternative to capitalism appear utopian indeed. For this very reason it is important to bear in mind that the Bolshevik tradition was not the only one in the history of socialist movements; and that the particular form that socialism took in Russia was closely linked to the Leninist conception of the revolutionary project. As early as 1904 Rosa Luxemburg had criticized Lenin's prescriptions on the need for a centralised party in the following terms:

> "It is a mistake to believe that it is possible to substitute 'provisionally' the absolute power of a Central Committee (acting somehow by' tacit delegation') for the yet unrealizable rule of the majority of conscious workers in the party, and in this way replace the open control of the working masses over the party organs with the reverse control by the Central Committee over the revolutionary proletariat."

She went on to point out, in a rather prophetic passage, that the "*attempt to exorcise opportunism by means of a scrap of paper may turn out to be extremely harmful—not to opportunism but to the socialist movement*" and ended her critique with that ringing admonition:

> "Let us speak plainly. Historically, the errors committed by a truly revolutionary movement are infinitely more fruitful than the infallibility of the cleverest Central Committee."[12]

Unfortunately the German revolution of 1918-19 did not succeed and Rosa Luxemburg paid for that failure with her life. In Russia the Bolsheviks ensconced themselves in the seats of power vacated by the Czarist régime and proceeded to impose their hegemony on the international working class movement, thereby attempting to bury, as effectively as capital, alternative revolutionary traditions. They could not bury them completely, any more than capital could, without annihilating the proletariat itself; yet the overwhelming presence of these two social orders has made the conception of an alternative more difficult and increased the doubts many entertain regarding such a possibility. These doubts usually express two generalized disbeliefs: one, that a libertarian socialist society is materially, technically possible, the other, that it is politically possible for people to govern themselves. The historical irony of this situation lies in the fact that whereas previously the working class has demonstrated its capacity for autonomous action, its ultimate failure to carry through a libertarian socialist revolution lay with the relative underdevelopment of productive forces such that scarcity remained a dominant concern. Today, on the other hand, where the forces of production have developed to the point where scarcity can technically be dispensed with, the weight of previous failures, together with the force of the existing order, lead people to wonder whether in fact people can run their own affairs. In his evaluation of the Spanish anarchist movement, Bookchin suggested that even had the generals been defeated in 1936, many anarchists considered that Spain's narrow technological base ruled out the possibility of a truly libertarian society. The material want it engendered would have reinforced capitalist social relations and denied workers the free time necessary "to transform the totality of society". This limitation was reflected in the puritan injunctions that circumscribed the Spanish anarchists' celebration of conviviality, a conviviality based nonetheless on the factory, and the scarcity and toil which underpinned it. Given these limitations, their revolutionary activity was all the more audacious and their legacy all the more significant for revealing

> "how far proletarian socialism could press toward an ideal of freedom on moral premises alone. Given a favorable conjunction of events, a revolutionary workers' and peasants' movement had indeed been able to make a libertarian revolution, collectivize industry, and create historically unprecedented possibilities for the management of the factories and land by those who worked them. Indeed, the revolutionary act of crushing the military rebellion in key cities of Spain, of taking direct control of the economy, even if under the mere compulsion of external events, had acted as a powerful spiritual impulse in its own right, appre-

ciably altering the attitudes and views of less committed sectors of the oppressed. Thus proletarian socialism had pushed Spanish society beyond any materially delimiting barriers into a utopian experiment of astonishing proportions—into what Burnett Bolloten has aptly described as a 'far-reaching social revolution. . . more profound in some respects than the Bolshevik revolution in its early stages. . .' Not only had workers established control over industry and peasants formed free collectives on the land, but in many instances even money had been abolished and the most radical communistic precepts had replaced bourgeois concepts of work, distribution, and administration."[13]

That the Spanish anarchists succeeded, under conditions of material scarcity, to such an extend in their efforts to establish an anarchist or libertarian communist society ought to demystify the notion that the working class is incapable of autonomous revolutionary political action. By looking at the history of revolution from below, of which Spanish anarchism was but one example, we might open up once again the belief in the possibility of a revolutionary alternative and widen our understanding of the nature of that alternative, as well as the dynamic and significance of contemporary struggles. Before doing that, however, it is equally important to examine the changed material conditions of today's society, to see to what extent and in what manner the expanded wealth and technological transformations have laid the basis for a truly libertarian society; and in that way too reestablish the belief in the possibility of a revolutionary alternative.

The libertarian socialist project has little to do with centralised planning, which tends to reinforce many of the structural characteristics of the commodity/money system. In the centrally planned economies of contemporary socialist societies key economic decisions are taken by state planners instead of large corporations, as in capitalist economies. The consequences in each case are the same. Workers have no control over what is produced or the manner in which work is organised. The criteria for allocating resources, even in centrally planned economies, retain the form of generalised measures much like money in capitalist economies. In the libertarian socialist project, planning is decentralised, consisting of coordinated economic activities decided upon by basic units of workers and consumers. The criteria for determining the production and distribution of goods would no longer be exchange value but use value and the satisfaction of basic human needs. For money to no longer mediate social relations implies the free distribution of goods and services, both to liberate people from the necessity of work and to free human energies from the antagonistic interactions which the struggle to survive under capitalism engenders. The expansion of wealth unleashed by the scientific revolution and the technological advances to which it has led has made this free distribution of goods, and most certainly those relating to the basic necessities of life, an immediate possibility. Already certain goods in society are provided free of charge—water, for example—and in times of emergencies other goods, like food and shelter, are too. In previous eras, droughts and floods would have wreaked their natural havoc, which gives some measure of the wealth we command today; yet under normal conditions we subordinate this readily available wealth to the dictates of the commodity market economy. Indeed, under capitalism science itself has become transformed into capital, while the technological transformations it has engendered have been used to reinforce the domination of capital in the labour process. At the same time, the increasing automation of the labour process and the growing role of science in the cheapening of production has drastically reduced the component of labour in the production process and thereby ruptured, to all intents and purposes, the relation between wages and prices. Under such conditions there are no technical reasons for maintaining scarcity and drudgery, however necessary they may be to the continued domination of capital.

The growing importance of science-based production and use of automation has reduced the size of work-teams in the basic productive units such that

> "the basis for the organisation of people as producers probably already exists in the work teams of a modern economy. In a pit, in a unit of a factory, in a hospital, in a school, on a railway, people are naturally combined together in a work team by the requirements of the job they are doing. From time to time they are given specific objects of work, determined by some outside authority or by a manager or owner. Such teams, even as they are today, provide in a certain sense the basic units in socially linked production processes and other economic activities that encompass the whole world. A form of more direct control over the economic apparatus could emerge if these work teams operated not merely as work teams but also as small scale 'parliaments of the people' deliberating on the manner and the direction of their economic activity. And, in fact, the struggles that are proliferating in the name of 'workers' control' are evidence of people moving in this direction."[14]

Obviously these basic work-teams are quite capable of taking many decisions related to the production process, and are in many ways more qualified than the planners and managers of the modern corporation and state apparatus. In many respects the current forms of centralised decision-making are highly inefficient and productive of severe imbalances in social life, but persist because they are governed by the rationality "of producing commodities (exchange values) for the market" instead of "producing things for use". Under the rationality of the market money functions to coordinate economic activity. There are, however, other ways of coordinating economic activity, most notably through the

> "establishment of manifold information flows between consumers and producers. For example, it is technically possible for individuals and groups of consumers to communicate their requirements through computerised information exchanges; to which producers would communicate their availabilities and from which they would receive suitably processed information about demands. This would not be barter, but a form of reaching understandings, a new model of social relations to replace the market."[15]

Today, of course, information tends to be centrally monopolised because of the competition between large corporations and the need of capital and the bureaucratic state to maintain their domination over the working class. In a society based on workers' control and governed by the rationality of production for use, the incentive would exist for the decentralisation of information, a process made possible by the development of computer technology. Already,

> "the memory and analytical capacity of the computer could be made available to all and universal electronic communications, linking anyone to anyone, are becoming technically and cost-wise feasible."[16]

Money works as a coordinator of economic decisions in a market economy because production for exchange requires an abstract expression of exchange relations. Similarly in centrally planned economies generalised indices of input/output serve to allocate economic resources. In an economy based on production for use, free distribution and democratic control, the criteria used for the allocation of resources will have to find a much more concrete expression. Democratic planning is dependent upon people's concrete specifications of their use needs, which in turn "will require constant analysis of complex patterns of interrelated productive systems, massive up-to-date data, detailed modelling and much else that before the electronic revolution it would have been possible to do only crudely and slowly." The capacity of computers to store vast amounts of information in incredibly small spaces and to put that information at people's disposal in incredibly short time periods makes it technically feasible to deal with the problems posed by democratic planning. Arrangements freely negotiated by contracting parties could be continuously evaluated to make sure they continued to be equitable. The future implications of current investment policies could be clearly delineated so that people could make a more informed and rational choice between policy alternatives in accordance with generally elaborated social priorities. Computers are used today by the corporations and the state to formulate policy alternatives or determine consumer demand, but the parameters governing policy options are severely circumscribed by the dictates of capitalist accumulation. Nowhere is this clearer than in current policies on energy resources. This is not to suggest that all problems will disappear in democratically planned economies, but the decentralisation of decision-making, coupled with the use of computer technology, would enable people to zero in on the real subjects and causes of disagreement by eliminating those that arise from class stratification and monopoly of information.

Of course there are fundamental political questions that will have to be dealt with relating to efficiency, fairness, the demarcation of freely provided goods and services, the problem of transition from market to non-market economies, and many others. If these issues are not confronted, then the computers will prove to be of little value, since the information flows which computers provide are useful only to the extent that information is socially defined and organised. These questions assume their full importance only to the extent that they are raised by people in the context of a radically different socio-economic structure marked by democratic planning and production for use. The question of the technical possibility of a libertarian society thus leads inevitably to the questions of power, of politics and of social revolution.[17]

Clearly the material basis for a libertarian socialist society exists today, but people will first have to overthrow the shackles of domination inherent in the contemporary social orders of monopoly and state capitalism. The dominant classes will not cede their powers without a fight and the people will not wrest theirs without a revolution. The very nature of this revolutionary alternative, rooted in the process of control from below, suggests that the only form of revolutionary politics compatible with this social alternative is autonomous working class action. Yet just as the realisation that this social alternative is a material possibility contributes to the revolutionary process by making it clearer to people where they are heading, so too does the confidence that comes from the conviction that revolution from below is a political possibility. The analysis of that revolutionary tradition should help strengthen that conviction.

NOTES:

(1.)   G. Barker, J. Penney, W. Seecombe, *High Rise and Superprofits*, Kitchener, Ontario, 1973; Leonard Lessard, op. cit., p. 257.

(2.)   S. Rowbotham, *Women, Resistance and Revolution*, Penguin, London, 1974; R. Sennett and J. Cobb, *The Hidden Injuries of Class*, N.Y., 1973.

(3.)   Montano, *op. cit.*, p. 33-5; Cherki, Wieviorka, *op. cit.*, p. 1795.

(4.)   Demac, Mattera, *op. cit.*, p. 130, 135-6; Taylor, *op. cit.*, p. 100-13; Mollenkopf, "The Fragile Giant. . .", *op. cit.*, p. 30; O'Connor, *op. cit.*; Deaton, *op. cit.*, p. 47-8.

(5.)   Markusen, *op. cit.*, p. 58-62; E. Cherki, D. Mehl, "Quelles luttes? quels acteurs? quels résultats?" in Autrement, No. 6, Sept., 1976, p. 11-12.

(6.)   Meynaud, Léveillée, *op. cit.*, p. 144-52; R.C. Hill, "State capitalism and the urban fiscal crisis in the United States" in *International Journal of Urban and Regional Research*, vol. 1, No. 1, p. 96.

(7.)   Cottereau, *op. cit.*, p. 793 (my translation—S.S.); Pelletier, Vaillancourt, *op. cit.*, cahier IV, p. 195, cahier III, p. 50, cahier I, p. 47-51; Thompson, *op. cit.*; Copp, *op. cit.*; Schecter, op. cit., p. 393; O'Connor, *op. cit.*; Editorial Collective, *Zerowork, Political Materials 1*, op. cit., p. 1-6; P. Mailer, *Portugal, The Impossible Revolution?*, Montréal, 1977, p. 139.

(8.)   R.-C. Hill, "Fiscal Crisis and Political Struggle in the Decaying U.S. Central City", in *Kapitalistate*, 4-5, summer 1976, p. 42-8.

(9.)   The Taborite Chiliast Articles of 1420 cited in P. Anderson, *Passages from Antiquity to Feudalism*, London, 1974, p. 250, f 6.

(10.)   M. Bookchin, *The Spanish Anarchists: The Heroic Years 1868-1936*, N.Y., 1977, p. 4-5, 55-9, 270-1, 291-5.

(11.)   M. Brinton, *The Bolsheviks and Workers' Control*, Montréal, 1975, p. xi, xii, 22, 29-35, 38-41.

(12.)   R. Luxemburg, *Organisational Question of Social Democracy*, in M.-A. Waters (ed.), *Rosa Luxemburg Speaks*, N.Y., 1970, p. 120, 129-30.

(13.)   Bookchin, *op. cit.*, p. 308, and more generally, p. 307-12.

(14.)   Bodington, *op. cit.*, p. 150, also p. 115, 122-3, 176, 144; Braverman, *op. cit.*, chs. 7 and 8, especially p. 166-7.

(15.)   Bodington, *op. cit.*, p. 175-6, also p. 166-7, 185-6, 189-97.

(16.)   *Ibid.*, p. 166.

(17.)   *Ibid.*, p. 179-203.

CHAPTER THREE

REVOLUTION FROM BELOW: THE HISTORICAL EXPERIENCE

"On the Sunday afternoon, a march the like of which the city had rarely seen before, took to the streets of Budapest. Some put the number as high as two hundred thousand. In the Kerepesi Cemetery, where many of Hungary's most famous literary and political figures lie buried, speaker after speaker demanded to know why Laszlo Rajk had died innocent, and one of them, a fellow prisoner of Rajk, declared: 'We shall not forget!'

By the end of the day, members of the opposition just as much as leaders of the party were staggered by the fact that so many people had so easily been mobilised. As one of the intellectuals remarked later:

'It was then that we realised, that everybody realised, that this wasn't just an affair of a few communist intellectuals, but that everyone felt as strongly, the same way, against the régime.'

More than one person left with the opinion that 'perhaps if it had not rained, there would have been a revolution that day.'"[1]

"On May 28 **Diario de Lisboa** *carries a manifesto by the prostitutes of Lisbon (who work mainly in the dock area). After pointing out that they 'had to practice, illegally, what was the most ancient profession in the world' and that although their lives were generally considered 'easy' this was far from being the case, the manifesto went on to demand the creation of a union where 'free from all puritan pressures, they could discuss the problems of their class'. Their main concerns were their exploitation by pimps, the need to protect minors, the determination of a scale of charges, the promotion of a 'free pavement' aimed at 'developing tourism' and opposition to 'the scandalous activities of conservative colleagues who only practice in expensive nightclubs'. They offered their support to the MFA. For a period of a year, all ranks below that of lieutenant would only be charged half price.*

Some three weeks earlier **Diario de Lisboa** *had carried a manifesto of the 'Movement of Revolutionary Homosexuals'. They had been severely persecuted during the old regime, their bars and clubs being repeatedly raided. They now asked for an end to discrimination.*

These and other manifestos cause General Galvão de Melo, a member of the Junta, to bemoan the 'debasement of April 25th'. 'Our glorious revolution' he said, 'is turning into a movement of prostitutes and homosexuals'."[2]

Leninism vs. Social-Democracy: Russia and Germany

SINCE SO MUCH OF HISTORY tends to be written from the perspective of who won political power, we tend to forget the richness of the social process itself; and the conclusions we draw about the possibilities of ordering social life tend to be dominated by that perspective. Nowhere is this truer than in considerations dealing with the problem of revolution. The history of peasant jacqueries and working class insurrections that have failed to overthrow the dominant social order become grist for the mill of those who argue the impossibility of people ever carrying through the revolution to a successful conclusion. Even those instances of success, like the Russian Revolution, are used to justify this position, for without the historical agency of the revolutionary party, it is claimed, the Kerensky régime would not have been overthrown; while the subsequent degeneration of the Bolshevik Revolution is adduced as further evidence of the impossibility of the workers' themselves being able to govern society. What this reading of history tends to obscure is that the failure of the working class to overthrow oppressive social orders, or to carry through the democratic control of social life when it does, is to a large extent the fault of the working class parties themselves, even and often especially those that proclaim themselves the most revolutionary. Instead, the opposite conclusions are drawn. The class power of the bourgeoisie and its readiness to use violence to safeguard its interests, the lack of 'revolutionary consciousness' on the part of the working class, the need to coordinate workers' struggles all become arguments to justify the need for a revolutionary party, while the failure of previous such attempts is ascribed to unpropitious material conditions or an incorrect line. The social democratic reading of the historical experience is really much the same, only it turns the Leninist arguments around against the Leninists to justify the abandonment of all revolutionary efforts.

A deeper analysis of the history of working class movements would yield a considerably different picture. It was the workers themselves who unleashed revolutionary situations. Far from lacking 'revolutionary consciousness' they displayed an acute awareness of the interplay of social forces, made attempts to coordinate their forces and expressed a readiness to arm themselves. In the process they developed their own institutions, which not only became organs of revolutionary struggle but embryos of the future democratic, socialist order. In each case it was the social democratic or Leninist parties who, in the name of their correct assessment of the situation, hampered the workers' revolutionary efforts and crushed their autonomous institutions. The postmortems that inevitably followed led people further and further away from the possibility of autonomous working-class action, while a closer scrutiny of events reveals a much greater complexity that, without minimizing the difficulties of such a project, demands a rereading and a new understanding of the revolutionary process.

In many ways the best place to start with this rereading is the Russian Revolution itself, for it was the first socialist revolution and as such, marked indelibly the subsequent course of working class struggles. The Bolshevik seizure of state power occurred in October, 1917, but the revolution which toppled the Czarist régime transpired in the preceding February following a prolonged strike movement, in which autonomous working class organisations and unled and "unorganised" workers and mutineers played an important part. The Soviets which had first emerged in the 1905 uprising of Russian workers reappeared in February 1917 and following the formation of the Provisional Government, Factory Committees and Workers' Councils arose in every major industrial centre. As early as May the Mencheviks, who participated in the Provisional Government, had come out against the Factory Committees, arguing that "the control of industry was a task for the State" and suggesting that the Committees become "subordinate units in a state-wide network of trade unions". At that time and up until they themselves seized state power, the Bolsheviks supported the Factory Committees, since they saw them as key instruments in pushing the revolution to its completion and containing the capitalists whose cooperation would be needed subsequent to the seizure of state power. Besides, the Mencheviks controlled the trade unions. Yet even then the Bolsheviks did not equate socialism with workers' control expressed through their autonomous institutions, but rather reduced workers' control to functions of accountancy in a centralised state, which they always identified with the dictatorship of the proletariat.

On October 25, 1917 the Bolsheviks overthrew Kerensky's Provisional Government. On November 3 Pravda published Lenin's Draft Decree on Workers' Control which stipulated that the decision of the workers' elected delegates could be annulled by trade unions and congresses, and in enterprises of state importance the delegates were to be "answerable to the State for the maintenance of the strictest order and discipline and for the protection of property". In the decree finally adopted on November 14 by the Bolshevik dominated All-Russian Central Executive Committee of the Soviets and ratified by the Bolshevik government on the 15th, the Factory Committees were to be surbordinated to an All-Russian Council of Workers' Control, which did not emerge from the Factory Committees but which was imposed by the Bolshevik Party. The latter decided on the composition of the higher organs, which turned out to be dominated by the trade unions that the Bolsheviks now more easily controlled and were subsequently to integrate into the state apparatus. When the Factory Committees did try to coordinate their activities on a national level in the weeks following the October Revolution, the trade unions blocked all attempts to convoke a national congress. The Bolshevik sponsored All-Russian Council of Workers' Control "never really functioned at all." When it did meet once in November, 1917, the Bolshevik representatives made it clear that they regarded the Factory Committees as representative of particular interests that required subordination, while the Factory Committee movement spokesmen regarded them as sovereign institutions which should control production and then "establish coordination on a regional level".[3]

The workers, then, were not unaware of the need for coordination if the national economy were to function effectively and the revolution defended. For the Bolsheviks coordination meant the imposition of centralised control, which made the autonomous efforts of the working class at national coordination difficult. This difficulty was in turn seized on to justify a policy of centralised control, an argument onto which later were grafted others citing the civil war, backwardness, etc. In this version the workers emerge as lacking consciousness and needing to be organised, while in fact they demonstrated very clear consciousness and a capacity for autonomous organisation. As early as April, 1917 the workers indicated by their actions that they meant to go far beyond what the Provisional Government had conceded in terms of workers' control. At the Second Conference of the Petrograd region Factory Committees in August, 1917, the workers adopted a series of statutes which made the Committees de facto rulers in the factories in the name of "customary revolutionary right". At the Third Conference of Factory Committees in September, 1917, which opposed a government circular affirming that the right to hire and fire belonged to the employers,

> "a worker called Afinogenev asserted that 'all parties, not excluding the Bolsheviks, entice the workers with the promise of the Kingdom of God on earth a hundred years from now. . . We don't need improvement in a hundred years time, but now, immediately.'"[4]

In December, 1917 the Central Council of the Petrograd Factory Committees published their own manual on the implementation of workers' control. There they made it clear that they meant to take over management functions and exercise full control over all aspects of the production process, while the counter-manual produced by the Bolsheviks made it equally clear that workers' control had nothing to do with management except in so far as it meant the execution of nationally determined economic activities.[5]

According to some twisted logic it could be said that the workers' inability to resist the Bolsheviks' suppression of the movement for workers' control ultimately reflects the futility of the revolutionary project based on the autonomous action of the working class. There is a kernel of truth to the assertion, in the sense that revolution belongs to the realm of praxis, to the process whereby men and women create their own history and as such are ultimately responsible for their own actions. In that sense it is somewhat contradictory to argue that the Bolsheviks betrayed the Russian workers. On the other hand, it would be fallacious to argue, in the face of the evidence, that the workers were, or are, incapable of autonomous political action, and misleading to ignore the important role the Bolshevik Party played in curbing the revolutionary practice of the working class when in fact it could have helped to extend it. In that sense the obstacle to the revolutionary transformation of Russian society was not the workers' incapacity for autonomous revolutionary action but the Leninist conception of the revolutionary project.

In that conception, elaborated by Lenin in part as early as 1903 in *What Is To Be Done* ?, the proletariat was regarded as incapable of revolutionary consciousness and action whithout the leadership of a politically conscious vanguard party. The organisational structure of the party which emerged from this conception led to the separation between the Bolsheviks and the working masses upon whom they relied, a separation which the political conditions of Czarist Russia reinforced, but which resulted after October, 1917 in the inability of the Russian working class to control the party. The conception of class consciousness upon which this organisational model rested—with its emphasis on the professional revolutionary, armed with the correct, revolutionary theory that so easily led the party to substitute itself for the working class—also underlay the Leninist equation of the revolution with the overthrow of the bourgeoisie, the seizure of state power and the nationalisation of the means of production, rather than with the transformation of capitalist relations of production which only workers' control could realise.[6]

This conception of the revolutionary project was to destroy not only the revolution but the party itself, shared as it was even by those like Trotsky who, years earlier, had warned the party of the dangers of substitutionism which such a model presaged. As early as April, 1918, when the party was discussing the issue of workers' control, some communists warned that failure to allow the proletariat to find its own way to the socialist organisation of labour will lead not to socialism, which can only "be set up by the proletariat itself", but to "state capitalism". The response of the party was to remove publication of the journal in which these comments appeared from the control of these party militants. This was followed by the suppression of anarchist journals and Lenin's defence of state capitalism. In 1919 Trotsky proposed the militarisation of labour, which Lenin supported. At the Ninth Party Congress in 1920 the party opted for one-man management and reinforced the powers of the highest and most restricted party organs. By the Tenth Party Congress in 1921 strikes had broken out in the Petrograd area and the Kronstadt sailors were up in arms against the Party's dictatorship. The Bolsheviks crushed the revolt, voted the New Economic Policy and banned factions within the party, giving the Central Committee secret disciplinary powers. Even those with severe misgivings voted for these measures, trapped as they were by the primacy they accorded the party over the working class itself. This conception of revolutionary organisation had very deep roots, reflecting

"the unrecognised influence of bourgeois ideology, even on the minds of those who were relentlessly seeking to overthrow bourgeois society. The concept that society must necessarily be divided into 'leaders' and 'led', the notion that there are some born to rule while others cannot really develop beyond a certain stage have from time immemorial been the tacit assumption of every ruling class in history."[7]

Precisely because the Leninist tradition serves to reinforce this belief it is important to demystify it and confront it with the reality of working class experience and alternative revolutionary traditions. One such tradition was that represented by Rosa Luxemburg, and only her "death prevented her from developing and defending her leadership of an alternative, revolutionary Marxist tradition against other claimants".[8] This tradition was reflected in part in the critique of the Russian Revolution which she wrote from her prison cell in Germany in 1917-18. In it she criticised and condemned the suppression of democratic institutions, the refusal to convoke universal popular elections, the limitation of the right to vote, the destruction of the rights to free speech and assembly, and the use of terror. Luxemburg also criticised the Bolsheviks for the grounds on which they justified these measures, not because she was committeed to an abstract, formal democracy, but because she was committed to a conception of revolution in which the action of the masses played the central role. Hence she pointed out that

> "Freedom only for the supporters of the government, only for the members of one party—however numerous they may be—is no freedom at all. Freedom is always and exclusively freedom for the one who thinks differently.";

but her defence of these freedoms rested ultimately on the fact that without them, "the rule of the broad mass of the people is entirely unthinkable." When Trotsky justified the dissolution of the Constituent Assembly by a general theory about the "cumbersome mechanism of democratic institutions" which makes them unable to keep up with political changes in a revolutionary period, Luxemburg pointed out that the historical experience of England's Long Parliament, the French Revolutions and even the Fourth Russian Duma contradicted this assertion, precisely because "the living movement of the masses" subjected these representative bodies to "their unending pressure." Her very description of the revolution as creating

> "by its glowing heat that delicate, vibrant, sensitive political atmosphere in which the waves of popular feeling, the pulse of popular life, work for the moment on the representative bodies in most wonderful fashion"

indicates the difference which separated Luxemburg from the Bolsheviks. As she herself pointed out,

> "The tacit assumption underlying the Lenin-Trotsky theory of the dictatorship is this: that the socialist transformation is something for which a ready-made formula lies completed in the pocket of the revolutionary party, which needs only to be carried out energetically in

practice. This is, unfortunately—or perhaps fortunately—not the case. Far from being a sum of ready-made prescriptions which have only to be applied, the practical realization of socialism as an economic, social and juridical system is something which lies hidden in the mists of the future. What we possess in our program is nothing but a few main signposts which indicate the general direction in which to look for the necessary measures, and the indications are mainly negative in character. . . The negative, the tearing down, can be decreed; the building up, the positive, cannot. New territory. A thousand problems. Only experience is capable of correcting and opening new ways. Only unobstructed, effervescing life falls into a thousand new forms and improvisations, brings to light creative force, itself corrects all mistaken attempts. The public life of countries with limited freedom is so poverty-stricken, so miserable, so rigid, so unfruitful, precisely because, through the exclusion of democracy, it cuts off the living sources of all spiritual riches and progress. (Proof: the year 1905 and the months from February to October 1917.) There it was political in character; the same thing applies to economic and social life also. The whole mass of the people must take part in it. Otherwise, socialism will be decreed from behind a few official desks by a dozen intellectuals."[9]

Whatever her strictures on the Bolsheviks, Luxemburg remained fiercely critical of the Social Democrats, whom she regarded as merely the other side of the coin without even the Bolsheviks' saving grace of having dared to act. Her conception of a majority was not that of the SPD (the German Social-Democratic Party), defined numerically by the counting of ballots, but the product of mass action. In the German Revolution of 1918-19 that was the conception she opposed to the SPD government who she knew, from years of struggle, had not only resisted mass action, but behind their elaborate justification of their 'attentiste' policy, had also abandoned the revolution itself.[10]

On November 3, 1918 the sailors at the Kiel Naval Base had revolted and within days delegations of workers and sailors had spread the revolution to other ports. Workers' and Soldiers' Councils sprang up in most major German cities. The Independent Socialists and the Spartacists (led by Liebknecht and Luxemburg) called a general strike in Berlin for November 9, while the SPD Leaders negotiated with the Imperial government. While the forces of both reaction and revolution tried to plan strategy, the mass uprisings all over Germany finally determined the situation and forced the resignation of the Imperial government and the abdication of the emperor. Throughout the ensuing months, however, the SPD refused to recognize the importance of the revolutionary impulses that surged up from below and sought by all means to channel this initiative into the narrow limits of bourgeois democracy. Characteristically, the SPD leadership did not even want to proclaim a republic without first convoking a Constituent Assembly. It was only when one of the leaders returned to the Reichstag for a bowl of soup following the transfer of office, and found himself confronted by a throng assembled outside that he proclaimed "almost as an after-thought" the republic, a proclamation which drew down upon him the rage of the new chancellor, Ebert. Worker and soldier demonstrations did not cease. Arms circulated freely. Left-wing forces took over the Berlin police headquarters and installed one of their membres, Eichhorn, as its president, and occupied newspaper offices. On November 10, 3000 delegates assembled to form the Executive Council of the Berlin Workers' and Soldiers' Councils.

The Spartakus group, through their newspaper *Rote Fahne* which Rosa Luxemburg edited, proposed a series of radical measures, including the dissolution of parliamentary institutions and their re-placement by elected Workers' and Soldiers' Councils which would exercise political and economic sovereignty. The SPD, on the other hand, had just negotiated the formation of a government of People's Commissioners with the Independent Socialists (USPD) and pushed for its ratification. The irony of the situation was that the very body which the Spartakists defended as the political basis of a socialist republic refused to accord the Spartakist leaders seats on the Berlin Executive Council and approved the formation of the provisional government. This situation was repeated a little over a month later at the National Congress of Workers' and Soldiers' Councils, which refused Luxemburg and Liebknecht the right to speak and voted its approval for general elections to a National Assembly.[11]

The contradiction confronting the Spartakist group was seized upon by the Social Democrats to distort the position of Luxemburg and her colleagues even more and to elaborate a historical defence of Social Democracy as only a response to the democratic wishes of the masses. If the Spartakists persisted in their opposition after the resounding defeat they experienced at the National Congress of Workers' and Soldiers' Councils, it only showed that they were Bolsheviks at heart. Indeed, when the uprising broke out in January, 1919, in which Spartakus participated over Luxemburg's objections, the SPD attacked them on these grounds, singling out Luxemburg and Liebknecht for endangering the achievements of the revolution and strangling "with their dirty fists the right of free expression". The SPD, on the other hand, as true democrats, were only carrying out the expressed wishes of the workers. This argument formed the core of subsequent social-democratic ideol-ogy, justifying the reformist and at times anti-proletarian character of social democratic governments on the grounds that such policies only reflect the workers' own desires. The implication at the end of this argument is, once again, the impossibility of the workers' ever carrying through their own revolution. After all, when offered the choice in Germany in 1918, did they not throw it away?

In one sense, the answer is yes, and no one knew that better than Luxemburg, which is why she opposed the uprising proclaimed by the parties on the left on January 6:

> "Only the week before she had written: 'It would be a criminal error to seize power now. The German working class is not ready for such an act. . . It is useless, it is childish to overthrow it (the Ebert government) and replace it by another if the masses are not ready and able to organize Germany.' Agitation and propaganda were both well short of their goals. Even if this uprising succeeded—and Luxemburg was sure it would not—it could be sustained only by Leninist policies of terror."[12]

Precisely because she saw that "the battle for Socialism can only be carried on by the masses", Luxemburg did not hesitate to confront the German working class with its historic responsibility. In her analysis of the Russian Revolution she pointed out at the end that everything that happened in Russia eventually came round to "the failure of the German proletariat" to act. Yet no one knew better than Rosa the debilitating effect that years of stodgy SPD leadership, with its radical rhetoric and conservative practice, had on the German working class. Hence when Luxemburg supported participation in the elections to the Constituent Assembly at the founding congress of the KPD (German Communist Party) at the end of December, 1918, she did so not as a tactical adjustment but out of profound recognition of the import of the decision by the National Congress of Workers' and Soldiers' Councils. Her acceptance of the decision of the workers stemmed not only from her understanding of the point the workers had reached but also from her conception of the revolution as fundamentally a long process, and long because of its democratic essence. Hence she had meant what she had told the KPD congress:

> "Spartakus will never undertake to govern other than through the clear and unmistakable wish of the great majority of the proletarian masses of Germany, and never without their conscious agreement with the ideas, aims, and methods of Spartakus."

It was precisely because Rosa's concept of revolution was anchored in the masses that once the January uprising occurred, she and the other Communist leaders refused to abandon them. Radek, Lenin's plenipotentiary to the KPD, had urged the party to pull out of the revolt and cut their losses, in view of the inadequate organisation of the revolutionary forces. Luxemburg argued on the other hand that "it was a matter of honour for the revolution to ward off this attack with all its energy". In her view, the leadership had failed the masses, but to abandon them now would only sow greater confusion and postpone even longer the day when "a future victory will blossom from this 'defeat'" In the end, it was the masses who "are crucial, they are the rock on which the final victory of revolution will be built."[13]

This reliance on the masses was not ill-placed, for the masses did in fact act throughout this revolutionary period; and had the SPD leadership proved revolutionary instead of reactionary, the workers' manifest capacity for autonomous revolutionary action would have grown instead of shrunk. After all, it was the workers and sailors of Kiel who launched the revolt in November and the SPD Leader Noske who was dispatched to maintain order. At the meeting of workers and soldiers in Berlin on November 10, the delegates did not only ratify the provisional government; they also called for a National Congress of Workers' and Sailors' Councils, reflecting thereby the dialectical possibilities of the situation. The workers themselves were aware of the need for national representation in the government, yet had they seen the government's taking the form of a resurrected Reichstag they would not have issued the call for a national congress of councils. It was the SPD that pushed for that form of representation and their organisational majority at the national congress secured its adoption. At that same congress, however, the delegates also voted a number of radical measures, including a series of measures regarding the army known as "the Hamburg Points". These called for

> "the abolition of all insignia of rank, for the election of all officers by vote of the soldiers, for matters of discipline and punishment to be handled by the soldiers' councils, and for the speedy replacement of the regular Army by a new 'People's Army'."[14]

No resolution could have been more revolutionary, for it implied the abolition of the officer corps and the destruction of the most important remaining pillar of the ancien régime. Its enforcement would have paved the way for a successful mass uprising. Its adoption testifies to the profound class instincts of the workers, to the dialectical nature of the revolutionary process and to the mistake and danger of regarding that process in static terms. It is not as if the working class is inherently reformist or revolutionary, but that it has the capacity to be either and, indeed, both at the same time. It was the friction that came from conflict with capitalist society that unleashed the workers' radical potential in Luxemburg's view, a view which the reality of revolutionary situations would seem to confirm. Under conditions of capitalist normalcy little may be seen of the workers' revolutionary capacity, yet for all that it has not disappeared, but waits for the propitious moment to explode. That is why under revolutionary situations the working class becomes transformed, and what has appeared impossible in the routine of everyday life becomes suddenly within immediate reach. Those who view social life in static terms cannot see this and work instead to convert every revolutionary situation back into the grooves of normalcy. To them it is inconceivable that the working class itself is revolutionary. To recognize that would require a revolutionary perspective on their part, which is why they devote their efforts to reinforcing the static and conservative manifestations of working class consciousness, which they later seize on to justify their own contribution to the repression of revolutionary situations.

It was the SPD leadership that ignored the congress resolution on the army and relied instead on the army to quell the revolutionary upsurge of the masses. When the decision of the Ebert government became known Berlin was up in arms. Although the dispute centred around the People's Naval Division's demand for pay, the government soon found itself prisoner of the sailors and called on the Supreme Command to keep the promise Ebert had secretly and originally concluded with it to defend the government if the government defended Germany from Bolshevism. The troops sent in by the military forced the sailors to surrender, but in the truce arranged for negotiating the surrender large crowds of civilians gathered and persuaded the soldiers to abandon their attack. In the last week of December and the first week of January power slipped from the Ebert government to the masses in the streets. Strikes and riots grew apace. When the Independent Socialists quit the government, Ebert and his colleagues decided to counterattack, starting with the firing of the left-wing president of the Berlin police. The Independent Socialists, the Revolutionary Shop Stewards and the Communists issued a call for a mass demonstration and the workers responded on an unprecedented scale, leading the revolutionary groups to call for a general strike and an armed uprising. In the end, the Revolutionary Executive formed by these three groups displayed a faltering leadership and ineffectual organisation, and the Ebert government put down the insurrection with the aid of the army, suppressing in the process "even the relatively harmless Workers' and Soldiers' Councils as undesirable revolutionary institutions".[15]

The Social-Democrats, like the Bolsheviks, were victorious, and like the Bosheviks their victory enabled them to stamp their version on the events. The result was that subsequent working class movements were confronted with the choice between Social Democracy or Bolshevism, both of which, from different perspectives, left no room for autonomous revolutionary action by the working class. The Social Democrats argued that they saved the German Revolution from Bolshevik terror; the Bolsheviks ascribed its defeat to organisational inadequacy. This process was repeated over and over with disastrous and debilitating effects on subsequent working class movements. Not only did the official parties of the working class, Social-Democratic or Communist, impede the development of autonomous working class revolutionary forces in subsequent insurrectionary periods; they also consigned them to the same fate which Rosa Luxemburg's ideas met. As the debate narrowed over the years it was forgotten that Rosa Luxemburg represented a very real alternative which placed mass revolutionary action from below at its core. From Italy in 1920 to Portugal in 1975 these parties, even when they did not hold state power, have acted to contain the revolutionary initiative of the masses. As the debate between Social Democracy and Bolshevism continues to occupy front stage, the historical reality of this revolutionary tradition is ignored, thereby dimming its prospects even further. As people continue to debate the question of revolution in terms of the relative merits of Social Democracy or Bolshevism it becomes more difficult to assess the real problems posed by the commitment to revolution from below. Yet revolution from below does form an historical tradition that has its own continuity. Each successive struggle raised certain questions and came up with certain responses that together helped advance this tradition and form a different legacy for the international working class.

Italy, 1920

ITALY, 1920 was a struggle where metalworkers occupied the factories in response to a lockout by employers at the end of August. What began as a dispute around wages, hours and working conditions soon mushroomed into a full scale political crisis, as the occupations which began in Milan soon spread to other cities and eventually to non-metallurgical industries as well. For those who doubt the capacity of the working class to coordinate its own revolutionary dynamic, they need only look at the unfolding of the factory council movement. In Milan, FIOM, the metalworkers' union, ordered the occupation of the gas plant, which was carried out at once. The council of workers' leagues promised to extend the occupation if other employers' groups helped the metal-based industrialists. The railway workers supplied the occupied factories with the necessary raw materials to enable the workers to carry on production without the bosses. The organising committees of the workers' councils which emerged in the factories dealt with problems of production, supply, distribution and defence. Through the labour institutions in the cities they arranged for food to be supplied to the factories:

> "Urgent needs were met by subsidies from the cooperatives, above all by popular solidarity, in 'communist kitchens' and a thousand gestures of aid and fraternity."[16]

Everywhere the atmosphere was euphoric, as befitting a revolutionary situation, but nowhere more so than in Turin, Milan and Genoa where "the occupation grew into a mass popular movement", reflecting the crucial role which major industrial cities have continued to play in working-class insurrections. Provisions were made, especially in Turin, for the armed defence of the factories. Of course contradictions abounded. The factory council movement had difficulty in linking up on a national level. Workers in some plants proved incapable of running production; in others they could not maintain the struggle. Only in Turin did the factory council exhibit really effective leadreship. Yet many of the difficulties experienced by the factory councils were due to the influence of the unions. Significantly, only in Turin did the factory councils have their own tradition independent of the unions. Elsewhere, they were

> "more obviously the product of collusion between internal commission and local FIOM section. This in itself explains why the movement had no national organization, no political platform of its own."[17]

Nonetheless, the working class was poised for an advance. Everywhere the struggles in the factories intensified. Land occupations in the South, which had been going on for months, increased. Anarchist and socialist groups were pushing for a radicalisation of the struggle from below. It was clear that a political solution was required, yet the CGL (the General Confederation of Labour), the major trade union, and the PSI (the Italian Socialist Party), the main workers' party, both shrunk from extending the struggle and launching an armed insurrectionary movement. Instead the CGL executive made union control over industry the principal goal of the struggle and succeeded in getting it adopted at the CGL congress of September 10-11. In effect what union control amounted to was union collaboration in the reimposition of capitalist discipline over the labour force.

Much was made by the leaders of both the CGL and the PSI of the military unpreparedness of the workers in the event of an armed confrontation. In fact, as the Turin delegates pointed out, the workers in the factories could defend them, but for an armed confrontation with the bourgeoisie to succeed it would require an uprising on a national level. The military organisation of the workers in the factories was essentially defensive, such that

> "it would be very difficult for the workers to make a sortie from their fortresses unless a general popular insurrection had altered the balance of military force."[18]

What this indicates is that the determining factor was not military but political. Had the party and trade union leadership issued a firm call to extend the struggle and had it been endorsed by the CGL congress, the political conditions would have been created in which the bourgeoisie would have been placed very much on the defensive. The military position of the state was far from solid, which was reflected in the government's preference to rely on the ideological subordination of the working class. By leaning on the moderate leaders in both the workers' and the industrialists' camps the government hoped to bring about a negotiated settlement to the crisis. The disarray in the industrialists' ranks after Giolitti, the prime minister, had proposed a negotiated settlement in which he endorsed the principle of union control "conveys the exasperation, the fear, the sense of impotence which had gripped conservative circles." A combative political strategy was far from ruled out by the analysis of objective conditions alone, a fact which was reflected in the closeness of the vote at the CGL congress which endorsed the leadership's proposal: 591,245 for, 409,569 in favour of the revolutionary motion. 93,623 abstained, including many FIOM sections, while the revolutionary syndicalists had not even been invited to the convention.

Although the leadership justified their action by an analysis that anticipated the slaughter of the Italian proletariat in the event of an armed insurrection, their position reflected their own political timidity and lack of understanding of the revolutionary process. As one supporter of the radical resolution commented:

> "We felt the revolution could not be made. Because a revolution is not made by first calling a convention to decide whether there is going to be a revolution or not."[19]

The bureaucratic perspective of the trade union leadership was deeply rooted in their own experience and the organisational structure they had helped build. Already in the spring or 1920 this attitude had clearly emerged in FIOM's opposition to the factory council movement:

> "The attitude of FIOM towards the Turin movement of 'factory councils' was typical: deep suspicion of an experiment in workers' democracy which broke the hold of the traditional union over the masses, which shifted the focus of organization inside the factory, made the productive unit the fulcrum of a new proletarian union structure and gave voice and representation to the unorganized. The national leaders of FIOM feared all this as a new version of anarcho-syndicalism. They were afraid that the intellectual attractions of the ordinovisti, with their impulsive experiments, would undercut the union's authority. Hence the condemnation of the factory council movement at the Genoa congress of FIOM in May 1920."[20]

Given that this was the perspective with which the trade union leadership entered the fray in the autumn, their handling of the CGL congress is not all that surprising. The result was that the revolutionary movement started to collapse almost at once and flowed back into reformist channels. A negotiated settlement was soon reached and in the referendum organised by FIOM, overwhelmingly ratified, although only a minority of metalworkers took part in the referendum. At an extraordinary congress convoked by FIOM to approve the federation's conduct, only the anarchists were critical.

For those like myself who could not understand how the workers in France could go out on an extensive general strike in May 1968 and a month later vote in a Gaullist government, the Italian experience of 1920 is instructive. As with the German events of 1918-19, we see once again that the revolutionary movement must advance or fail. There is no intermediate solution; and the workers' consciousness and actions correspond quite accurately to the different moments. Under the dynamic of a revolutionary moment workers will occupy factories, exercise their capacity for autonomy and radicalised by their own struggle, be prepared for further action. When that revolutionary moment is broken and the normal politics of capitalist society are reasserted, they fold up shop and return to previous patterns. The conclusion drawn by the Russian dominated Third International, and even by Gramsci himself, was that the events highlighted the need for a vanguard party "to work for 'a tighter, more disciplined, better-organized activity' in the future". This conclusion led to the split in the PSI and the founding of the Italian Communist Party, a schism which Gramsci characterised as "reaction's greatest victory", but only because the PCI did not win over the majority of the PSI rank and file. In the future the Italian working class would be presented with the choice between the social-democratic or Leninist options. The workers themselves, however, drew a different conclusion, reflecting by their actions a perspective that acknowledged the much greater importance of the revolutionary dynamic itself and their role within it:

> "In many factories, particularly in Turin, the communist workers who had organized armed defence hid the weapons in the countryside or walled them up in warehouses. Some were to be used against fascist expeditions later. Others were rounded up by the police. The booty was sparse."[21]

This perspective had quite different organisational implications from those developed by the Leninist assessment of the 1920 crisis in Italy, implications that can be more clearly seen in the history of the Spanish anarchist movement.

Spain: the anarchist tradition

TO THE SPANISH ANARCHISTS re-
volution meant a total transformation of the relations of social life, a
conception which they tried to build into their organisational structure.
Driven by a fierce ethical concern, their struggle.

> "became a struggle for the integrity of the working class, a validation of
> its moral capacity to reorganize society and manage it on a libertarian
> basis in an era of material scarcity."[22]

This ethical concern led them to develop a form of organisation which
stressed the individual responsibility of its members and the sovereignty
of its base groups. Both the Spanish Regional Federation, the Spanish
section of the First International, and the CNT, the National Confederation of Labour set up in 1911, were marked with the stamp of the
anarchists who predominated at their founding. These syndicalist
organisations grouped together, on a federated basis, trade and local
federations, thus ensuring that all workers in a given locality were
represented, irrespective of occupation. This was in keeping with the
Spanish anarchists' attempts to mobilise the masses of landless peasants
and labourers who streamed into the cities rather than concentrate
solely on the industrial working class. In doing so they differed with
Marxists who argued, as did Marx himself, that only the industrial
proletariat would manifest revolutionary élan; and indeed, the recently
arrived rural migrants who constituted the bulk of the urban poor provided a revolutionary spark to the Spanish proletariat. This concern
with the urban poor also reflected the anarchist conception of the
revolutionary process itself: open to all, resting on the recognition that

the source of oppression and corruption lay in capitalist society, yet demanding a high degree of moral commitment to transform one's relationship with others now. Although some of the founders of the Spanish anarchist movement were intellectuals, the vast majority of its members were ordinary workers and peasants. For them anarchism became an important alternative way of life, a source of dignity in the face of capitalist society which was reflected in their changed attitudes and habits in such basic areas of social life as diet, smoking, child-rearing, relations between the sexes. This conviction led them to spread "the Idea", as it was called, throughout Spain, travelling from place to place, living off more prosperous workers, organising strikes and gaining adherents to their vision. The expansion of the Spanish anarchist movement depended on these voluntary workers, for the organisations which they set up made it a mark of pride not to have any paid officials. In the CNT, for example,

> "The general secretary of the National Committee and the secretaries of the Regional Committees were the only paid officials. . . In contrast to its Socialist rival, the CNT shunned any manifestation of bureaucracy and centralization. It relied primarily on the initiative of its local bodies, *comarca*, and regional confederations to carry out the work of the organization. No strike funds were established. Strikes were expected to be short, and if necessary, violent as befitted a revolutionary organization whose primary aim was the overthrow of capitalism. The purpose of the CNT—or so its Anarchist militants believed—was to keep alive the spirit of revolt, not to quench it with piecemeal reforms and long, attritive strikes. Regular funds were established, however, for aid to prisoners and their families, and to some degree for 'rationalist schools'. There have been few unions more concerned than the CNT with the defense of its imprisoned members and the cultural, spiritual, and moral elevation of the working class. The phrase *emancipacion integral de los trabajadores* (integral emancipation of the workers) recurs in all the leading documents of this extraordinary organization."[23]

The organization was highly decentralised, depending on the voluntary participation of its members for the success of its actions. Local and trade federations, not the annual congresses, were the sovereign institutions, for if the annual congress decided upon an action, "none of the delegations which disagreed with it or felt it was beyond the capacity of its membership was obliged to abide by the decision." This did not mean that there were no ideological battles within the CNT. In the 1930s, for example, the FAI (the Iberian Anarchist Federation) led a sustained attack on the moderates in the CNT leadership, but they did so by conducting a number of strikes and uprisings which revealed the class bias of the Liberal republic and the poverty of the Socialists' policies. In the end,

> "The popularity the FAI enjoyed among the more militant *cenetistas* in the early 1930s was not merely the product of social and economic instability in Spain, but stemmed in no small measure from the FAI's willingness to do many of the risky and thankless tasks which the staid CNT leaders were reluctant to undertake on behalf of their own syndicates."[24]

Although decried as ineffectual and adventurist, the organizational practices of the Spanish anarchists only recognized the fact that revolution was not the product of bureaucratic organisation but the result of direct action by workers inspired by a revolutionary outlook. They therefore stressed voluntary participation and sought, through their patient efforts, to win over adherents who would then function autonomously, not to build an organisation strong in numbers alone. Hence they sought not to moderate their action, but to pose the revolutionary alternative inherent in every situation, to release the creative capacities of the workers and to drive home the truths that came from conflict with capitalist society. In that way they built not only an organisation, but a revolutionary organisation, that expanded and contracted with the ebb and flow of revolutionary moments themselves. In the period 1918-20 a wave of general strikes spread across Spain in the north and insurrection in the south. The anarchist movement swept across Andalusia:

> "Then would come the strikes. Many of them exploded spontaneously, sweeping in everyone from day laborers and craftsmen to the house servants and wet nurses of the privileged classes. Stores would close, the cafés would empty, and the fields would go untended. If provoked by the *Guardia* there might be violence—rioting, acts of incendiarism, the killing of watch dogs and cattle. Quite often, however, nothing would stir; an eerie silence would descend upon the entire town. Although many of these strikes would raise specific demands (and in 1918, Diaz del Moral tells us, the majority of them were successful), others were strictly revolutionary. The strikes would pose no demands. Their purpose was to achieve *communismo libertario*. When at last it was clear that this was not to come, the strikes would end as suddenly as they had begun, and everyone would quietly return to work. Then the town would wait for the next opportunity. The swollen groups would shrivel back to a small nucleus of devoted revolutionaries until another upsurge swept across the land."[25]

The anarchists were not averse to organisation or to the need for cadres, but they assigned them different meanings and invested them with different functions. In providing cohesion to local strikes and uprisings the CNT established workers' centers in every town which became not only union meeting places, but centers of political and cultural activity for workers and peasants throughout the locality. Official union meetings were held much less frequently than cultural and festive activities which permitted the workers to learn and exchange anarchist ideas and develop a solidarity that "was so intense that it was not always possible to maintain an isolated strike in a locality. There was always a tendency for one strike to trigger off others in its support or generate active aid by other *sindicatos*." In Andalusia and the Levant especially, the single unions, which united skilled and unskilled workers on an industrial basis and which formed the basis of the CNT after 1918, often embraced the entire town such that "any strike involved everyone to some degree and usually took on the proportions of a general strike". As a result, "during periods of upheaval, the *sindicato* as a whole became a 'dual power' in the full sense of the word, often completely undercutting the authority of the official municipality." Responsibility for organising these local activities and managing the affairs of the workers' centers was placed in the hands of ordinary workers, in keeping with the stress on developing autonomous organisations wedded to revolutionary activity rather than maintaining an apparatus. For this reason strike funds and paid officials were kept at a minimum.

These practices characterised not only the CNT, which was an anarcho-syndicalist organisation, but the anarcho-communist FAI as well, which linked together small action groups based on an affinity that went beyond politics. In many ways the FAI represents the most distilled attempt by the Spanish anarchists to practice in a revolutionary organisation those principles which they felt characterised the kind of revolutionary society they sought to bring about. In contrast to the Communist or Socialist Parties which stressed primarily loyalty "to the party, that is to say, to its apparatus", the anarchists

> "tried to build an organic movement in which individuals were drawn to each other by a sense of 'affinity,' by like interests and proclivities, not held together by bureaucratic tendons and ideological abstractions. And just as individual revolutionaries were drawn together into groups freely, by 'affinity,' so too the individual groups federated by voluntary agreement, never impairing the exercise of initiative and independence of will." [26]

These anarchist organisations provided the leaven which, more than anything else, prevented the bureaucratisation of the Spanish workers' movement. The FAI, like its precursors in the nineteenth century, did not shrink from violence and provided the underground network which kept up resistance in periods of severe repression by the capitalist state. Its violent actions, however, were not an aim in itself. Their success, like that of the organisation itself, rested ultimately on the political capacity and initiative of the masses in whose name they fought. Their faith and energy were not misplaced. The history of the Spanish workers' movement bore quite distinctly the mark of the anarchists' praxis.[27]

Once of the most striking successes of the Spanish workers was their capacity to conduct strikes without having to rely on a leadership, underlining thereby the anarchists' stress on autonomy. In 1901, for example, the Barcelona metalworkers walked out and struck for three months in order to obtain an eight-hour day. As it became clear that the issue was a test of strength between the workers and employers, the rest of the Barcelona proletariat went out on a one week general strike, without any leadership and without any demands, merely to demonstrate their solidarity with the metalworkers. In 1909 conflict broke out anew between the Barcelona textile workers and the manufacturers. The anarchists tried to turn the strike into an insurrection but were quickly arrested. The Socialists tried to contain the movement. Nonetheless, a social revolution broke out. Crowds roamed the streets, won the soldiers over to the workers' side. Railroad lines were blown up, barricades erected and arms distributed. Women joined in the struggle which "aroused not only the workers and *Murcianos* but also elements of Barcelona's déclassés, especially prostitutes". The insurrection was suppressed not because the working class was too spontaneous, but because no support came from outside Catalonia. The UGT, which was the only national labour federation in Spain at the time, dominated by the Socialists, did not call for a general strike until two days after the Barcelona uprising and scheduled it for two days after its suppression.

In 1919 a strike which began as a minor dispute in the Anglo-Canadian hydroelectric company soon spread to the entire Barcelona proletariat, as workers from sectors having nothing to do with the electricity workers expressed their solidarity. Printers refused to print proclamations detrimental to the workers' cause. When the government tried to press the workers into military service, the railway and trolley workers struck and the majority of those called-up refused to answer. Thousands were arrested, but the solidarity of the workers was not broken. In the end those imprisoned for 'social questions' were released and Spain became the first country to enact the eight-hour day. The general strike had lasted forty-four days and reflected the tremendous capacity of the Barcelona proletariat, schooled in anarchist principles, for initiative, direct action, and solidarity far beyond questions of wages or the sectoral interests of any given group of workers. This emphasis on political and moral issues in strike actions was part of the anarchist tradition. In the spring of 1933 the CNT launched a series of strikes and demonstrations in a campaign to release 9,000 imprisoned CNT-FAI militants, which reached its peak in a 60,000 strong rally in Barcelona in September. In November of that year the CNT and FAI joined forces to hold an anti-electoral rally which drew 75,000 workers.[28]

By that time the CNT had taken a marked turn to the left under the stimulus of the FAI and in response to attempts by the Socialists to use their position in the government to foster the UGT at the expense of the CNT. Once again the anarchists took a leading role in this battle, just as they had done in the previous decade in the conflicts within the CNT. There the moderates had tried to turn the anarchists' own beliefs against them, arguing that since a large number of workers did not yet share the anarchist belief in *communismo libertario*, the immediate emphasis on revolutionary politics would ultimately lead to dictatorship. Instead of developing this argument into a strategy for revolutionary education, "the moderates used it as a springboard for opportunistic politics". This same kind of social-democratic logic was taken up by the Popular Front government in 1936, with the CNT leading waves of strikes and the government trying to repress them in order to prevent civil war. Hence instead of preparing the workers for revolutionary combat the government helped prepare them for defeat. Only in anarchist Barcelona did the workers ignore government blandishments and take the initiative to arm themselves.[29]

As was the case in Italy, the revolutionary movement must move forward or flow back; and while the Communist and Socialist Parties in the government, intent on 'leading' the workers, tried to contain the moment, the workers, under the influence of a different tradition, sought to push the moment forward. The contrast had already been seen in the Asturian insurrection of two year earlier. There the revolution had taken the form of hundreds of small revolutionary committees, with the Socialists through the UGT functioning through tightly knit, centralized committees and the anarchists favouring "looser structures, often quasi-councils composed of factory workers and assemblies composed of peasants". But the difference was not only in the form of revolutionary organisation, council or committee, as much as in the whole dynamic which surrounded it. The difference was vividly conveyed by one observer,

Mellada, who companed two towns separated only by a river, the anarchist-controlled La Felguera and the Marxist-controlled Sama:

> "Sama was organized along military lines. Dictatorship of the proletariat, red army, Central Committee, discipline, authority. . . La Felguera opted for communismo libertario: the people in arms, liberty to come and go, respect for the technicians of the Duro-Felguera metallurgical plant, public deliberation of all issues, aboliton of money, the rational distribution of food and clothing. Enthusiasm and gaiety in La Felguera; the sullenness of the barracks in Sama. The bridges (of Sama) were held by a corp of guards complete with officers and all. No one could enter or leave Sama without a safe-conduct pass, or walk through the streets without passwords. All of this was ridiculously useless, because the government troops were far away and the Sama bourgeoisie was disarmed and neutralized. . . The workers of Sama who did not adhere to the Marxist religion preferred to go to La Felguera, where at least they could breathe. Side by side there were two concepts of socialism: the authoritarian and the libertarian; on each bank of the Nalon, two populations of brothers began a new life: with a dictatorship in Sama; with liberty in La Felguera. . ."[30]

Hungary, 1956

IF THERE IS one strand that runs through the whole tradition of revolution from below it is precisely that great liberating feeling of workers' prefering to breathe. Everyday life under capitalism is organised so as to deny this feeling and the possibility of its expression, and the situation is no different in the socialist societies of the Soviet Bloc, as the following testimony on the effects of piece-work in Hungary indicates:

> "Ultimately, the only thing that helps is if I turn into a machine myself. The best workers excel at this. Their eyes are veiled whatever the work, as if they wore impenetrable masks on their faces, yet they never miss a thing. Their movements don't seem to require any effort. They follow the unfailing trajectories of magnetically controlled, emotionless bodies. They average the fastest possible pace over the day as a whole, as they do not rush at things when they are still fresh and do not slow down when they are tired. Truly, just like machines. They only give way to nerves when the ratio of 'good' work goes haywire; otherwise their attitude reflects the reality, which is that 'good' and 'bad', 'paid' and 'unpaid' work run together to make a working day. The profit which is generated and the wages that come their way are both equally indifferent to such distinctions."[31]

The attempt by capital, including its state-socialist varieties, to transform the worker into a machine is reproduced in the very discourse of the Communist Parties and their latter-day self-proclaimed successors. Workers, in their eyes, are not individual actors on the stage of history, moved by passion, daring and the desire to affirm life, but masses, heterogeneous elements of a working class that needs to be organised, mobilised and marched toward a revolution. Yet the workers are individuals, not machines, and the masks they wear at work reflect their daily resistance to the domination they must endure, a resistance that explodes in revolutionary moments into a challenge to the entire system, revealing a daring and affirmation beyond the capacity of the forces of order and orderly change to anticipate. Hence in the Hungarian Revolution of 1956, even the most radical of the intellectual dissidents to the régime, organised in the Petofi Circle, did not expect and did not welcome the mass uprising which occurred on October 23. Throughout the revolution they tried to steer the uprising into conventional channels. After the Soviet Union had invaded Hungary, the workers responded by declaring a general strike, setting up workers' councils in the factories and revolutionary committees in the provincial towns. The Nagy government, instead of reinforcing the workers' combativity, sought to reach a negotiated settlement with the Russians by calling on the workers to go back to work. The effect was to reinforce those within the workers' own groups who still entertained illusions about the possibility of effecting significant change within the existing social order and so weaken the political force of the only organs which were to prove capable of withstanding the second Soviet invasion—the workers' councils themselves. Although the intellectual opposition displayed considerable moral courage—Nagy and others paid for their actions with their lives—in the end they were prisoners of their Leninist heritage. Wedded to transforming the party and the state, they could not see that what the revolution required was the abolition of the party-state and its replacement by the autonomous organs of the working class, an outlook that implied continuous support for the workers' councils that sprang up everywhere.[32]

It was not only a question of the intellectual opposition's commitment to the party-state formula; it was also their incapacity to envisage the possibility of autonomous action by a working-class which seemed politically untutored. Yet it was precisely the "rough, working-class youths of the Budapest slums, the tough-guys, leather-jacketed 'yobos' and hooligans from Angyafold and Ferencvaros" who took up the fight against Russian tanks. When asked why they had risked their lives, many of these youngsters "who knew nothing about the Petofi Circle" and little else of official politics responded with such answers as, "'Well, is it really worth living for six hundred forints a month?'."[33] Their answer speaks volumes about the very sharp political consciousness that workers have, their understanding that so much of what passes for politics is but the machinations of the dominant class, which explains why they ignore it so much. That kind of politics is very much like working for six hundred forints a month, a state of affairs to be endured but also one to be overthrown when the moment presents itself. The incapacity of intellectuals who dominate so much of official politics to understand this reflects the division between manual and intellectual labour produced by capitalist social relations. It should not blind us, however, to the very different and very real definition of politics which workers have, in which they do invest their energies and exercise their political capacities, as the many examples of the Hungarian Revolution of 1956 make clear.

It is sometimes the very small details which are most revealing of this distinction. When the Central Workers' Council of Greater Budapest attempted to publish their own newspaper the Hungarian authorities raided the printing works. The Council responded by duplicating an Information Bulletin which they managed to relay to provincial towns over the telephone, despite the government's attempts to suppress it by seizing the duplicating machines in the larger factories. In turn the Central Workers' Council called on the workers to boycott all official government newspapers except for the *Sports News*. The selectivity of the boycott was highly political, for while official news was an outright distortion of social reality, sport still retained a vestige of truth and social meaning.

This distinction between the official and popular definition of what really constitutes politics was reflected in the dual structures that emerged during the revolution. The reformers understood democracy as the dismantling of the one-party state, but the general public saw in the return of the old-time parties and politicians it made possible another form of domination which they thought they had already done away with. Against it the workers posited the idea of workers' councils. As the Parliament of Workers' Councils which met on October 31 in Budapest made clear, this form of political organisation meant workers' control of the production process, including the determination of wage levels, their means of assessment, and the amount of profits to be paid to the state. This last stipulation was important, for it reflected the workers' awareness of the need for future investment and national coordination within a context of workers' control. Twelve years later the party and state technocrats in Czechoslovakia were to invoke the workers' incapacity to think in terms of the general interest as a justification for the suppression of the workers' councils which emerged in the Prague Spring. As was the case in Hungary, the workers' councils were suppressed in Czechoslovakia because they represented another centre of political power opposed to the domination exercised by the party through the state.[34]

The workers were not unaware of the political power which control of the production process gave them, while the network of workers' councils which they set up enabled them to exercise it, through strikes and other forms of resistance, for two months following the second Soviet invasion of Hungary in November, 1956. Although the Kadar government imposed by Soviet bayonets controlled the state apparatus, it did not exercise effective power, which it had "to seize back" from the workers. To do this it had to suppress the workers' councils, a task which it achieved in the end only through the use of arrest, intimidation, and military force. Up to the very end the workers resisted with attempts at clandestine national conferences of workers' councils, strikes and demonstrations. Even their final act of disbanding themselves bore witness to their deep awareness of their own power and their refusal to accord the government the legitimacy it so obviously craved. The workers' council of the Csepel iron and steel works, for example, announced its resignation in the following terms:

> "Under the presently prevailing circumstances, we are no longer able to carry out our obligations . . .and for this reason, we are returning our mandate into the hands of the workers."[35]

The Central Workers' Council disbanded exhorting the workers to sabotage and passive resistance, those traditional forms of opposition which had characterized the years of normalcy preceding the revolutionary outbreak of 1956. The revolutionary moment had died down, the workers' political energies flowed into different channels; but the consciousness which had produced that moment, and the political achievements to which it gave rise, did not disappear. As with previous situations of working-class insurrection, the Hungarian Revolution demonstrated the workers' capacity for autonomy, initiative, coordination, and clarity, in short, for that revolutionary praxis which their official parties have so long denied them. It was the workers who knew, from bitter experience, that the Communists "promised us everything, at the same time subjugating us and pulling us down to the greatest misery conceivable." It was the workers who were the first to procure the arms that would be needed to defend the revolution. It was the workers who, spontaneously and independently of what transpired in the different urban centres, instituted the political form of workers' councils which subsequently took over the direction of social life. Even in the more isolated towns where the Stalinist functionaries tried to control information the workers succeeded in overthrowing the government's institutions and replacing them with their own.

The revolution unleashed its own dynamic. The workers' council of Miskolc, the country's largest industrial complex outside Budapest, called for "free and general elections with several competing political parties" on October 28. By November 1, the workers' council formed for the whole of Borsod County, of which Miskolc was the main town, demanded that Parliament be replaced "by a National Assembly made up of delegates from the workers' councils, and declared that the land, the factories and the mines must remain in the hands of the people." Early on the workers' councils in the provinces called for national coordination and radical action to defend the revolution, a position which they maintained well into December:

> "When the Russian leaders talked of a counter-revolutionary danger in Budapest, of threats to the workers' power, and of capitalist restoration, delegates from the Borsod Workers' Council told the Nagy government that they would lead the workers of Borsod to Budapest to demonstrate just who was leading the revolution. 'You only have to pick up the telephone,' they promised, 'and in three hours we will be there, the workers of Ozd, Diosgyor and Miskolc, all twenty thousand and armed.'"[36]

The Nagy government, trapped by its reformist illusions and possibly by its fear of a bloodbath, never called them. Its refusal to link up with the workers' council movement did not prevent the arrest, imprisonment and death which met many of the Hungarian revolutionaries as the Stalinists reimposed order in the country, much as Allende's refusal to arm the workers in Chile a quarter of a century later did not prevent the bloodbath which he thought his refusal would avert. Not only did the Nagy government prove in the end to be powerless to protect the workers from reprisals; its refusal to call them into action robbed even the death which many of them met of the sense which the workers, by their revolutionary stance, wished to accord it. Substitutionism comes in many forms, and not only in its original Leninist appearance, but its effect is everywhere the same: the denial of the workers' right to affirm their own existence.

This desire for self-affirmation, to assert themselves as political actors making their own history, marked the Hungarian workers' actions throughout the course of the revolution. Once the fighting died down after November 4, the factory workers' councils in Budapest took the initiative in setting up district workers' councils in their local neighbourhoods, whose task was mainly political: to defend the achievements of the revolution, including workers' control over the production process. Thus the workers successfully made the link between factory and commune without diluting the radical thrust at the heart of the factory council movement. At the same time they displayed quite clearly the understanding that the workers' council movement had to expand or die. By November 14 the founding meeting of the Central Workers' Council of Greater Budapest took place. Of course there were conflicts and problems, about the formal structure the Central Council should take, about the accountability of its leaders, about the attitude to adopt vis-a-vis the Kadar government, about the means to effect national coordination, about the decision to continue the general strike. In each case, however, the workers arrived at their own solution, even if in some cases the policies eventually adopted were moderate rather than radical. On the strike issue, for example, the Central Workers' Council decided to call off the strike in exchange for concessions from the Kadar government, and though the negotiations proved unproductive, the Council decided to call for a resumption of work for November 19. Many of the workers were angry with this decision. Provincial delegates to the national conference of workers' councils angrily criticised the Budapest leaders for calling off the strike. The Budapest leaders persisted in their moderate policy and succeeded in explaining their position to their provincial colleagues, to the point where the national conference decided not to constitute itself as a National Workers' Council, so as not to provide the Kadar government with a pretext to ban the Central Workers' Council too.

The workers of Budapest, however, propelled by the dynamic of a revolutionary situation, had other ideas. When it became known that the original site for the conference had been surrounded by Soviet troops, the workers of Budapest launched a protest strike, "and by the time the Central Workers' Council learned about it, the strike was almost total throughout the city." The Central Workers' Council then gave the strike its support and even the more moderate members, such as the Csepel Workers' Council, joined in. Although the executive of the Csepel Workers' Council originally opposed the protest strike, the workers of Csepel threw out their leaders and replaced them with a more militant executive. In some ways it is not surprising that the leadership of the Central Workers' Council adopted a more moderate policy; it was in keeping with the logic of responsibility they expressed that seems to characterise the office of leadership itself. What is significant is that the democratic structure which the workers adopted, including the right of immediate recall of elected delegates, made their leadership bodies responsive to the workers at the base, who were inevitably radicalised by the dynamic of the revolutionary movement. As the government hardened its position in the face of attempts by the Central Workers' Council to arrive at a compromise, the position of that latter body stiffened too, for "the confrontation hardened the views of the workers' leaders, and strengthened the arguments of those calling upon the Central Workers' Council to act as an independent political force."[37]

The Hungarian experience indicates once again that whatever the difficulties encountered by the workers in a revolutionary situation, the presence of a vanguard party will only help to compound rather than overcome them. The solutions can only come from the workers themselves; and in this sense the valiant struggle of the Hungarian workers, like those of their predecessors and successors, bequeath us a legacy which points us in the right direction, if we only learn from the past.

Portugal: 1974-75

          RECENT EVENTS in Portugal would indicate that this is a lesson that is hard to learn. In the vacuum that followed the military overthrow of the Caetano dictatorship on April 25, 1974, the workers threw up their own autonomous organisations in the form of Workers' Committees elected by the general assemblies of workers in a factory and subject to recall:

> "Although the Committees were not revolutionary organisations (very few of them called for the abolition of wage labour or for an end to the capitalist mode of production), they showed an extreme distrust of the unions and, in many cases, of the new institutions created by the MFA. This is not to say that the MFA was unpopular. Workers just wanted things to move faster. By the end of October 1974 some 2,000 such Committees existed throughout Portugal."[38]

The Committees and Assemblies had to deal with a whole range of problems that stemmed from their efforts to transform social relations in an environment which was dominated, politically and economically, by capitalism. One of their first problems was to decide whether or not to take part in management if a factory remained in private hands. In cases where they took over a factory they had to face the obstacles posed by international capital to the distribution of their products. Workers' Committees in smaller companies or in affiliates of giant monopolies were isolated. Conflicts existed among the workers between the young and the old, between men and women, between those with work and those ready to scab, between the better-paid, specialised categories of workers and the more unskilled labourers. The conflicts surfaced around how to distribute wages more equitably, how to reorganise the work process, how fast to go in their political demands and many other issues. In the process of dealing with these problems the workers experienced a growing awareness of the difficulties inherent in the transition to socialism and of the global nature of capitalism. Nonetheless, the workers' control movement continued and by March 1975 over 200 such situations existed. The workers also came up with imaginative solutions to some of these problems. When unemployed workers marched on some building workers in July, 1974, for example, the latter collected funds and gave out money to the unemployed. In January, 1975, on the initiative of workers in the Lisbon electrical engineering company of Efacec-Inel, a Federation of Workers' Committees was set up under the name of Inter-Empresas. The Ministry of Labour and the main trade union federation, Intersindical, both dominated by the Portugese Communist Party (PCP), opposed it. When Inter-Empresas called a demonstration to protest the landing of NATO forces in February 1975, the government, Intersindical and the PCP attacked it. The demonstration took place despite the ban and 40,000 people took part.[39]

The incident reflected the biggest problem, in many ways, facing the workers: their own institutions and those purporting to represent their interests—the unions, the parties, the government, the MFA and even the far left groups so critical of the traditional parties. As early as May, 1974, the Timex workers occupied the factory, issued a radical proclamation to the nation, called for working class solidarity and sought to coordinate the struggle by setting up their own committee, rejecting "all attempts by the Maoists to take over their struggle." Such actions began to spread, but the unions, dominated by the PCP, cautioned against them as 'adventurous'. In September, the Lisnave dockworkers decided to march on the Ministry of Labour to demand the purging of their fascist director and to protest the anti-strike law recently passed. The MFA banned the demonstration and the PCP denounced the workers for 'adventurism'. The march took place anyway and "was applauded all the way." When the workers extended direct action and autonomous organisation to the neighbourhood, such that by April, 1975, 20,000 house occupations had been reported throughout Portugal, the government passed a law legalising collective occupations like crèches but forbidding squatters, and thereby hoped to defuse the movement.

The Neighbourhood Committees that sprang up in the Portugese Revolution reflected the extension of the popular movement to a concern with issues beyond the workplace, but the attempts by the various political parties, including the formations to the left of the Communists, to use these committees to build 'the Party' only reinforced the divisions within the working class. Unionised factory workers and public employees were more present in the body that federated these Neighbourhood Committees, but these workers already had a roof over their heads. The occupants of the shanty towns had different preoccupations which the left, bound by its traditional concern with the party, the factory and the organised proletariat, could not come to grips with:

> "The shanties were the 'great shame' of Portugese capitalism. They were an obvious eyesore and everyone was intent on 'getting rid of them at all costs'. But thinking seldom went beyond this. What would the shanties be replaced by? What would the new communities be like? Such problems were hardly ever aired in the Assemblies. There was here a universal paralysis of imagination. Would the 'pressures' in the new houses (if and when shanty dwellers ever got them) really be less than in the old huts—or merely of a different kind? These questions were never openly discussed, because never openly admitted as relevant. The silence of the left on these issues could be heard for miles around."[40]

As the workers developed their own organisations and defied the injunctions of the official bodies, the parties tried to capture them from within. After the demonstration of February, 1975 made it clear that Inter-Empresas was a force to reckon with, the PCP sought to dominate it by pushing certain delegates from Intersindical to form a block within it. As a result, many Workers' Committees (CTs)

> "stopped sending delegates to general meetings. This facilitated the manipulation of the Inter-Empresas skeleton by PCP delegates or other leninists (PRP-BR, MES, MRPP, FEC ml) and contributed to its further dessication."[41]

Although the Maoists worked hard on the Workers' Committees, they also used them "for purposes of propaganda and recruitment" and by raising factional disputes, "detracted from the discussion of real issues, wasted working class time and effort, and created mystification." In the end they differed little from the Communist Party they criticized, except that they

> "wanted their own, more 'radical' version of Intersindical. To achieve this they needed a stepping stone. And if one wasn't immediately to hand they would create one, by capturing certain CTs and using them as an instrument in their power struggle. While the PCP used the most populist language imaginable, the MRPP used more worker-oriented slogans. In the last analysis both approaches were very similar."[42]

Nontheless the workers continued to try and coordinate their struggles at the base. By September 1975 they had started to form Popular Assemblies which consisted of delegates from the Workers' Committees, Nieghbourhood Committees and Soldiers' Committees, organised on a non-party basis. These Assemblies led struggles over issues involving all aspects of social life—economic sabotage, the occupation of houses, the creation of parks, etc., but "the most active militants in the Popular Assemblies were Leninists of one kind or another—with all that that implies in terms of behaviour and concerns." The insufficiency of worker participation in their own institutions, which was already a problem in the Workers' Committees, obviously hindered the advance of the Portugese revolution. The inability of the working class to go beyond the vanguards "was to remain the biggest problem of all. And it was to remain unsolved." Yet the solution proposed by the vanguard parties was no solution at all; on the contrary, it only further alienated the workers. When these militants got up to speak at meetings of Neighbourhood Committees, they would use "a specialised 'political' language which was off-putting for the others", with the result that ordinary members would refuse to speak. When the Maoists organised demonstrations they insisted on subordinating them to their political line, as the following story so painfully shows:

> "Some Maoists were demonstrating in Porto, shouting 'Viva o *Grito do Povo*' ('Long live the *Shout of the People*', the name of their paper). A group of workers join in, mishear things, and—no doubt voicing their hopes for the future—begin shouting 'Viva o Rico Povo' (Long live the people made rich). When the Party militants explain that this slogan is 'incorrect' the workers answer: 'Ah, what does it matter? It's good to be shouting!' They could have added: 'and which is the more real, anyway?'"[43]

Eventually the workers prohibited party banners on the demonstrations, as "the difference between those who attended on behalf of their party and those who came because they felt that a revolutionary movement was possible or necessary was almost palpable." Yet the voices of the latter were lost in the welter of leftist rhetoric propagated by the political groups and amplified by the media. Even the notion of popular power was fetishized. One Marxist-Leninist group, for example, kept pushing for the creation of workers' councils, even though the form of organisation which emerged out of the workers' own struggles was the Workers' Committees. The radio station controlled by the left, Radio Renascença, also

> "pushed the slogan of 'popular power'. But it was mainly wind. There was little discussion as to what it implied. No attempt was made to get to

grips with people's anxieties and fears of the unkown in order rationally to overcome them. Fundamental (yet immediately relevant) issues such as the structure of work, the internalisation of hierarchy, the relations of manual and intellectual labour and various other problems that would confront a communist society were all avoided. Instead: just revolutionary trumpet calls. At times it was even tiring: revolution, revolution, revolution. After a hard day's work one wanted to relax, just a little. One had to shut it off, get it out of one's ears, or treat it as background noise. People turned to other stations. Sad, because despite its shortcomings (ambigous attitudes to Third World issues and to the state capitalist countries for instance) it hit hard at the local technocrats and rulers. So hard that their only solution was to blow it up.''[(44)]

Indeed, the leftist mystification was so great that when the paratroopers blew up the station on November 7, the later claimed "they 'hadn't realised what they were doing'", having thought that "the orders had come 'from the left'."

The contradiction between word and deed which so typified the conduct of the Marxist-Leninist groups marked the behaviour of the parties they wished to supplant as well; and everywhere the effect on the workers was the same: confusion and demoralisation. In February, 1975, for example, workers in Casebres had taken over 4,000 hectares and set up an agricultural cooperative which was run on genuinely egalitarian lines:

"The workers were full-blooded communists; the land and everything on it was for everyone, they said. In March 1975 they erected a large sign at the entrance proclaiming 'the Dictatorship of the Proletariat'."[(45)]

When Cunhal, the leader of the PCP, was about to pay the cooperative a visit, the PCP workers who formed his advance party told the workers it would have to come down, because it harmed the PCP's chances in the elections. When the workers remonstrated that the quotation came from Marx and Engels, the PCP delegates merely answered that their Seventh Party Congress had voted against it. The answer reflected the deep-rooted elitist bias which was shared by the entire technocratic class which dominated Portugese politics and cut across their ideological divisions of Socialist or Communist:

"They acted as if they had the unique model of revolution and as if the rest (the 'inferior' revolutionaries) had to follow suit or be denied salvation. The proletariat could be saved, they seemed to be saying but only through *their* superior level of consciousness and *their* 'more significant' interpersonal relationships. There seemed to be a leninism of everyday life, relegating those who weren't of this or that political persuasion to a very primitive emotional consciousness."[(46)]

This Leninism of everyday life did not go unperceived by the workers, with disastrous consequences:

> "People were cruelly forced to make false choices: defend this or condemn that. The choices remained confined to the political sphere, despite the widespread non-party feeling which had come to the fore during recent months."[47]

When the army finally called a halt to the revolutionary process by staging the coup of November 25, 1975, calls for direct action and defense of the revolution went unheeded by the workers. In spite of the lively discussions, no one quite knew what was going on or what sense to make of events:

> "It might have been happening in another world. In no way were the workers going to support one side or the other. After 20 months of the 'revolutionary process' and of leftist talk they had drawn one conclusion: revolution and counter-revolution were jobs for specialists. And anyway, they had to work tomorrow."[48]

The lessons of the Portugese revolution are very much the lessons of earlier working-class insurrections. The choice between the Socialists and the Communists, the former waving the banner of "freedom" and the latter, the flag of "revolution", was really no choice at all. It was the same old confrontation between Social Democracy and Bolshevism that had emerged from the First World War and the Russian Revolution, reinforced by over a half century's historical experience in which each had become ever more fixedly the prisoner of the other's mythology. The mythologizing was greatest with respect to the working class and proved, in spite of violent disclaimers from both sides, their ultimate meeting point.

In the Portugese Revolution of 1974-5, for example, the workers at *Republica*, a newspaper with a long tradition of independence, took it over, claiming that they wanted it to retain its non-party character instead of the pro-Socialist position it was taking after April 25th. The Socialists accused the Communists of being behind the move and elevated the whole affair into a question of the freedom of the press. In fact, all sorts of political tendencies were represented on the Workers' Committee. The case became a focal point of autonomous working class struggle, as 40,000 workers in the Lisbon region answered the call of the *Republica* workers, thus forming the largest non-party demonstration since February 7, 1975. The government, forced to intervene, nationalised the paper, a decision supported by the Communists. The real lines of battle, however, were not between the Socialists and the

Communists, but between those committed to revolution from below and those committed to state capitalism. The *Republica* workers put it clearly themselves:

> "The organs of decision-making are either on the side of the dynamic elements of the revolutionary process: the Workers' Committees, the Neighbourhood Committees, the organisations of popular power. Or they relate to the political parties, are yoked to those parties which in most cases don't defend the interests of the workers at all. The question is *who* is to have political power in this country? Is the MFA interested in the construction of a socialist society? Or is it interested in bourgeois democracy?
>
> We are only 150 workers, but in a sense we are representative of our class, of millions like us. What is at stake is political power and knowing in whose hands it is.'"[49]

Revolutionary politics:
the libertarian alternative

IN EVERY SITUATION we examined, and in the many others that we did not, both the Social-Democrats and the Communists clamped down on the workers' movement as they struggled to find their own means of revolutionary organisation and expression. Sometimes the Social-Democrats and Communists waited until they seized state power; sometimes they did not, but their actions in the end always proved fundamentally anti-democratic and anti-revolutionary. Neither could get byond capitalist ways of thinking about the crucial issues of class, power and revolution; and nowhere did these limitations emerge more clearly than in their attitudes and actions with respect to the working class itself. What is both surprising and disheartening is the extent to which contemporary political thinking and action seem to be reproducing that very tradition which has proved to be a dead end, in which the distinctions between Social-Democrat and Communist, and more latterly, Marxist-Leninist too, blend in the face of the common assumption they share with capital—namely, that working people are incapable of running their own society.

The persistence of these ideas reflects in part the very real and continued subordination of the working class to capital, and the recognition that the emancipation of the working class requires political organisation and struggle that will eventually have to confront the violence and state power of capital. A critical reading of the history of working class movements, however, indicates that there are other ways to approach the problems of organisation, violence and class power that do not necessarily reproduce the very social relations which a truly revolutionary movement purports to abolish. In their struggle against capital workers have shown themselves to be quite aware of these alternatives. Significantly, in revolutionary moments they developed not parties or unions (with the exception of the anarcho-syndicalist tradition), but councils or committees which were far more revolutionary than even the most self-consciously avant-gardist political formations. These councils or committees were important not only as embryos of the future socialist society but as direct forms of revolutionary struggle. In them and through them workers raised their most revolutionary demands, confronted issues that their parties had always skirted, and developed strategies that the latter had never dared to conceive.

Take the question of violence, for example. In every situation the workers sought to neutralize the army, demanded arms for themselves and prepared for a violent clash with the dominant social forces who, they knew, would not peacefully abandon their privileges. The parties of the working class, on the other hand, in every insurrectionary situation subsequent to the Bolshevik Revolution, shrunk from such a confrontation and used their organisational strength to disarm the workers' movement and steer its revolutionary energy into reformist channels. The consequences for the workers have been calamitous, as the fascist reactions in Italy, Spain and more recently, Chile have shown. To the Marxist-Leninists the lessons to be drawn have been obvious, and differed little from the assessment Gramsci drew of the Italian crisis of 1921: more organisation, tighter discipline, the formation of professional revolutionaries linked in a clandestine hierarchy, who would be able to provide the force and leadership necessary to counter the violence of the bourgeoisie next time round. In their horror at the violence that the forces of capital have unleashed on the workers, they fall back on the one model of revolutionary organisation which succeeded in overthrowing the bourgeoisie, yet they ignore the extent to which subsequent Bolshevik terror emerged from that very model. The social-democrats seize on that terror, and the rather terrifying practice of the Marxist-Leninists, to justify a position of gradual reform that refuses to consider the problem of violence at all.

Both positions are mystifying, for they reduce the question of revolution to one of violence and terror, and the result is both poor history and poor strategy. Of course the problem of violence is quite real. Obviously the dominant classes will resort to force when all else fails. Yet the question of revolution cannot be reduced to the question of violence, any more than it can be reduced to the seizure of state power.

It is one thing to throw out the bourgeoisie; it is quite another matter to transcend capitalist social relations, as the history of the Bolshevik Revolution clearly showns. There the use of violence and terror to short-circuit the long process of revolutionary transformation only underscored the extent to which violent action is but one moment in the revolutionary process in no way coterminous with the exercise of power itself, which can only come from the concerted and solidary action of people struggling together and which must precede the violent confrontations with the dominant social forces. Hence in the Italian crisis of 1921 the leaders of the Socialist Party and the trade unions were right when they claimed that the extension of the struggle would lead to an armed confrontation with the state, but their assessment of the balance of forces in purely military terms overlooked the much more important political context and led them to defeatist conclusions. The problem was not organisational but conceptual; and the solution not the creation of a vanguard party but the extension of the movement to create and solidify the organs of popular power and workers' control which were the necessary prerequisites to military victory.

Working class autonomy implies neither inefficiency nor a lack of coordination. On the contrary, it implies a very definite form of organisation, in which coordination is the central concept and federalism, the principle on which it is based. The most far-reaching social revolution that has yet occurred took place in Spain from 1936-39. Peasants took over land and urban workers took over industry on an unprecedented scale. Eventually over 1700 agricultural collectives were set up, while in certain urban regions, such as those of Catalonia, all the industries and all transportation passed under the control of the workers. Urban collectives were established in areas ranging from munitions industries to hairdressing establishments. All this economic activity required coordination: between town and country for the provision of food and agricultural implements, between metal and munitions industries for the supply of tools and parts necessary for the manufacture of weapons, between the urban industries and the front lines for the transport of material to the troops, within industries to deal with the social problems of collectivization, etc. This economic coordination was carried out in the most trying of circumstances, namely those of the Civil War which was raging throughout Spain during that period. If the anarchists succeeded in carrying through their social revolution to the extent that they did during those years, it was because the principle of federated coordination which characterises the future organisation of society had already been firmly embedded in their practice.[50]

Subsequent attempts to cut the gordian knot of the revolutionary transformation of society with the formation of vanguard parties have only retarded, as the Portugese situation so poignantly revealed, the formation of those organs of popular power so indispensable to this process. The workers, on the other hand, have, by their actions, demonstrated the importance of such bodies to the revolutionary process, and thereby affirmed that power does indeed reside with the people, not with the party, the state or capital, who can only exercise domination by wresting power from the people through the use of violence. The Kadar regime in Hungary did not exercise power even though it commanded the state institutions as long as the workers' councils continued to exist; and even when it suppressed them with military force it did not succeed in regaining power, for the councils, wisely and appropriately, surrendered their power back to the people from whom they received it in the first place. In one sense, it is this very understanding of the nature of power which leads workers, once the revolutionary moment has been spent, to withdraw from official politics and wait for the next round. As the net of monopoly or state capital descends once again on everyday life the working class becomes enveloped in silence. Into the vacuum move the parties, jockeying for position, tilting at electoral jousts, building up the organisation, citing all the while the silence of the workers as justification for their bureaucratic politics.

Of course these parties are responding to something very real, namely the domination of capital which requires the reduction of workers to silence, an aim to which the organisation of all social life is directed. As a result they develop organisational models and engage in political activity based on their reading of working-class consciousness as it appears under the reign of capital. This understanding is highly partial. Dominated by capitalist categories of thought, it fails to take into account the very different consciousness which workers have manifested in periods of revolutionary upheaval and which has sustained working-class resistance during periods of political quiescence. In a sense, there is a calculus of revolutionary logic to working class politics common to both moments, which suggests that the tremendous unleashing of political energy only occurs when the stakes appear sufficiently high, when the total transformation of the social order, the implementation of *communismo libertario*, seems possible; otherwise people do their best trying to find meaning and happiness at six hundred forints a month and leave politics to the politicians. How else explain the fact that revolutions sometimes break out if the sun shines that day?

Yet the years of subordination and atomisation leave their mark, lulling people's political reflexes and reinforcing traditional patterns of social interaction—hierarchy, sexism and all the other values rooted in fear and death upon which capitalism so eagerly preys. To counter the debilitating effects of everyday life under capitalism organisation is clearly needed and useful, keeping critical politics alive, stiffening working-class resistance, accelerating the revolutionary moment and arming the people with an alternative set of values and forms of solidarity to deal with the problems that inevitably emerge in each revolutionary period, not least of which are the internal contradictions of the working class itself. Such organisation, however, bears little resemblance to the political parties as we traditionally know them. These parties, by their organisation and practice, have only masked the contradictions which the workers themselves have attempted to confront and thereby reinforced the silence with which capitalism has surrounded them. The disenchantment of the Portugese generals with the revolution of April 25 because it opened the door of liberation to prositutes and homosexuals found its parallel in the weak support and sometimes outright opposition which the Communists displayed in the face of women's attempts to escape their roles, and the "universal paralysis of the imagination" which the entire left showed on other urban issues, such as the problem of shanty-towns.[51]

Clearly, if the revolution requires organisation, then that organisation must be linked to a conception of revolution and modelled on the institutions and practices that the workers themselves have evolved in the course of their own revolutionary history. It is significant in this respect that those groups which stressed revolution from below, placed action by the masses at the core of their practice and accorded primacy to autonomous working-class organisation, developed, within their own organisations, social bonds and political practices quite different from those of traditional parties, yet quite similar to each other's. The affinity groups which characterised the Spanish Anarchist Federation, the FAI, resembled very much the Polish peer group which was so central to Rosa Luxemburg's politics. Both organisations stressed personal initiative and ability; preferred informal cooperation and consensus to the regulation of disputes by organisational manoeuvering; expressed intense solidarity vis-a-vis the outside world, whatever the internal differences. Both were societies more than parties, meshing the personal and public dimensions of their lives while according each member the lattitude, respect and acceptance which comes with "a group that makes no demands on its membership greater than are willingly accepted."[52]

If these groups organised on this basis, it was precisely because they understood that organisation was no substitute for the action of the working class, and that the task of cadres was, and is, to raise revolutionary ideas and provide political networks which would enable workers to develop alternative values, ways of living and political practices in the here and now compatible with a revolutionary, libertarian vision. How can people's doubts and fears be overcome, the very real contradictions confronted, unless radicals themselves refuse to comply with official politics and pose the most advance questions? The anarchists are attacked for raising impossible demands, for going too fast, yet in the end the workers responded to their revolutionary credibility, not to the reformism of the regular parties; and in the centres dominated by years of anarchist activity, workers in insurrectionary periods proceeded directly to the establishment of *communismo libertario*. Yet ideas do not exist in a vacuum, but draw life and breath from ongoing interaction and solidarity, whose organisational forms must correspond to the ideas their adherents raise. If the revolutionary society is to be characterised by democratic control, autonomy and affective solidarity, then revolutionary organisations must also run on the basis of voluntary adherence, the sovereignty of base groups and the primacy of friendship over political lines and rules. To do otherwise, as the history of working-class movements shows, is not only bad ethics; it is also bad politics. The organising principles of revolutionary, libertarian groups were also those of the workers' councils and committees that emerged in insurrectionary periods: autonomy, control from below, voluntary adherence, the consensual working out of problems, an openness regardless of party affiliation and position in the labour force, federated coordination, intense solidarity. When the head of the Budapest police was condemned to death for his role in the Hungarian Revolution the Borsod Workers' Council threatened the Kadar régime with an armed march on the capital, and he was speedily released. Their action was highly reminiscent of the reprisal with which Rosa Luxemburg's Polish friends threatened the Polish government when she was imprisoned in the revolution of 1905-6.[53]

Contrary to official disclaimers, revolutionary politics works, while the crushing of workers' revolts have had as much to do with the conduct of the parties of the working class as with the limitations of the workers themselves. No magic recipe exists to surpass these difficulties except revolutionary activity itself, the constant hammering away at the contradictions of society in order to create networks of free men and women committed to the total transformation of the social order and daring to attempt it. Such praxis, as all those engaged in revolution from below have known, is predicated on the understanding that revolution is ultimately an act of affirmation, in which individuals create their own history as opposed to being stamped into a class identity, a process of action rather than organisation, of life, not death; and hence better a thousand times the workers' own mistakes than the infallibility of a central committee.

The organisational forms which underpin such revolutionary praxis are intimately linked to the social vision it advances. Decentralisation is no more to be fetishised than any specific form that autonomous working class organisation has taken in the past; and certainly not within the confines of capitalist society. An organisation based on decentralisation without any revolutionary commitment is in much the same situation as the CNT reformists who invoked the absence of a majority of workers in favour of *communismo libertario* as grounds for abandoning the revolutionary project. If autonomy and voluntary participation guide the conduct of revolutionary cadres, it is because the vision to which they are trying to gain adherents has no room for any master, neither capital nor state. Significantly, such forms of revolutionary organisation emerged to the greatest extent where the revolutionary libertarian tradition sunk its deepest roots, reflecting thereby the totality of the revolutionary process such as groups like the anarchists conceived it, and as indeed it really is. Revolutionary praxis cannot be restricted to the organised proletariat alone, but reaches out ot the entire working class, just as its locus of activity extends beyond the factory to encompass the city itself, and all its social contradictions. To do less is to acquiesce in the role which life in the capitalist factories assigns to the workers, contained in the very notion of the proletariat: the submergence of individual distinction and the capacity for autonomous action to the class viewed as an object of command and manipulation. This latter approach shows up organisationally in the form of the party, strategically in the emphasis on the principal contradiction and teleologically in the restriction of revolution to the seizure of state power, followed more or less by the nationalisation of the means of production. One could say that the 'metro-boulot-dodo' formula encapsulating the capitalist project finds its parallel, on the traditional left, in the equation Factory-Proletariat-Party-State.

Against them both stands the alternative tradition of libertarian socialism, based on the understanding that revolution means first and foremost the transformation of social relations, a transformation that can limit itself neither to the seizure of state power nor to the factory gates, but, by virtue of its totality, includes all social relations, and most especially those we have internalized. Hence its focus on all relations of oppression—those between bosses and workers, young and old, teachers and students, parents and children, men and women, the list is almost endless—and its understanding that all the oppressed are potential actors in a process of liberation which demands the confrontation of their own contradictions. Hence too its emphasis on networks or federations oriented towards the autonomous organisation of working class power, towards those sovereign bodies of workers' struggle which will abolish capital, replace the state and liberate social life from the domination of toil and hierarchy. Such are the thematic and strategic implications of the history of revolution from below, in which cities have played a key role ever since the flag of the Paris Commune was raised over a century ago. Petrograd, Berlin, Turin, Barcelona, Budapest, Lisbon —the names resonate with the social revolutions that went on within them. The countryside was important, but if the cities did not fall to the workers, the cities which were at once the heart of society's power structure, the point of industrial concentration and the centre of autonomous working class power, then the social revolution could not advance. As the anarchists' equation of *communismo libertario* with the commune has made clear, and the experience of recent years confirmed, the struggle for the city is very much the struggle for revolution from below, that is to say *social revolution*.

NOTES

(1.)   B. Lomax, *Hungary, 1956*, London, 1976, p. 45.
(2.)   P. Mailer, *op. cit.*, p. 60-1.
(3.)   G. Katkov, *Russia 1917*, London, 1969, p. 377; Brinton, *op. cit.*, p. 1, 5, 12-21.
(4.)   Brinton, *op. cit.*, p. 11, also p. 2-3, 8-9.
(5.)   *Ibid.*, p. 25-7.
(6.)   *Ibid.*, p. x-xv; J.-P. Nettl, *Rosa Luxemburg*, 2 vols., London, 1966, p. 285-94.
(7.)   Brinton, *op. cit.*, p. xii-xiii, also p. 39, 41, 56-7, 61-4, 77-82.
(8.)   Nettl, *op. cit.*, p. 786, also p. 751.
(9.)   R. Luxemburg, *The Russian Revolution*, in Waters (ed.), *op. cit.*, p. 384-95.
(10.)   *Ibid.*, p. 393-5; Nettl, *op. cit.*, p. 749-51, 785-6.
(11.)   R. Watt, *The Kings Depart*, N.Y., 1968, p. 164-7, 192-200, 215-17, 227-30; Nettl, *op. cit.*, p. 710-13, 720-1, 745-6.
(12.)   Watt, *op. cit.*, p. 266, also p. 254.
(13.)   *Ibid.*, p. 266-7; Nettl, *op. cit.*, p. 750, 756, 765-8, 771-2; Luxemburg, *The Russian Revolution*, *op. cit.*, p. 394-5.
(14.)   Watt, *op. cit.*, p. 229, also p. 158-61, 178-82, 216-7, 227-30.
(15.)   Nettl, *op. cit.*, p. 769, also p. 290, 761-9; Watt, *op. cit.*, p. 199-200, 230-5, 254-73.
(16.)   P. Spriano, *The Occupation of the Factories: Italy 1920*, London, 1975, p. 83, also p. 52-5, 60-3, 66, 75-8, 81-2, 117-20.
(17.)   *Ibid.*, p. 84, 85.
(18.)   *Ibid.*, p. 77, also p. 71, 75, 77-80, 85-93, 106.
(19.)   *Ibid.*, p. 92, also p. 79-80, 105.
(20.)   *Ibid.*, p. 28-9.
(21.)   *Ibid.*, p. 122, also p. 101, 108, 120-2, 129-30.
(22.)   Bookchin, *op. cit.*, p. 59.
(23.)   *Ibid.*, p. 161, also p. 54-8, 69-71, 78-9, 160-2.
(24.)   *Ibid.*, p. 249, also p. 162, 241-50.
(25.)   *Ibid.*, p. 174.
(26.)   *Ibid.*, p. 197, also p. 162, 175, 196.
(27.)   *Ibid.*, p. 242, 82-3.
(28.)   *Ibid.*, p. 249-50, also p. 141, 149-50, 177-9.
(29.)   *Ibid.*, p. 210, 285-6, 298-9.
(30.)   *Ibid.*, p. 270, also p. 268-71.
(31.)   M. Haraszti, "I Have Heard the Iron Cry" in *New Left Review*, 91, May-June 1975, p. 21.
(32.)   Lomax, op cit., p. 47-50, 115-6, 140, 147-9, 166, 198-200.
(33.)   *Ibid.*, p. 11.
(34.)   J. Pelikan. "Workers' Councils in Czechoslovakia" in *Critique*, vol. 1, no. 1, Spring 1973, p. 7-19; Lomax, *op. cit.*, p. 133, 140-1, 163-4.
(35.)   *Ibid.*, p. 169, also p. 149, 166-9, 200-3.
(36.)   *Ibid.*, p. 97, also p. 37-8, 85-92, 95-7, 100-3, 116, 159, 167.
(37.)   *Ibid.*, p. 162, also p. 150-62.
(38.)   Mailer, *op. cit.*, p. 132.
(39.)   *Ibid.*, p. 132-45, 150-1.
(40.).   *Ibid.*, p. 216.
(41.)   *Ibid.*, p. 249, also p. 90-3, 115-6, 208-14.
(42.)   *Ibid.*, p. 249-50, also p. 133-4.
(43.)   *Ibid.*, p. 245, also p. 145, 215, 286-7, 298.
(44.)   *Ibid.*, p. 305-6, also p. 254-6, 298, 304.
(45.)   *Ibid.*, p. 287, also, p. 288, 317.
(46.)   *Ibid.*, p. 328.
(47.)   *Ibid.*, p. 326.
(48.)   *Ibid.*, p. 335.
(49.)   *Ibid.*, p. 231, also p. 227-36.
(50.)   S. Dolgoff (ed.), *The Anarchist Collectives*, Montréal, Black Rose Books, 1974.
(51.)   Mailer, *op. cit.*, p. 217-20, 288.
(52.)   Nettl, *op. cit.*, p. 268, also p. 256-69.
(53.)   *Ibid.*, p. 350; Lomax, *op. cit.*, p. 97.

CHAPTER FOUR

REVOLUTION FROM BELOW: CONTEMPORARY URBAN STRUGGLES

Chile

FROM SANTIAGO to Rome contemporary urban struggles have been addressing the central contradictions of modern capitalism and thereby connecting with the revolutionary tradition of libertarian socialism. The demands posed have amounted to nothing less than the direct appropriation of social life, while the organisations which have emerged have insisted on working-class autonomy. Like other working class movements in this tradition, however, they have had to deal not only with the problems posed by capital, but also with those posed by their own unions and parties.

Urban struggles in Chile grew out of the contradictions of Chilean capitalism and the attempts by the Frei government to deal with them, especially in the area of housing, with a series of liberal reform measures during the period 1964-70. The domination of the housing market by private enterprise, linked to monopoly U.S. capital, coupled with the massive rural migration to the cities, created a housing deficit of over half a million by the 1960s and extensive shantytowns which ringed Chile's major cities with revolutionary potential. The Frei government tried to respond to this situation by stimulating economic growth with the aid of American capital and using state funds and institutions to ameliorate the lot of the "pobladores", the urban poor. As part of its reform programme, the Frei government set about organising the urban poor by creating a number of different bodies within the shantytowns, through which housing and other social services were channelled to the dependent population. In this way it was hoped to contain a potentially explosive situation and integrate the urban poor into Chilean capitalist development. The subordination of Chilean development to its local bourgeoisie and U.S. imperialism, however, undermined economic growth, created tremendous inflation and forced the state to cut back on its social programme. The result was popular unrest, fanned by the left-wing organisations which had also moved into the shantytowns opened up by the government intervention and sought to encourage more autonomous community organisation, illegal occupations, etc. This was a large part of the social background in the pobladores leading to the electoral victory of the Popular Front government headed by Allende in 1970.

The Allende government used the control it could obtain on financial institutions and the construction industry to reorient the spatial and social distribution of housing in favour of the working class, including the urban poor. This led to much greater control of the production process by construction workers, who organised themselves into brigades in response to the employers' boycott of the government's housing policy. Within the shantytowns organisations of democratic self-management arose, starting with committees composed of residents and construction workers to make sure that the rate of construction proceeded apace and to counter ripostes from the bosses. These self-management institutions spread to other areas of social life: justice, education, health and self-defence, as the Allende government introduced reforms in these fields as well. Two significant traits marked this process. The first was that this self-management of social life, which led to other social transformations, like the participation of women in political life, was undertaken by that section of the working class always considered marginal, dependent and incapable of initiative and self-organisation. The second was the link-up made between the two fronts of production and consumption, a link-up that proved central not only to a new form of urban organisation but also to a new form of class power.

The upsurge of popular control of community life was paralleled in the workers' occupation of factories. When the bosses tried to counter this growing movement towards worker control with their strike of 1972, which hit at the weakest point in the government's strategy —the control of distribution—the entire working class responded with incredible energy, enlarging upon the measures they had already initiated to counter this threat. They occupied plants, requisitioned means of transport, set up their own distribution networks, and through committees which controlled supplies and prices, provided the materials needed in the factories and the goods and services required by the population. In the process coordinating committees between various firms were set up, while in many neighbourhoods and localities communal councils were established linking the industrial cordons with community organisations.

Although this self-initiated exercise of workers' power defeated the bosses' strike and saved the government, the latter, anxious to avoid a confrontation between the forces of capital and the people, resolved the crisis by bringing the military into the government and thereby froze the mass movement for the moment. Its action reflected the parliamentary limits to which it narrowed political combat and the way it used popular mobilisation to reinforce its parliamentay position. Such conduct is characteristic of social-democratic politics and indicative of its inability to conceive of a revolutionary project without the state. It is also self-defeating, weakening both the popular movement and its parliamentary expression.

The entry of the military into the Allende government did not lead the Right to abate its attacks, but on the contrary, encouraged them in their campaign of political and economic sabotage. The conservative wing of the Popular Unity government succumbed to this pressure and suggested handing back some of the factories occupied by the workers in the fall of 1972. The workers mobilised against this proposal and succeeded in pressuring the Popular Union to go to the polls in March, 1973 on a radical platform committed to workers' control and popular power. The result was a "victory" for the revolutionary movement, but the lessons were lost once again on the government as it refused to arm the workers in the face of mounting pressure from the Right, who understood only too well the import of the electoral results. The rest in history, bloody and tragic.[1]

If urban struggles are very much part of the wider class struggle, their limitations are also those of the wider revolutionary movement that emerges from the contradictions of capitalism and unfolds in dialectical opposition to its institutions. The initial victory of the Popular Unity government created a space within which the movement for revolution from below could develop. The government's use of certain state institutions encouraged this process, yet the primacy accorded to electoral and parliamentary politics in the end doomed the revolutionary movement. This dialectic of urban struggles in Chile also characterised those that emerged elsewhere, notably in France and Italy, throwing the strategic implications of the current crisis and their contradictions into sharp relief.

France

URBAN MOVEMENTS in the Paris region in the 1970s, both in their practice and in their demands, challenged the dominant class' organisation of social life. Sometimes the challenge remained implicit, directed at a very immediate and specific issue, like the increase in public transport fares in 1971. Yet the form opposition to the fare hike took—people collectively riding the metro free—was itself a radical challenge to the dominant order. This form of opposition has become part of daily life in Paris, while the immediate demand has led to a questioning of the role that automobiles and autoroutes play in fashioning urban space. Housing struggles also took the form of direct action —illegal occupations, squatting and rent strikes, especially among young and immigrant workers, but over the years the focus of their protest changed from shoddy and expensive housing to the nature of the housing itself. Immigrants challenged the racism which surrounded them and both denounced the repressive and authoritarian management summed up in the slogan 'non aux foyers-casernes'. Resistance by inner-city residents to the central power's renovation projects and the deportation to the suburbs which awaits them, has opened up a wider debate about the quality of urban life which has surfaced in more recent conflicts. At heart these struggles

> "put into question a conception of urban development, a type of relation between time at work and time outside work, a form of management of daily life. They reveal the decisive place which the sphere of consumption occupies in contemporary capitalism, as well as the central role played by the state, as much in the consumption field as in the regulation of social relations. In this sense, they represent much more than a symptom of the urban crisis."[2]

These struggles have been especially successful where linkups have been made with workers at the point of production. The notable case in the Paris region where the unions participated actively was the fight against public transport fare increases. Although the demand for free public transport, paid for by the employers and usable throughout the Paris region, which arose during the struggle has not been attained, the most important part of the fare hike, the weekly travel card to work, was prevented. As a result, the Paris rapid transit authority is running a deficit which shows no signs of being borne by its users. The political combativity of the working class directed at a point of consumption thus reinforces the class struggle as much as contests in the workplace, hitting out at the circulation of capital and exacerbating its contradictions in the form of the fiscal crisis of the state.

Nonetheless, urban movements modelled on the trade unions, a sort of unionism of collective consumption, run the risk of falling into the reformist practice of the trade unions, limiting the struggles to the immediate satisfaction of specific demands rather than the transformation of social relations. Such movements have also tended to be dependent on the political parties whom they have often propelled into municipal office, but who, once encumbered with the responsibility of managing the local version of the state's fiscal crisis, dampen the combative élan of the movements and opt for a bureaucratic, rather than a mobilising orientation. This dialectic was clearly present in Sarcelles, one of the large development projects in the Paris region, where an active residents' association contributed to the electoral victory of the left in the 1965 municipal elections. The left-wing government then negotiated a development plan with the Central Building Society of the Investment Fund, since in the past they had attacked the piece-meal manner in which the commune was constructed. The accord confirmed the developer's original density estimates, which the residents' association had strongly opposed. The government's calculations were that the higher density would generate increased revenue, which it could then use to finance other services demanded by the residents. Yet in so doing, they had to accept the dominant form of urbanism which the residents rejected and opposed the citizens' right to determine the nature of their urban environment. The result was the weakening of the residents' association and the subordination of the extra-parliamentary groups to the municipal government, with all that that implies.

Such an outcome, in general, is all the more likely given the reformist orientation of the PCF, the French Communist Party and the left-wing party often at the head of local administrations. Young immigrants, living in Paris in dwellings run by Sonacotra, withheld their rent and set up a coordinating committee independent of the trade unions and political parties, with whom Sonacotra refused to negotiate. On the other hand, it did accept to negotiate with delegates from the three buildings out of the sixty on strike where the PCF and the CNL, the National Housing Committee dominated by the PCF, controlled the struggle. In general, although the PCF has supported urban struggles, it has also channelled them into the framework of capitalist everyday life precisely at the point they have tried to get beyond it. When women in one Parisian ghetto, Villejuif, chased out the cops with the aid of PCF militants and sat down to discuss their own problems, all the PCF militants could offer was a discussion of the left's common programme and party membership. When committees of young unemployed demanded guaranteed incomes and free services, the PCF denounced them as leftists, since they were beyond the control of the official trade union movement. At the same time the PCF sought to recuperate their demands in order to denounce the government's and capital's inability to deal with unemployment and offered, as an example of a possible solution, the industrial development project put forward by the communist mayor of Champigny. In so doing the PCF translated the refusal to work into a demand for work, kept the young insurgents in a state of dependency and revealed its very traditional conception of social change.[3]

In opposition to the orientation of some urban movements and the reformism of the traditional left-wing parties a number of groups have emerged linking immediate reforms with a political challenge to the dominant order, participating in both issue-specific struggles and electoral politics to advance their radical demands for direct democracy and the appropriation of social wealth. Some of these struggles, like the squatters' movement in Paris in the early seventies, have been dominated by the Maoists, with much the same results as in the Portugese situation: a rather mechanistic application of a tactic regardless of the particular circumstances of the district, a failure to broaden the movement to include other struggles of other sections of the working class, a tendency to regulate the internal contradictions of the groups they worked with and so maintain the latter in a state of dependency. The subordination of the immediate issue to the political concerns of the militants reduced their support among the population and opened them up to the repression by the state which followed. Because the squatters' movement did not follow the traditional reformist pattern of urban struggles, but raised political demands which could explode in the present crisis, the state intervened swiftly and brutally; yet the ease with which the latter managed to repress the movement had much to do with the failure of a popular base to emerge autonomous from the political militants, a failure to which avant-gardist practice offers little redress.

Nonetheless, the problem posed by the experience of the squatters' movement is quite real. If the success of urban struggles depends on the emergence of a strong, autonomous popular force linking different sections of the working class, what kind of praxis is required such that the radical political implications of specific issues can be raised without the movement's being repressed by the state before such a force can emerge? The more radical urban movements that have emerged in the big development projects in the Paris region have encountered only limited electoral success and have not yet won, to any significant extent, the support of the factory and office workers living in these areas. The class segmentation of these suburbs seems to have been reproduced in the political movements which the contradictions of urban life have thrown up. At the same time, the attempts by the developer to soak up potential discontent which had surfaced earlier in similar residential agglomerations, by diversifying its social composition and offering a range of social activities, met with resistance on the part of the residents themselves. The residents' council set up by the developer to limit potential conflict was dominated at Sarcelles by the residents' association, which used it to demand effective control over rents, services and the administration of the project, with the long-term aim of self-management. A similar logic of turning the residents' council against its intended purpose was at work in the neighbouring agglomeration of Val d'Yerres, although the predominance of the CNL did not lead it in the direction of self-management. Even the residents of supposedly the ritziest part of the complex organised counter-forms of leisure activities to those offered by the developer.

Their resistance shows the extent to which opposition to the social control inherent in the capitalist organisation of urban space surpasses the strict categories of class that emerge at the point of production. This resistance also shows the radical potential inherent in urban struggles despite the dilemma posed above. As yet this resistance has taken a defensive form, resulting in the drift to the left among the municipal governments of the large agglomerations and the state's decision to abandon further construction in light of their failure as tools of social integration.[4] For this resistance to develop its revolutionary potential, urban movements will have to connect with the radical tradition of libertarian socialism implicit in this terrain of struggle. The French experience poses the need for a long-term perspective even as it raises the dilemma of its practicability. To see the unthinkable and the impossible in action one has to turn towards Italy.

Italy

URBAN STRUGGLES in Italy emerged out
of the crisis of Italian capitalism, itself the product of the increasingly
revolutionary militancy of Italian workers at the point of production.
More pay for less work, the suppression of wage differentials, the
emergence of internal commissions based on shop floor and assembly-
line delegates as parallel bodies to the trade unions, sabotage, absenteeism, wildcat strikes and work stoppages characterised the struggles
of Italian workers in the factories of monopoly capital throughout the
seventies. The lessons are salutary and significant. In the first place,
such radical action was common to very different groups of workers,
reflecting once again that popular militancy is not the prerogative of any
one section of the working class. In 1969 immigrants from the south of
Italy formed a large proportion of Fiat workers. The management,
feeling their recent arrival gave them little attachment to the factory,
saw in them a major cause of the upsurge of working class militancy and
sought therefore to isolate or cashier them. In the years that followed
they recruited their workers from the Turin labour force, but in 1972 and
1973 conflict broke out again with renewed vigor and even greater
displays of working class autonomy. In March 1973, tired of lagging
negotiations and the union strategy which called for limited strikes by
different sectors within the plant, the workers took matters into their
own hands, organised processions throughout the Fiat factory and in
little over a week succeeded in occupying the entire plant at Mirafiori.
This was no small feat given the tremendous area over which the plant
extended. As one worker pointed out looking back at the occupation,
had the idea been suggested in 1968 or 1969, the reaction would have
been one of incredulity:

"We would have been told: 'It's not possible, there are too many doors, there is a sea of doors.' This time the occupation seemed like child's play."[5]

It succeeded precisely because no one raised it in advance; rather the strategy emerged in the course of the action, reflecting once again how revolutionary moments cannot be "organised", but once they emerge the workers come up with the appropriate action. In this case it consisted of workers from different sections going to block doors in other areas of the plant, an action itself inconceivable without the initiative taken by workers on the shop floor.

As usual, the unions and the PCI, the Italian Communist Party, denounced the workers' initiative as adventurous and came out in favour of wage differentials. Forced to recognize the delegates' movement, they sought to institutionalise it in the form of factory councils. In exchange for the imposition of social order demanded by the capitalists, they proposed a series of structural reforms in line with their state capitalist thinking, amounting to a more rational use of productive capacities and investment funds. The negotiated settlements were always much less than what the workers demanded, involving considerable wage increases but not touching on the issues pertaining to workers' control. In a sense, however, this was a victory, which only the autonomous organisation of the working class guaranteed. On the one hand, the profits squeeze on Italian capitalists was maintained; on the other, the unions were forced to resist capital's attempts to link recognition of the delegates' movement to productivity increases. The return to work did not lead to any let-up in the workers' opposition, which amounted to no more and no less than the refusal to work, thus driving even Fiat to have recourse to the Cassa Integrazione, that system, now expanded, whereby the state covers, for an indefinite period, 80-100% of the salaries of workers laid off by private enterprise for almost any reason.

Although the massive layoffs diminished somewhat the force of the delegates' movement, it merely displaced the struggle from the factory to the city. The crisis of Italian capitalism, coupled with the strains it placed on the state's finances, led the state to try and recoup from the workers via the social wage what capital could not impose at the workplace. From 1974 on increases in transport, electricity and telephone rates were announced, provoking a series of urban struggles characterised by the same kind of autonomous working class militancy that marked the conflicts in the factories. The merging of contradictions in the workplace and the community found its strategic parallel in the linkups made between workers from both social spaces, while the dialectic between organisations at the base and the official organs of the working class was reproduced here as well.[6]

The history of urban struggles goes back many years in Italy. Housing was a major area of class conflict in Rome in the immediate post-war period and continued to be so in the fifties and sixties. The development of Rome as a bureaucratic and financial capital and a corridor for migrant labour, subordinated to land speculation and the private construction industry, produced a housing crisis such that by 1969 70,000 workers lived in abysmal conditions while 40,000 apartments stood empty because of their prohibitive cost. In a generally volatile political context created by workers and students' struggles, citizens' groups, aided by left-wing militants, started to occupy flats and reduce rents on their own (self-reduction). The occupations gave rise to Suburban Agitation Committees composed of delegates from each group of occupiers in the working class and poorer districts of Rome. An attempt was made to get each group to assume responsibility for its own struggle and through the struggle, to enlarge the number of cadres in the movement. This effort met with only partial success, given the disperal and divisions of workers in the shantytowns. These problems were reinforced by the PCI, who condemned the direct action of the workers and sought to turn the struggle, as it had done on earlier occasions, into reformist and parliamentary channels. The PCI claimed that the occupation of public housing set the occupiers against those workers on the waiting list for dwellings, yet the PCI's subordination of popular struggles to a demand for a rational urban policy in the past did not succeed in curbing the ruling Christian Democrats' use of public housing to build up a political clientele.

The Suburban Agitation Committee's efforts at the autonomous organisation of workers around the housing issue did succeed somewhat. Three to four thousand inhabitants of the shantytowns demonstrated around the capitol and five hundred newly constructed apartments slated for civil servants were occupied. In Turin housing occupations and the self reduction of rents did lead to the autonomous organisation of tenants and the poorly housed in certain districts. When IACP, the public housing construction authority, tried to play off the occupiers against the workers on the list for those dwellings, a joint committee of the two groups was formed, in which it was agreed that the workers waiting for those apartments would not move in until the squatters had obtained assurances of a dwelling. Once again the workers in direct struggle found an answer to what the reformist parties could only see as an insurmountable problem. Nonetheless, when the extreme left tried to push these local struggles into a wider political movement, linking up with other areas of collective consumption like the schools, health services, etc., and with factory struggles, they ran into considerable difficulty. In the years 1970-74 the struggles remained confined more or less to the political and ideological boundary of the neighbourhood, into which moved the PCI and the organisations like SUNIA, the national tenants' union, which it controlled.

In part the inability of urban struggles to get beyond their specific and local character in the period 1969-71 was a response to their being caught between the hammer of left-wing avant-gardism and the anvil of PCI reformism; but in part it also reflected that the moment was simply not right. This does not mean that urban struggles are inevitably doomed to 'neighbourhoodism', or that the principles of direct action and autonomous organisation are impractical. Rather it suggests that the moments of popular upsurge are not predictable, that no political line can guarantee a revolutionary outburst or account totally for its failure, and that hammering away in the intervals of political quiet at the contradictions of capitalism, advancing revolutionary ideas, pushing for autonomous working class mobilisation are not wasted efforts. When urban struggles exploded once again in 1974 they extended to areas beyond housing and made linkups with the unions. Those tenant groups and neighbourhood committees who had already been involved in housing occupations, who had not ceased to reduce their rents, who had some history of political combat provided the most persistent support in this next wave of self-reduction struggles. In Rome two new features stood out in this round of housing occupations: the direct participation of factory workers and the extension of the movement to include dwellings built by the private sector, giving the struggle a dynamism similar to that exhibited by the workers of Santiago and Lisbon. The combativity of the workers produced tangible results, the occupation movement spread to Naples and Milan, and the state found itself faced with an intensified fiscal crisis. In 1974 delays in rent payments had reached the 20% level and the deficit of the public low-income housing office, 5 billion lire. By the autumn of 1975 the movement had become enriched:

"with a new form of communist appropriation of the city: groups of young workers had installed themselves in dilapidated factories and transformed them into places for encounters, life and combat."[7]

The self-reduction struggles that emerged around the transport and electricity increases in 1974 also bore all the hallmarks of revolution from below—spontaneous and direct action organised by the workers independent of their unions and parties; linkups between the factory and the city; demands and forms of organisation that represented attempts to appropriate and transform the direction of social life; the development of strategies that required the practice of revolutionary principles. In the process the workers showed that the limitations encountered by urban movements in France, and previously in Italy, could be surpassed, and that the contradictions underlying their emergence were very real indeed. When the increases in transport fares were announced in 1974 in different parts of Italy, the first reaction on the part of workers was spontaneous and unorganised. In the Turin region cars were blocked, leaflets distributed and delegations descended on the municipalities. In the Milan region workers' committees in the factories went out on wildcat strikes opposing the fare increases. The PCI and the national unions opposed such action. The Milan strike was attacked on the grounds that the workers were confounding the role of their organisations with that of the mayor and the government. Under the impulse of popular pressure, however, the Turin steelworkers' union (FLM) undertook to organise the struggle on the basis of self-reduction. Their example, combined with the initiative taken by workers who did not wait for their unions to give the order, helped the movement spread.

The struggle was organised in the following manner. Union militants took up positions in front of the wickets where workers usually bought their weekly pass and distributed leaflets outlining their position calling on the users of public transport to pay only the old fare. Delegates appointed to each car of a bus or train then collected the fare at the old rate, issued a receipt prepared by the unions, who then handed over the money to the company concerned. This form of action was decided upon in part because protest in the factory was useless, a boycott was difficult to organise and a total refusal to pay would have led the companies to stop operating. Significantly, however, it was the extension of the class struggle beyond the factory gates that led the unions to break with tradition and place themselves at the center of a strategy of civil disobedience, an action that even three years earlier appeared unthinkable. This development was not only the result of popular pressure, but also of the sharpening of the contradictions of capitalism in the areas of collective consumption. As urban transport worsened, the unions of the FLM began to take a stance on issues other than wages. For a number of years they had been demanding public management of the interregional transport systems, the gradual implementation of free public transport paid for by the employers and, in the meantime, more equitable fare rates, especially for those having to travel longer distances, which was often the case for tens of thousands of workers.

Similar forces were at work in the self-reduction of electricity rate increases. In Turin the example of the transport struggles led the unions to take the initiative this time. The union in the state electricity corporation proposed a 50% self-reduction and the Turin FLM, uniting workers from the three union federations, undertook to organise it. Elsewhere the union leadership often proved refractory, as did factory councils dominated by the PCI; but wherever the base was strong the leadership had to fall in line, as even PCI militants joined in the struggle. There were also other pressures. Since 1973 the combative workers in ENEL, the state electricity corporation, had been meeting to figure out a riposte to the freeze on hiring and the letting go of 12,000 workers which had been part of ENEL policy since 1970. The struggle of some women in Rome in 1972 against electricity increases taught them the importance of linking up with consumers, while the hike which followed intense struggles at the workplace made it clear to workers in general that the defense of their living standards could not be limited to the factory.

Direct action thus appeared as a viable strategy, but it was also politically significant. It permitted the workers to practice, in their actions, the aim of the struggle itself and thereby signified their refusal to accord capital or the state the right to determine how society should run. The demands of the autonomous assembly of workers in ENEL on the transport issue were eloquent in this respect:

> "We have had enough of cattle cars, troop transports, rigid schedules put in place to control us, wage discrimination, the bigwigs of private transport. We want to travel for free, comfortably, quickly; we want our travelling time to be included in our work hours and paid for by the bosses. Our lives, our health, the possibility to spend a few hours in the company of our wives, to take care of our children, to meet with friends and comrades are matters which do not have a price. The struggle around transport is important precisely in that it concerns us all at that level. For this reason the struggle against the bosses is above all a struggle on our part to take back our time and our health. We do not want to settle this question cheaply or even sell it for a little more. Travel time is work time; we want to have the time to be with ourselves."[8]

In line with the principles of direct action and the reappropriation of social life that it implied each participant in the electricity struggle was required to take a certain initiative. First a petition was circulated which obliged each signatory to deduct 50% from his bill and send, along with his payment, a letter to ENEL explaining he or she was acting in line with the directives of the three Turin labour unions. The signatories had also to indicate their account number and the amount, thus obliging them to read their bill and giving the unions some measure of the dimensions of the struggle. The electricity workers' unions helped out by supplying all the information concerning the dates on which bills were issued, district by district, thus enabling the factory or community committees to set up pickets in front of the local post office on the appropriate day and hand out prepared forms for the workers to fill out in paying their bills.

The organisation of such a struggle led inevitably to the emergence of autonomous forms of workers' power, which explains more than anything else the tepid support, if not outright opposition, of the PCI and the national unions. For example, in the Milan region a number of struggles emerged around the poor service of commuter trains, leading to the formation of a commuters' committee composed of delegates from each station and train, who demanded a complete re-vamping of the service and recognition of their committee, and pro-ceeded to block the trains in support of their claims. At this point the PCI regional organisation intervened, denouncing their spontaneity and promising help in mobilising support, which turned out to be the organisation of a meeting where they talked about the problems of freight transport and the need to develop a new rail system.

The conduct of the PCI in Milan regarding the electricity struggle was little different. The regional executives of the unions, in line with the national leadership dominated by the PCI-affiliated CGIL, held back the self-reduction movement; and the same was true of Rome. Nonethe-less the movement spread. 150,000 households practised self-reduction in the Turin area and estimates for all of Italy ran to 280,000. The majority were workers, but the numbers included some families of the petite bourgeoisie, thus indicating, in contrast to the French experience, the possibility of conducting a radical, massive urban struggle under the leadership of the working class. In some areas, such as Naples, the movement exploded without any union participation, as local district committees helped organise the self-reduction of more than 60,000 bills.

The participation of the unions, however, was very important, especially in the electricity struggle where the electricity workers' union refused to cut off the current from those dwellings where self-reduction was practised, thereby providing the movement with one of the guaran-tees of its success. Conversely, the abstention of the unions from the struggle, outside of Turin, prevented the movement from growing and developing into a more significant political challenge to the state. In both the transport and electricity struggles, moreover, the unions saw in the self-reduction movement only a tactic to force a negotiated agreement to the dispute; and in each case the negotiated agreement could only be described as a partial victory at best. In the case of the electricity increases, for example, the rates agreed upon after the struggle represented a considerable improvement for those who consumed the least amount of electricity, by implication the lowest income groups.

On the other hand, for the vast majority of working class families, the new rates were as high or higher than those previously announced, amounting to a 60-70% increase. Once the agreement was signed, the unions made every effort to bring the movement to a halt; and in the face of their opposition, attempts by the extreme left to keep it going did not prove overly fruitful. The movement did continue, but on a reduced scale and forced back into the community.

The unions' decision to call a halt to the movement and settle for a negotiated agreement was motivated in part by tactical considerations specific to its own functioning. On the transport issue the Turin unions in the FLM found the organisation of the struggle a considerable burden which would be difficult to support over a very long time, especially in view of other struggles and other negotiations that loomed. In the case of the electricity struggle, the Turin unions felt more isolated as the date for the second round of self-reductions approached, while in the meantime the economic crisis worsened and a new government appeared, suggesting that a negotiated agreement was possible. The problem, however, went deeper than the tactical constraints inherent in union activity. It was also a question of the revolutionary conception and the historic role to which the unions and parties of the working class subscribed. The Turin unions and the Turin PC were always more radical than their national counterparts, reflecting thereby the much more militant tradition of the Turin working class. Both participated actively in the self-reduction movement around electricity, just as the PCI and the CGIL opposed it at the national level. What the latter feared most was the autonomous organisation of the working class implicit in the form of direct action which the movement assumed. Self-reduction represented not only the workers' refusal to foot the bill of the contemporary crisis of capitalism, but also their refusal to accept the social control exercised by the state as it attempts to resolve that crisis. The refusal to work spills over into the area of social consumption, leading workers in the course of their struggles to appropriate directly the control of social life:

> "Self-reduction puts into question, almost always directly, the state, the public authorities; one of its principal dimensions consists in the political idea of which it is the instrument, namely the idea of a social control, of popular control of so-called collective consumption, the idea of 'political' prices for public services . . . going against the policy of 'the true cost' of public services put forward by the Carli plan."[9]

This confrontation with the state is reinforced by the practice of civil disobedience inherent in self-reduction struggles, a practice that can only weaken the state which the PCI wants to manage. Indeed, the whole of PCI policy, its historic compromise with the Christian Democrats, is predicated on its capacity to transform Italian society through its control of the state—a fitting, if sad, dénouement to a revolutionary tradition that over sixty years ago also saw social revolution in terms of the seizure of state power.

Ironically, it was the wave of popular struggles that contributed so much to the electoral victory of the left-wing coalitions at the municipal level throughout Italy by the mid-seventies. With the left installed in government, the whole dialectic between electoral politics and extra-parliamentary struggles, between state power and autonomous working class organisation, between reform and revolution reasserted itself. For the urban movements the problem was how to use and maintain this new leverage to advance the movement without getting coopted. For the parties in government the question hardly presented itself in this way. Their traditional reformist orientation was reinforced by the situation in which they found themselves: in short, forced to govern the fiscal crisis of the state at the local level with no resources, while the Christian-Democrats who controlled the national government starved them for funds. The dilemma they faced could have led them to different conclusions, namely the need to reinforce the popular struggles and autonomous workers' organisations whenever possible, but such a strategy went against the grain of their entire political project. When a self-reduction movement emerged in June-July 1975 to contest the telephone rate increases, the left-wing parties and the unions kept their distance. Instead, in the context of the municipal elections of June, they picked up some of the movement's demands and defended them through very traditional, parliamentary forms of action.

The pressures acting on the unions were much the same as in the electricity struggle, and this time the threat of the government and SIP, the telephone monopoly, that failure to increase the rates would lead to cutbacks in salaries and jobs made a dent on the workers. The extra-parliamentary left tried to join the demand for lower rates with that of workers' control, especially regarding the company's investment and reconversion policies. Yet the general reformist orientation of the PCI and the unions only reinforced the corporatist reaction of the workers. In the end the agreement negotiated, itself a result mainly of the pressure kept up by the self-reduction movement which had reached on its own 150,000, proved to be weak, in line with the strategy pursued by the official left, and highly similar to the outcome of the electricity struggle.

There was one new wrinkle to the self-reduction movement that emerged around the telephone increase: the role played by radical lawyers and judges in helping the movement advance. In the payments sent to the company, those who practised self-reduction explained that they would settle the rest of their account should the increase prove legal. A number of judges agreed that this was a perfectly legitimate action and thereby gave the movement a breathing space, especially as the unions were approaching the government for a negotiated settlement. In the meantime a number of radical lawyers investigated the SIP case and found it to be full of errors and abuses which, according to the Italian Constitution, did not justify the increase. Their dossier caused a scandal, undermining the legitimacy of the monopoly and of the state which had defended it. Some claimed that the involvement of the judges and lawyers made the movement too dependent on the professionals, but this was not in fact the case; while the dependence that did arise could be traced directly to the absence of union participation, which had lent previous such struggles their legitimacy.

The history of these radical lawyers and judges is itself an interesting sidelight and sheds further light on the radically different nature of the reformist and revolutionary outlooks. Radicalised by the class conflict of the sixties, these radical magistrates formed their own association within the National Association of Magistrates called Magistratura Democratica, MD, which subsequently split in 1969 with the more reformist members close to the PCI leaving to form their own group. The significance of MD lies precisely in the refusal of these radical magistrates to separate their politics and their work, and their decision to fight the battle, as Marxists, not in the factory but in the legal arena. The dismissal of such a position sometimes found among the Marxist-Leninist left fails to understand the revolutionary significance of such action. Not only did MD help spread revolutionary ideas in contexts outside traditional areas of class struggle; they also confronted bourgeois democracy on its own terrain and showed how weak its commitment to liberal values really is. Although MD has not yet dealt with the question of the role of a judicial system in the transition to socialism, its actions clearly raise the question and thus make it more difficult for it to be ignored, a prospect which past experience has shown to be fraught with disaster. Their investigation of SIP in the telephone struggle indicated the importance of liberal values and liberal institutions for the socialist movement. The attitude of the PCI to MD, on the other hand, has shown it to be conformist in the extreme and its pretensions to liberal values as limited as those of the bourgeois democracy it criticizes. When MD tried in 1971 to initiate a referendum against the provisions in the fascist code still in effect regarding offences pertaining to the expression of opinions, the PCI kept its distance, a practice which has only increased as its chances of electoral succes seem greater.[10]

In spite of the reformism of the parties of the left, the popular movement in Italy moves forward. Self-reduction of rents and housing occupations still go on. Consumer groups have passed from food boycotts to the direct seizure of goods in supermarkets in the heart of working- class Milan. Women's movements have exploded around the issues of day-care, divorce and abortion. Urban struggles in Italy represent in many ways the most recent and most advanced expression of the libertarian tradition of social revolution, but their unfolding has not been free of that dialectic between the reformism of official parties and the revolutionary politics of the base. However advanced they may appear to situations in other countries, they have emerged from a crisis which is common to all of advanced capitalism and have raised demands which workers in other countries, in one way or another, have also raised, thereby producing "a political crisis of consensus in the face of which 'economic' measures remain powerless."[11] It is worth remembering too that many of the features which urban struggles have assumed in Italy would have been unthinkable at an earlier date, such that the questions we might pose about the Montréal experience would best be looked at with this caveat in mind. The 'failures' of the struggles around the east-west autoroute, Milton-Park, St-Norbert are part of the same open-ended process and debate as the Italian self-reduction struggles around the electricity and telephone rates.[12] The lessons are there to learn from, but there is no magic formula. Bearing in mind, however, our understanding of urban contradictions and the lessons of the historical and contemporary experience of revolution from below, we can try and develop strategies that will lead urban struggles further than recent analyses indicate they have gone.

NOTES

(1.) P. Donovan et al, *Des conseils de quartier pour Montréal ?*, Montréal, Centre de Recherches et d'Innovation Urbaines, September, 1974, ch. 3, "Les organisations populaires et le mouvement ouvrier chilien", p. 71-100; P.G. P. Allende, R. Cheetham Price, "Politique du logement et lutte de classes au Chili (1970-75)" in *International Journal of Urban and Regional Research*, vol. 1, no. 3, 1977, p. 474-507; M. Raptis, "What Kind of Socialism in Chile?" in *Our Generation*, vol. 10, no. 2, summer 1974, p. 3-47.

(2.) Cherki, Mehl, *op. cit.*, p. 10-11; E. Cherki, "Populisme et idéologie révolutionnaire dans le mouvement des squatters: Région parisienne 1972-1973" in *Sociologie du travail*, 2, 1976, p. 192-215. (My translation—S.S.)

(3.) Collonges, Randal, *op. cit.*, p. 126-31; Cherki, Mehl, *op. cit.*, p. 17-19; D. Mehl, "Les luttes des résidents dans les grands ensembles" in *Sociologie du travail*, 4, 1975, p. 357-9, 366-8.

(4.) Mehl, *op. cit.*, p. 368-71, also p. 360-1; Cherki, *op. cit.*, p. 205, 207, 212-5.

(5.) Collonges, Randal, *op. cit.*, p. 42. (My translation—S.S.)

(6.) *Ibid.*, p. 31-50.

(7.) *Ibid.*, p. 73, also p. 53-73 (My translation—S.S.); Cherki, Wieviorka, *op. cit.*, p. 1793-1807.

(8.) Collonges, Randal, *op. cit.*, p. 78-9. (My translation—S.S.)

(9.) Cherki, Wieviorka, *op. cit.*, p. 1830 (My translation—S.S.), also p. 1807-31; Collonges, Randal, *op. cit.*, p. 75-89, 97-114.

(10.) E. Cherki, M. Wieviroka, "Luttes sociales en Italie (2): magistrats et autoréducteurs" in *Les Temps Modernes*, nov., 1976, p. 635-73.

(11.) Collonges, Randal, *op. cit.*, p. 123 (My translation—S.S.), also p. 93-5, 122; Cherki, Wieviorka, "Luttes sociales en Italie (2)", *op. cit.*, p. 639-40, 673.

(12.) Hamel, Léonard, *op. cit.*, p. 73-6.

CHAPTER FIVE

ELEMENTS OF A SOCIALIST STRATEGY ON THE URBAN QUESTION

The dialectic of revolution and reform

IT IS CLEAR that the urban politics cannot be divorced from the wider class struggle; in many respects it lies at its heart. The contradictions of contemporary capitalism, the implications of the revolutionary project raised by urban struggles, the historical lessons of the libertarian tradition in which this project is embedded—all point to the need to link struggles of production with those of reproduction, the work place with the community, and redefine the latter terrain so as to embrace all the points of contradiction and oppression in the organisation of social life. It is not only that struggles emerging in the community around the issues of collective consumption need support of workers at the point of production in order to succeed; nor simply a question that only their joint demands against capital can prevent the movement from taking a very narrow and particularist turn. It is also that the transformation of social relations, the thorough democratisation of social life cannot be limited to one area of social life. Workers' control of the production process goes hand in hand with the control of community life, of which the ordering of land development, the control of the schools and the patterning of leisure activities are all part, just as their common subordination to the imperatives of capital create multiple points of oppression and resistance.

In the course of urban struggles, therefore, there is a need to forge a broad unity around these various issues, but a unity that takes revolutionary form only in working class organisations independent of the state, the party and our present type of union. Such institutions, be they neighbourhood councils or workplace councils serve both as organs of revolutionary struggle and as the basis of a new federated society to replace the rule of capital and the state. Yet such organisations emerge from struggles around specific issues, whose conduct often requires alliances with citizens' groups and trade unions which have different and sometimes very limited objectives, and which occur in an institutional framework weighted towards the political integration of opposition to the dominant social order. These constraints pose a strategic dilemma to urban struggles: how to move through the reformist channel of everyday life towards a revolutionary perspective and organisation.

The first such problem arises around the issue of specific reforms. Urban struggles emerge out of immediate grievances and specific contradictions. Buildings are destroyed, rents go up, transit fares are increased. As the Italian experience shows, however, if urban struggles are to succeed and their revolutionary implications emerge, then those engaged in them must go beyond the immediate reforms to raise the most revolutionary demands implicit in the very nature of these struggles. Resistance to transit fare increases is also a critique of the capitalist organisation of time, and must be seen as such. By making the claim explicit, those engaged in such a struggle succeed in translating a specific reform into one of the most revolutionary claims of *communismo libertario*: the right to dispose freely of one's own time.

The raising of the revolutionary project does not go on only at the level of ideas, but works itself out in practice as well. Forms of struggle that lead people to challenge the domination of capital, that oblige them to participate, that permit them to exercise their power directly by putting their demands into immediate effect have their own revolutionising effect, carrying the people involved far beyond the specific issue that sparked the conflicts in the first place. It was precisely for this reason that the extra-parliamentary left in Italy and Chile favoured direct action and self-reduction struggles, an approach which even the Italian unions who supported the self-reduction movement did not share. For the latter self-reduction was a useful tactic in winning a skirmish over a specific grievance; for the extra-parliamentary left it was a strategic principle, leading to the formation of those autonomous working-class organisations which are a necessary part of the revolutionary dialectic.

This fundamental difference in approach to the question of direct action reflects the tension between revolution and reform that is bound to emerge in the process of creating broad unity around issues of urban conflict. Not all unions and not all citizen groups are inherently reformist, although they are more often than they are not in the countries of advanced capitalism. In the process of defending their members' interests trade unions have come to accept the logic of political negotiation and the model of bureaucratic organisation imposed by their adversary. As contradictions sharpen in the areas of social life outside the factory, the state drawing upon its experience in containing class conflict at the point of production, has itself moved to integrate potential opposition by incorporating citizens' groups into local levels of the state apparatus and channelling protest into the discourse of urban planning. Neither trade unions nor citizens' groups, however, can shed their oppositional relation to capital. Both therefore remain open to pressure from their membership, as the Italian experience well demonstrates. This suggests that the linkup between the various urban struggles, and between urban and factory struggles, should be made not at the level of the executives of the organisations involved, but at the base. Of course workers on the shop floor or squatters in a housing project have their own immediate interests to defend and, like the Italian telephone company workers, often see these interests in a narrow perspective. Yet their reaction is quite different from the reformist orientation of the union leadership which is reacting much more to the pressures exerted by the office itself, a pressure which gets stronger the farther the leadership is from the base. Hence, while radical alliances may be made between community groups and unions at the local level, the national leadership is apt to remain more insulated from popular pressure and more conservative, as was the case with the Italian self-reduction movement around electricity. The workers at the base are much more open to a radicalising experience, as the dynamic of the Hungarian council movement showed, and more likely to resolve their internal contradictions when given the chance, as the Turin squatters so ably demonstrated.

The real danger comes not from raising revolutionary demands, but from hiding them, even if posing them requires the working class to face their own internal contradictions, their own sectional interests, for only out of such a confrontation can the alliances so necessary to the success of urban struggles emerge. Such confrontations can only occur, and such alliances only emerge, in a context where different groups are put into face-to-face contact, forced to come to grips with each other's needs and, having devised a common strategy, given the chance to put it into practice. Hence the importance of bringing residents in the community and workers in the factory, public employees and the users of public services into direct contact. Hence too the importance of encouraging the formation of autonomous workers' organisations to conduct these struggles independently of the established parties, unions and associations upon which capital usually leans to defuse the workers' opposition. In the course of the 1975 transit strikes in Montréal and the citizens' protest that marked the increase in fares that followed, the alliance between urban workers and consumers never got beyond the expressions of mutual support exchanged between the unions and the opposition party, the Montréal Citizens' Movement, although one of the unions was very combative and the opposition party called for civil disobedience. As a result the unions got what they could bargain for, the fare increase was maintained and the workers shouldered the blame. Had the bus drivers collaborated in the call for self-reduction, the outcome would most likely have been different, but such collaboration would only have been possible had the bus drivers been forced to account for their stance to those who, having earlier supported them in their strike, were waging the fight against the fare increase.

The insistence on contact at the base, on face-to-face confrontation, on autonomous working-class organisation and direct action is every bit as important as the advocacy of the most radical and libertarian ideas in unleashing the revolutionary dialectic inherent in urban struggles. On the one hand such forms of struggle make room for a truly revolutionary movement to emerge, allow workers to press their diverse interests and needs as a joint claim against capital and develop effective means of mutual support. On the other hand these forms of solidarity which emerge in the course of urban struggles become the basis for the reorganisation of social life. Much like the neighbourhood councils that emerged in the course of the Hungarian revolution, they consist of elected delegates from the streets and factories in a given locality, subject to immediate recall, through whom the workers conduct and coordinate their struggle with capital and the state and exercise an alternative form of economic and political power. The historical experience suggests that the existence of organs of dual power in any society over a long period is not a likely prospect, but a long-term perspective on urban struggles would indicate that one of their key organisational objectives lies in the development of the workplace and street committees which form the base of those organs of dual power, when they do emerge. In that sense, the organisational forms of revolutionary urban struggles are also their aims, and resemble very much those of the anarchists—the creation of networks of political solidarity that would blossom into organs of working-class sovereignty in periods of insurrection and continue as such in the establishment of a new social order.

Although such networks could provide working class struggles in the community and in the workplace with much of their leadership and combativity, they remain distinct from those political institutions which could emerge within the framework of capitalist society as a result of these struggles. Radical urban movements pose not only a series of demands on the state for more and better goods and services in the field of collective consumption, on behalf of the working class. They also advance a set of claims for structural reform of the state apparatus which would permit much greater popular control of urban development and local government. If self-reduction challenges the legitimacy of the state, it is because it joins equality with decentralisation, showing that political prices for public services is impossible without popular control over those services. This linking of demands for political decentralisation with the issue of class inequality marks off the radical from the conservative response to the centralisation of the state in fiscal crisis. Demands for the control of urban land use, for the reorganisation of municipal services, for local control of the police and many similar reforms, to be truly effective, must result in new forms of local government, such as community or neighbourhood councils, organised on the principles of direct democracy—elected delegates from streets and the workplace, with revocable mandates at all times, rotation of office, etc. The alacrity with which the French state repressed the Paris squatters' movement, the severity of the bourgeoisie's counter-attack in New York give some indication of the resistance capital would put up to such demands. The Chilean and Italian experience, however, suggests that under conditions of combative class struggle, capital might be willing or forced to concede certain structural reforms in order to maintain its overall position. Such structural reforms should not be confused with the organs of dual power that emerge in a revolutionary situation. Rather they should be seen as potential organs of working-class power in the community in its war of opposition against capital, similar to factory councils and trade unions at the point of production, with all of the contradictions attendant on oppositional institutions that operate within the confines of capitalist society.

Would it be possible, for example, for such neighbourhood councils simultaneously to act as institutions of local government and to provide support for working class struggles in the workplace and the community such as strikes, occupations, etc.? What guarantee is there that their behaviour in this area would be any different from the traditional practice of trade unions? How would such organs of local government avoid being coopted into the state apparatus, bogged down in administering the reforms wrested from capital, squandering revolutionary energies and ultimately providing a means of integrating urban discontent? In short, is a strategy of non-reformist reforms possible? Can they unleash a revolutionary dynamic, leading to a veritable situation of dual power, or is the fissure between everyday life and the revolutionary moment absolute and immediate?

Recent events in Chile indicate that use can be made of capitalist institutions and limited reforms to reinforce working-class power and push the contradictions of capitalism to their revolutionary confrontation, but the long march through capitalist institutions rapidly proves short as the mounting class struggle makes it clear that there is no half-way house between capitalist normalcy and *communismo libertario*. The history of the anarchist movement is even more pertinent to understanding this question. On the one hand the Spanish anarchists spent over fifty years mobilising around the Idea, focusing on the revolutionary moment and disdaining all attempts at working through intermediate reforms, with the result that every revolutionary moment became a question of *communismo libertario* or bust. On the other hand, in the periods between insurrectionary outbursts they dealt with immediate issues, built up an anarcho-syndicalist union and grappled with the problem of parliamentary electoralism, indirectly supporting the Popular Front government of 1936. The balance sheet of their praxis underlines the importance of concentrating on revolutionary mobilisation at the expense of intermediate reforms, for the social revolution of 1936-39 would have been unthinkable without the years of political education that preceded it, much of it carried on by the CNT. This priority accorded to revolutionary agitation made it possible for them to develop a trade union with a singularly revolutionary orientation and to conduct struggles on terrain that had traditionally produced reformist practice. Yet the CNT remained a trade union, and the Spanish anarchists never lost sight of the distinction between that body and the FAI networks. To a large extent the distinction they maintained between a revolutionary network beholden to no one and a trade union engaged in daily negotiation with capital enabled them to stamp on the latter body a revolutionary character, even though it could not completely escape the tug of reformist pressures.

Much the same distinction would have to be maintained between the revolutionary networks that could emerge and expand in the course of urban struggles and the neighbourhood councils that could be established in their wake. Such councils could give the working-class limited experience in self-management. They could provide workers with definite powers that would weaken the capitalist state, such as control of the police, and disrupt the circulation of capital, such as the control and suppression of rent. Their local and decentralised nature would make them more vulnerable to popular pressure than higher levels of government, thus turning them into potential sources of support for working-class struggles beyond the issues of local government. At the limit they contain the possibility of becoming transformed into revolutionary councils during periods of insurrection. Yet however much they organise on the principles of direct democracy and however firm they remain in keeping independent of the state, they can never totally escape the reformist pressures emanating from the state functions they must inevitably assume as institutions of local government. The call for their establishment must therefore be tempered with critical participation in their functioning. The role of revolutionaries in such a situation is to remind, by word and by deed, those involved in such institutions of non-reformist reforms that the cause to which adherents are sought is social revolution, not the reform of local government—a task facilitated somewhat by guarding the autonomy and integrity of their revolutionary network of affinity groups.

This task highlights the nub of the debate surrounding the strategy of non-reformist changes, for the choice is rarely one between total abstention or total participation in struggles for immediate reforms on the terrain of capitalist society. The contradictions of capitalism are everywhere present, the points of friction endless; one has only to listen to the murmurings of discontent rippling beneath the surface of everyday life and the struggles to which they give rise. The real questions are which struggles to engage in and how to conduct them so that they contribute to the advance of the revolutionary movement. Nowhere is this challenge more acutely posed than in the question of electoral participation. Even the Spanish anarchists, for all their hatred of the state, found it necessary at certain points to support the Republic, and even for some to participate in government, although such collaboration cost them dearly.

The dilemma facing urban movements is much the same. On the one hand, capturing municipal office provides them with a temporary buffer against other levels of the state and a platform from which to raise issues and mobilise support. On the other hand, the subordination of municipal governments to other levels of the state and to the power of corporate capital, coupled with the fiscal crisis of the state, allows little room for manouever. In such a situation strong pressures exist for municipal governments to carry out the dirty work of capital as, strapped for funds, they rationalise jobs and services and thereby undercut the radical thrust of the movement. These specific constraints only add to the more general risk that electoral participation entails, namely the channeling of revolutionary energies into the administration of capitalism's contradictions and the legitimation of its institutions. In the face of these competing pulls, the participation of radical urban movements in parliamentary struggles should only occur if it is viewed as a means of advancing the revolutionary movement and if an extra-parliamentary base exists to keep their revolutionary priorities straight.

The prior emergence of a revolutionary, libertarian network thus remains the initial, immediate aim of urban struggles and the sine qua non of their extension to the parliamentary arena. The purpose of a radical city government is not to set the revolutionary process in motion by passing a series of reforms, but to support and extend the initiatives already undertaken by the popular movement that has propelled such a government into office. The distinction may seem a fine one, much like that posed by the age-old question about which came first, the chicken or the egg. Yet the distinction has far-reaching implications. The Chilean experience may reveal the way in which the radical control of the state apparatus, or even part of it, can help open up the space within which the popular movement can develop at an accelerated pace. It also reveals the error of conceiving of fundamental change as a process that starts with the state rather than with the popular movement. Such a conception, however well-intentioned, leads ultimately to "revolution" from above, not from below. The preoccupation with state-initiated reforms occurs, in one way or another, at the expense of the popular movement and thereby renders the revolutionary process very vulnerable to the capitalist counter-attack that must eventually come. A thorough-going social transformation requires not only the dismantling of capital but also the dismantling of the state, a process in which the assumption of political office should be the culminating, not the starting point.

The political subordination of the city only underscores the importance of looking at the revolutionary dialectic from this perspective. The task of a radical city government, therefore is to dissolve City Hall and preside over the recomposition of the commune, transforming it into a body that coordinates the economic and political activities of the workplace and neighbourhood councils. City council is no longer a representative institution of elected councillors but an assembly of delegates mandated by autonomous working-class institutions, re-grouped on a federated basis and engaged in discussions which the use of modern technology can promote to every corner of the city. In this process urban politics is no longer the government of people but the administration of things, the revolutionary outcome of the contradictions inherent in the current management of the fiscal crisis at the municipal level.

Such an outcome presupposes the existence of collectives of people who have put forward far-reaching demands and have actively engaged in the process of seizing control of social life in its many forms. It is to the building up of that popular movement that the energies of those engaged in urban struggles should be directed. The political economy of the city indicates some of the major points of contradiction in the process of capitalist urbanism upon which such struggles could focus: the city's role in patterning the organisation of urban life in line with the social control needs of capital, its locus in the circulation of capital and the consumption of goods and services, and its importance in regulating the fiscal crisis of the state. Demands put forward in these areas would challenge the domination of capital, provide alternative arrangements for the organisation of urban life and rally people to the revolutionary project.

For example, radical urban movements could work towards the development of alternative patterns of leisure activities to the amuse-ment palaces of consumer capitalism, run on the principles of free access, community control and self-initiated activity. In and around community centers which would offer their facilities free of charge to people who desired to use them, they could open up natural food restaurants, radical cinemas, popular day-care centres, summer camps, thereby permitting a truly libertarian counter-culture to arise and de-monstrating the possibility of organising social life on principles other than those of exchange value and bureaucratic control. Demands for rent freezes, strictly enforced housing codes, and a ban on demolitions would interrupt the circuits of capital in the area of housing and make it an unprofitable venture for private profit. The call for free and expanded public transport financed by the large corporations could be linked to the support of municipal workers' struggles. This would throw a monkey wrench into capital's plans for fiscal retrenchment and centralisation in the face of the fiscal crisis and promote the alliance between public sector employees and the users of public services so necessary to the advance of the revolutionary project. In a similar vein, the establishment of food cooperatives would create alternatives to agribusiness and reorient food consumption and production along ecological lines, bringing farmers and urban workers together around joint claims against capital.

Although these struggles focus on specific issues, they form part of that larger process of struggle through which working people will come to settle no longer for what capital seems to allow. In that process counter institutions will form and the revolutionary alliances between town and country, production and reproduction, will emerge, alliances implicit in the struggles already waged by the working class which have fueled the present crisis. Given this perspective, radical urban movements must move beyond the institutional definition of urban politics to embrace and support those people contesting the right of capital and the state to order and distort the social relations of everyday life in all its aspects: movements for abortion on demand, gay rights, free schools, etc. Parliamentary politics, to the extent that they are engaged in as one more terrain of struggle, must be inserted into this revolutionary dialectic and used to support the initiatives of the popular movement at whatever stage they may have reached. Given the generally corrosive effect that participation in parliamentary institutions has generally had on the revolutionary élan of movements, parliamentary politics must be undertaken with a view to demystifying it, much as the state must be penetrated with a view to dissolving it. A revolutionary approach to electoral politics requires the development of an anti-politics, a practice based on the refusal of the dominant class' ground rules—shirt and tie, loyal opposition, successive tenure of office, the professionalisation of politicians and politics. Ultimately, such an approach demands on the part of its practitioners a commitment to abandon office rather than justify measures imposed by capitalist logic.

Take office to demystify it and abandon it—a contradiction in terms? Yes, but just like the entire dynamic of the dialectic between revolution and reform which characterizes urban struggles. That dynamic is in some ways unavoidable, for it is the immediate contradictions of capital and the struggles they provoke which provide the points of friction upon which a revolutionary perspective can be grafted, while even the reformist pressures of working-class struggles have led to the current crisis. The name of the game, however, is revolution, not reform; and waging it, and winning it, calls for a new kind of revolutionary politics.

Revolutionary politics: theory, organisation and the new praxis

IF THE STRUGGLES of the workers during the sixties provoked the present crisis, attacked capital at the points of production and consumption, demanded implicitly more money for less work and unleashed an upsurge of rank and file action, they did not take a self-consciously revolutionary cast; nor, in the absence of a revolutionary organisation of their own, are they likely to take one in the future. It could be argued that such a position, implicit in many of the points raised in the preceding section, contains a fundamental contradiction for the libertarian approach. How can one argue that revolution is the product of autonomous working-class action and posit, at the same time, the need for a revolutionary organisation? Is the latter not the thin edge of the wedge that will reproduce the same kind of praxis that libertarian socialists so vigorously denounced in the Communist and Social-Democratic parties?

The history of working class movements indicates that it is very much the workers who make the revolution, or the revolution is not made; just as contemporary workers' struggles have made clear that the present crisis is very much about the abolition of toil and the transformation of social relations. Yet the history of workers' struggles also makes clear that such a revolutionary perspective and its concrete practice are more likely to work their way into an insurrectionary period and push that moment to its most radical limits if they have already formed part of the workers' political culture. The anarchists, to take most pertinent example, did not eschew organisation and spent years building theirs up and fomenting revolutionary ideas, but both the organisation and education they fostered were radically different from those of competing socialist and communist movements. The difference could be clearly seen in the practice of workers' and peasants' movements in areas of strong anarchist influence during every insurrection up to and including the Spanish Civil War.

The commitment to abandon municipal office when it no longer offers the possibility of revolutionary exploitation is one indication of this different approach, very much like the action of the Hungarian council movement which, when forced to fold up shop, handed their mandate back to the people. Its tactical necessity stems from the larger commitment to the priority of mass mobilisation over parliamentary struggles which revolutionary urban politics demands. Such mobilisation requires some kind of organisation, whose members share a set of ideas around which they mobilise others, and distinct forms of political struggle. The question in each case is: what kind?

The demands raised by contemporary urban struggles, together with their organisational objectives, point us in the direction of an answer which owes much to the libertarian tradition to which such struggles are linked. The revolutionary politics called for by urban struggles requires first and foremost the creation and enlargement of a revolutionary network, but this network differs from traditional forms of organisation in two basic ways. In the first place the revolutionary conception to which their members are wedded is defined as the transformation of capitalist social relations in all their aspects, marked by a commitment to the abolition of the state, to freedom from toil, to the self-management of the workplace and the communities on the basis of political federation and direct democracy, in short to the principles of *communismo libertario*. In the second place, the network is a federation of societies of friends, in the profoundly political sense of the term, not a bureaucratic organisation or a party machine. Hence it is characterised by an absence of paid officials, voluntary adherence, a strong degree of moral commitment, the consensual resolution of conflict, autonomy of the base groups, social relations marked by love and trust, intense solidarity, joy and spontaneity in the conduct of political struggles. Both these theoretical and organisational elements must be present if this revolutionary network is to emerge and expand. People must be won over to ideas, to a social vision, not only to organisational principles, or the contradictions of urban struggles will never develop their revolutionary potential. The critical thrust of immediate demands will remain implicit, the internal contradictions of the working class avoided, decentralisation subverted into the reform of local government. The groups themselves will not hold together, especially in periods of political quiescence, unless there is a common commitment which binds their members. At the same time such revolutionary ideas must result in some kind of different organisational practice if they are to have a social meaning and impact, and the power to attracts adherents, while these ideas, in turn, can only spread to the extent that they are picked up by an ever-widening group of people. The patterns of social interaction which go into making an organisation are as important as a common set of ideas in making this process possible.

Both organisation and theory are essential components in the process of mobilisation; and the specific characteristics of libertarian theory and organisation govern very much the expansion of this revolutionary network, as well as its distinctive praxis. In this sense these characteristics point to certain strategic principles in the conduct of urban struggles. In initiating certain struggles, for example, or supporting others, revolutionaries must zero in one those issues and develop those aspects of a conflict which explode capital's contradictions and allow them to raise revolutionary ideas. If they fail to articulate the revolutionary truths inherent in those struggles, some reforms may be won, especially those that capital can tolerate, but the revolutionary movement will not advance, for no one will have had the chance to confront and possibly embrace a revolutionary outlook. Such an outcome would not be intolerable for nor incompatible with a movement that defined organisation in fairly conventional terms, such as its capacity to contest and win elections, or even to push through limited reforms. Such an organisation would measure its strength by the number of people it could turn out on a given issue, its electoral support, its party membership, the number of full-time paid officials on staff, its financial reserves, etc. For a revolutionary libertarian movement such an outcome would be a disaster, precisely because it sees organisation in terms of a federation of affinity groups who share a social revolutionary vision, participate in struggles on the basis of direct action and autonomous workers' organisation, and propagate its ideas. Its aim is to enlarge the number of people committed to its vision of a self-managed society and ready to exercise their capacities for autonomous action in the course of struggles waged towards that goal. Struggles therefore are not only fertile terrain in which to sow revolutionary ideas, on the understanding that the numerical strength of the movement follows the ebb and flow of the revolutionary moment, but also occasions on which to win over new, active adherents who will enlarge the movement and accelerate the revolutionary process even in the intervals of insurrectionary periods.

For the movement to grow in this manner its most revolutionary ideas must be posed with the greatest clarity; and this is all the more true given that the high degree of commitment demanded of its members requires, in true libertarian fashion, a strictly voluntary adherence that can only be undertaken in full cognizance of its meaning.

The way in which these ideas are raised is itself linked to the revolutionary conception of those who advance them. There is a world of difference between the libertarian socialists and the Marxist-Leninists on this score, a difference which extends beyond content to the ambience which suffuses their relationship to the world. It is not only that traditional revolutionary ideas have offered workers a more refined and disciplined version of what capitalism has already dished up, reflected even in current Marxist-Leninist demands for more work, state planning, the dictatorship of the proletariat. It is also that they convey through their wooden slogans calling on workers to smash capitalism and build the party that oppressive Leninism of everyday life which awaits us all on the morrow of their revolution. Against it stands the praxis of libertarian socialists, who dare to go beyond the limits of state capitalism and raise those truly revolutionary demands embedded in the original Marxist project. In the face of capitalist-induced unemployment they demand not more work, but the abolition of work; in the face of growing state power, the abolition of the state; instead of building the party, the direct control of social life. Like the Paris students in the uprising of May 1968, they urge people to be realistic and demand the impossible, but they do so in imaginative language and pithy statements that are full of the humour and irony which characterize their own brand of everyday life.

The difference in styles is unmistakable, but there is no recipe through which to convey the latter, for it comes out of an understanding of the revolutionary libertarian project and the experience of living it. That style, however, and the message which accompanies it, are crucial elements in the process of political mobilisation. The social-democrats try to soft pedal these issues on the grounds that they are too advanced for the workers, while the Marxist-Leninists dismiss them as lacking in proletarian character. Thus do both these political stances merge into a tepid reformism, bound by the common assertion that there are always issues that should not be raised, though capital in its own way does not shrink from handling them. For these issues lie at the heart of urban struggles defined as the politics of everyday life; the rearing and schooling of children, sexual identities and relations, the use of commodities and public facilities, the patterning of our social interaction, the need for free time and space. In the end these issues prove to have the greatest mobilising force, for they touch people at those points where they try and give meaning to their lives. Reich understood this long ago when he attacked the German Communist Party in the 1930s for refusing to acknowledge what the Church had long understood: masturbation is politics; and so are its modern counterparts.

This does not mean that most people share a revolutionary outlook on these issues, or even the revolutionary commitment to working towards it; but it does indicate an awareness, on a very profound level, that something is rotten in the state of Denmark. It is to that awareness that the language of revolutionary mobilisation must address itself, in order to confront people with the contradictions of their own subordination as a first step in the process of liberation. Yet that confrontation, if it is to lead in that direction, must occur with the warmth and gaiety that anticipate the future revolutionary order; and for that very reason such qualities must find expression in the revolutionary discourse of those who raise it. For capital also understands the revolutionary potential of such a confrontation, as did fascism, and in their own ways, the official parties of the working class, East and West, do too. Yet their treatment of the theme was and is governed by the projects of domination which have remained their goal.

Such a revolutionary discourse underlines the importance of not fetishizing the proletariat, neither by presuming that only the workers possess revolutionary virtue, nor by dismissing their views as inherently reformist. Such a position strategically implies accepting workers at the point where they are, but meeting them with the ideas of libertarian socialism, for beneath the reproduction of everyday, customary logic lie the revolutionary consciousness and initiative which workers have always demonstrated and which never disappear even under the sway of official politics. The internal contradictions of the working class are in many respects those of other social classes as well, which is another way of saying that people are people. Yet the options open to working people for resolving those contradictions within the confines of capitalist society are severely reduced by the nature of their class position. Posing their internal contradictions therefore affirms workers as individual actors, as historical agents, and not as the passive material out of which history is molded, capital's proletariat. Out of the resolution of these contradictions can emerge the revolutionary alliances which challenge the class domination of capital.

In the course of urban struggles revolutionaries must therefore raise those fundamental questions which permit and require those affected by the issues to develop alternative policies that deal with their very real and very diverse needs and fears. How indeed do working men deal with their own sexism? What shall happen to municipal employees as the government of people is replaced with the administration of things? What are the implications for teachers and social workers as the transformation of social life does away with the surveillance of the state? The Spanish social revolution of 1936-39 that anarchism initiated shows that there are answers to these questions perfectly, and one might add only, compatible with the libertarian reorganisation of social life, but the answers can only come from the workers as they grapple with them in face-to-face confrontation.

Direct action is an important organising principle precisely because it leads people to exercise their political capacities and gives them a taste of revolutionary power. A militant, extra-legal form of action, often initiated by small groups but also involving mass participation, direct action implies the defiance of bourgeois legality and ultimately the expropriation of capital. The atmosphere of mass civil disobedience it can create is important in breaking the psychology of fear and submission to alienated authority which leads people to acquiesce in their own subordination. In that respect the forms of praxis are as important as the content of ideas in building up a revolutionary network. The increase in the number of people ready to appropriate control of social life comes about in large measure from the experience of seizing it, and from the process of working through those contradictions that stand in the way. That is why it is important, in the conduct of urban struggles, to focus on forming the small-scale building blocks of the revolutionary network and the revolutionary society—the street and workplace committees which form the potential organs of dual power—and to insist on door knocking, face-to-face encounters, small group meetings and other forms of interaction which require direct contact, permit the exchange of ideas and the adherence of new supporters, and reinforce the solidarity of people engaged in revolutionary action.

It is not easy to work through these contradictions, nor, once having done so, to maintain a revolutionary outlook and conduct in the face of the grinding pressures of everyday life under capitalism. To do so requires continuous support and reinforcement from other people equally committed to these goals. Revolutionary groups must furnish this solidarity by offering an organisational model that permits their members to practise what they preach, by developing an alternative life style and counter culture to capitalism which takes into account the everyday lives of people, the constraints on their capacity to participate, their need for affective as well as intellectual support during the downswings of political activity and personal life. This means first and foremost that energies must be directed not into building and maintaining a bureaucratic apparatus but into conducting political struggles and developing new forms of social relations. It means that social relations within these groups must be marked by respect for others and the ideas they raise, but also by an unflinching commitment to transcending the social relations of capitalism—sexism, the separation between manual and intellectual labour, appeals to arbitrary authority, rivalry, hierarchy, the suppression of desire. This implies the equal sharing of tasks of all kinds and the mutual encouragement of individual freedom and personal initiative.

Such lofty aims require material underpinning in the form of common meeting places, cooperative day care centres, babysitting exchanges, food coops, common suppers, communal housing, free schools, libraries, newspapers, the pooling of money and other innovative arrangements in daily living over which members of the revolutionary network exercise direct control. They also require that activities be undertaken in line with the capacities of people to carry them out, or both active militants and new adherents will rapidly burn themselves out. These considerations are not inconsequential, for the attention paid to the emotional, interpersonal dimensions of people's lives reflects not only the recognition that people engage in the revolutionary dialectic under capitalism but also that the very nature of the revolutionary project, defined as the transformation of social relations, refuses to separate the personal from the political. Even the traditional parties understood the importance of building up their own cultural networks, although they used them, and still do use them, to maintain their hold over the working class. The German SPD was virtually a state within the state, offering its members everything from schools to taverns, while the PCF and the PCI have their own journals, their own newspapers, their own cultural centres, even their own picnics. So too, for that matter, did the Spanish anarchists, but their cultural network was linked to a radically different revolutionary project, reflected as much in the content as in the spirit which permeated their free schools and workers' centres. Today the anarchists carry on this tradition.

The spirit which animates the counter-culture of revolutionary libertarian movements should partake of the same joy, spontaneity and imagination which their members bring to the conduct of political struggles. This attitude is central to the great breath of life which runs throughout the course of revolution from below, reminding one that revolution in the end is an affair of the heart, the product of the voluntary desire to change things, which no one can do for others, and that those struggling towards it can also have fun on the way. Revolutionaries, in directing some of their political energies to these issues of immediate concern to themselves, affirm the centrality of this principle, yet signal too that such issues are the common property of the entire working class. The resolution of these issues can lapse into a new form of class privilege, but linked to a revolutionary perspective, it can also provoke the most far-reaching confrontation of the contradictions of the present crisis. The latter option demands that the issues be joined; and behind it lies the refusal to fetishize the working class once again.

This question is similar to the ambivalent possibilities opened up by the participation of radical jurists in the Italian self-reduction struggles around the telephone increases—on the one hand the recuperation of the movement, on the other its extension. Posed in a revolutionary perspective and subordinated to the maintenance of working class autnomy, such a gesture permitted the latter option to prevail, thereby reminding us that a revolutionary stance is no one's exclusive property. The conditions under which this stance had such an effect, however, also remind us that the organisational and theoretical components in the process of political mobilisation must be present, or the new praxis will fall into a vacuum. In the end, the points of strategic action upon which revolutionaries can press derive from an analysis of urban contradictions, but the principles of strategy ultimately rest on the tradition of libertarian socialism to which urban struggles are linked, and whose contradictions, in turn, once exploded, point to the creation of a libertarian and communal society.

CHAPTER SIX

THE EXPERIENCE OF THE MONTRÉAL CITIZENS MOVEMENT

A short history of the MCM: strategic difficulties and class contradictions

IN 1974 a municipal party was formed in Montréal called the Montréal Citizens' Movement. For the previous fourteen years Montréal had been governed by Mayor Jean Drapeau and his Civic Party, which was not really a party at all but a coterie of followers which provided him with the parliamentary facade for his one-man rule. His idiosyncrasies, French-Canadian nationalism and the reform movement out of which he emerged notwithstanding, Drapeau presided over the transformation of Montréal in line with the needs of monopoly capital, taking care at the same time to maintain his support among the local bourgeoisie and, in many cases, an electoral alliance with the Liberal Party that ran Québec for most of the same period.

Throughout the 1960s another movement was going on which addressed itself to the needs of the people of Montréal and led to a growing militancy and class consciousness in both the community and the workplace. On the one hand a far-flung community-organising movement developed. Largely focusing on organising the unorganised, this movement, which was inspired by the ideas of "animation sociale" on the francophone side and by the new left ideas of community-organising of the urban poor on the anglophone side, embraced a wide range of citizen groups engaged in a number of struggles. They included welfare struggles; the day-care movement; tenants' struggles against landlords; citizens' protest against demolitions, urban renewal, the growth of autoroutes, and the destruction of neighbourhoods; people's refusal to pay the municipal water-tax; etc. On the other hand, the labour movement in Québec, and especially in Montréal, underwent a radical transformation, with the CSN, the Confederation of National Trade Unions) leading the way. By the late 1960s, the alliance between labour and the state which had marked the initial stages of the Quiet Revolution in Québec had become severely strained, and the relationship more conflictual than harmonious. Strikes in the public and private sector were becoming increasingly bitter. Demonstrations, sit-ins, occupations, and other forms of direct action which had marked community struggles were now becoming part of union struggles. In 1968 the CSN adopted a manifesto called 'The Second Front' which committed the union to action in the field of collective consumption around such issues as unemployment, housing, credit, consumer cooperatives, health insurance, fiscal reform and the media. The document recognized that the workers' struggle had to extend beyond the workplace, acknowledged the existence of a radical community-organising movement and urged that unionized workers link up with these community groups.

This social ferment resulted in 1970 in the formation of FRAP, a radical municipal party. FRAP was put together by militant union officials, many of whom held staff positions with political functions, and community organisers in order to contest the elections, based on a programme entitled "power to the wage-earners" and built around a number of neighbourhood political action committees in those districts where FRAP presented candidates. The 1970 municipal elections were conducted in the midst of the FLQ crisis, in which members of the Québec Liberation Front abducted a member of the British consulate in Montréal and a Québec cabinet minister who was eventually found dead. The federal government under Prime Minister Trudeau invoked the War Measures Act. FRAP, in trying to work out a stand on the crisis, experienced its first serious split, which Drapeau, aided by some federal cabinet ministers, exacerbated by linking FRAP to the FLQ. Although Drapeau won every seat in the elections, FRAP succeeded in garnering considerable support in working class areas. Nonetheless, the strain put on it by the FLQ crisis was soon followed by a series of ideological divisions which resulted in the dismemberment of the organisation and the arrest of the popular movement.

The most important factor in this process was the collapse of the Québec General Strike of May, 1972, which involved over 200,000 workers from Québec's three major union federations, and which had formed a Common Front to negotiate salaries and working conditions for the public and para-public sectors with the government. They went out on a general strike, joined by other groups of workers. Workers took over radio stations and, in some places, entire towns. When the government passed Bill 19 forcing the workers back to their jobs, the Common Front leadership, after initially claiming they would defy the law, called on the workers to obey it and return to work.

Frustration and dismay set in among the rank and file. Many felt a sense of betrayal. The government profited from the labour movement's weakness and imprisoned its leaders, an act which itself evoked labour protest, but the movement had clearly been put on the defensive. Only a year later did social struggles appear once again on the Montréal scene. When they did, they were to be marked by the experience of the previous years. Some of the lessons, such as the need to link up struggles in the workplace and the community, especially in the public sector, were positive, but others, especially feelings of bitterness towards groups that had not gone out on strike in 1972, were not. In 1973 radicals in the Montréal area tried again. The Montreal labour councils of the three major trade unions—CSN, which regroups mainly public-sector employees, FTQ, mainly industrial workers in the private sector, and CEQ, the teachers' union—acting through their Inter-union Committee for the Montréal Region (CRIM), the Montréal branch of the independence-oriented Parti Québécois and progressive anglophones active in community colleges and citizens' groups joined together, supported towards the end by the Québec NDP (New Democratic Party), to form the Montréal Citizens' Movement.

The people who worked to put together this party were concerned to avoid the dissensions which ripped FRAP apart, but at the same time wanted to tap the forces on the left in Montréal, gather the energies of particular, local struggles and unite them around a wider political focus. Consequently the programme put forward avoided an explicit class analysis and an overall perspective of the urban question which situated urban struggles within the context of capitalist society. Instead it concentrated on a series of concrete measures whose content, it was felt, made clear the radical potential and working-class orientation of the party. Such an approach left considerable room for ambiguity, as one of the debates at the founding congress revealed. One district committee of the party had sent in a resolution calling for the replacement of the word 'worker' wherever it appeared in the party programme with the term 'citizen'. The motion was defeated. Those who helped to defeat it argued that they did not mean to assert that workers were not citizens, but rather to affirm the class dimension of the programme. That dimension was not clear to all, and the ambiguity of the programme was to surface time and again in the course of future struggles, while the theoretical weakness which marked its inception has continued to dog the MCM, making it difficult for the party to build an effective base. FRAP too had certain theoretical ambiguities, but its working-class orientation was much clearer and consequently, its base much more rooted in the popular groups active in Montréal at the time. The other major factor which governed the MCM's birth, and which has run through its subsequent history, until recently, like a fatal flaw, was the fact that it came into being around the 1974 municipal elections, such that despite its participation in a number of extra-parliamentary struggles, the electoralist mentality has always been strong in the party, making itself felt in diverse ways and introducing an additional level of ambiguity and strain.

To the surprise of many the MCM won 18 out of the 55 seats on City Council in the 1974 elections, with 45.3% of the popular vote, giving it a parliamentary wing that was much stronger than its base in the districts and presenting it with a host of problems inherent in the dialectic between parliamentary and extra-parliamentary politics, but reinforced by the MCM's own ambiguities. By 1978 that number was reduced to 13, after a series of resignations and splits that characterised not only the caucus but also the party. Although the MCM's conduct of the election was riddled with contradictions—the most notable case was one district association's decision to make an alliance with a defector from Drapeau's group, justified in the name of district committee autonomy—the ambiguities surrounding its birth emerged even more strongly afterwards. Interestingly, it was the conduct of its first extra-arliamentary struggle that provided the first such occasion. The MCM launched a campaign to obtain free public transport for senior citizens, but serious disagreements soon arose over the political discourse in which to frame the demand and the strategy to undertake to obtain it. On the one hand were those who wanted to limit the campaign to the immediate issue and focus strategically on the parliamentary arena; on the other were those who wanted to relate the issue to the contradictions of urban life in capitalist society and the need for extra-parliamentary mobilisation, which they considered the strategic aim. Both points of view worked their way into the public conduct of the struggle, as members at every level of the party subscribed to one or the other approach. Those responsible for carrying out the most salient aspects of the struggle, however, shared the first approach, resulting in a parliamentary dénouement of compromise marked by attempts to seduce the suburban mayors into supporting the measure.

The divergences articulated the ambiguities latent in the original MCM project and soon manifested themselves around every intervention the party was called upon to make, down to the wording of press communiqués. The consequences proved serious indeed when the MCM called for a campaign of civil disobedience in the face of the public transport fare hike announced in the fall of 1975. The electoralist orientation of some members led them to oppose such a strategy, while the lack of a radical approach to the question of power reinforced people's timidity in the face of authority and inexperience in the conduct of direct action. The district committees of the MCM never followed up the call, while the party as a whole never seriously debated the reasons for their failure to do so. The contradictions of a year and a half's practice led the executive of the party to submit to the 1975 congress a document which pinpointed these shortcomings, accounted for the tactical and strategic errors by the absence of a clear analysis, and called upon the party to opt for a socialist analysis of the urban question which would govern its interventions at every level. The party waffled and the congress eventually adopted a populist proposal which left most of its ambiguities unresolved. Although the congress rejected a commitment to socialism, it did commit itself to popular mobilisation, without a clear idea of what that entailed, put electoralism clearly as a second priority, and elected a radical executive. The socialist resolution was lost by a close vote, but the content of that socialism was never clearly defined.

The debate, or what little there was of it, revealed the political heterogeneity of the MCM activists—social democrats, left social-democrats, Stalinists, independent Marxists, populists and a large youthful constituency with sentiments in favour of many aspects of libertarian socialism. Other defied identification by any combination of traditional political positions. Nonetheless, the debate opened up the real divisions in the party. Henceforth the division in the party would take more and more the form of the independent socialists, libertarian Marxists and youthful constituency on the one hand, the social democrats and traditional politicians on the other, with an undefined populist base in the middle. In the year that followed the executive spent its energies trying to build up a base. A housing committee was formed, with representatives from different districts, to work out a common action and to provide a point where experiences could be exchanged and evaluated. The theoretical weakness of the MCM, which often surfaced as anti-intellectual bias, made it difficult for the different district committees to focus on a common point of attack. A proposal was submitted to the housing committee calling on the party to launch a campaign around the demand for the immediate freezing of rents, on the grounds that such a demand permitted the visible manifestations of the housing crisis in different districts — demolitions, rent increases, skyrocketing property taxes—to be linked around a goal which challenged the logic of capitalist urban development. The proposal was rejected on the grounds that it did not represent the particular problems of each district, but no alternative strategy was proposed other than mobilising around specific cases—evictions, demolitions, etc.—as they came to the attention of the district committees. Although such an approach has its own logic and potential if it were used to undertake direct action, build base committees and raise radical demands, the rejection of the first proposal implied the rejection of such a radical perspective at the same time as it veiled the class interests of the professional technocrats which prevailed in a certain number of district committees of the MCM.

In the light of the debate at the previous congress the executive felt it best not to press the issue but to wait for people to try out this approach and come to their own conclusions as to the need for a radical perspective. The respect for people and the process of their radicalisation implicit in this stance proved ineffectual in the face of the combination of class interest, electoralism and populism which predominated in the party and got buried in the sterility of the ensuing debates. Those district committees willing to countenance urban reform but not at the expense of their class privilege often invoked district committee autonomy and the need to respect the rate at which people moved on issues in order to resist an all-party struggle which ran the risk of raising a radical perspective. The same reasons were invoked by populists who proved refractory to any serious theoretical debate. As a result the party's proposed extra-parliamentary struggles on housing rarely got off the ground, while many district committees never even undertook them. The confrontation between different experiences, so vital to people's political evolution, never really took place within the housing committee, while the few district committee representatives left by the fall of 1976 prepared a report for the 1976 congress presenting a socialist analysis of the housing question and calling on the party to engage in a common struggle around the collective negotiation of leases.

The results of that congress were as frustrating and ambiguous as those of a year earlier. The party rejected the socialist analysis but embraced the proposed strategy which flowed out of it. It also adopted many of the specific proposals of the housing committee's reports, but many of them differed little from those already contained in the party's programme. As a result, some congress delegates who formed part of the party's populist base, motivated by a vague commitment to an alternative radical politics, could not see what all the fuss was about. To them the MCM left's position seemed to be one of ideological posturing which they felt justified in opposing on moral or practical grounds. Their opposition, however, was no more productive of a debate and clarification of the issues than the opposition of other groups in the party. To the left the distinctions between these different groups blurred into a common reformist position which took on an electoralist hue, especially as the commitment to extra-parliamentary struggle in practice proved to be a paper one, while many of those that were undertaken took on an electoralist perspective. For instance, the MCM's opposition to the city's extension of the metro system in order to satisfy the interests of a development corporation did not develop very far. To some extent this was a result of a lack of human resources, but this lack itself pointed to a deeper problem: the weakness of the priority accorded to mobilisation at the base and the direction of energies into maintaining a party apparatus which substituted for the politics of mobilisation.

The MCM left itself bears considerable responsibility for this situation. It kept exhorting the party to undertake extra-parliamentary struggles without providing the ideas and tools which a membership that had never done much community organising badly needed. Even when it did, as in meetings conducted subsequent to the adoption of the housing committee's strategic recommendations, many of the elements essential to successful community organising were lacking: the geographic concentration of resources, the emphasis on social as well as political activities, etc. To a large extent these errors reflect the political inexperience of the youthful constituency which formed the core of the MCM left, especially an inexperience in working on an ongoing basis in movement building. In insisting that those members in each district committee committed to extra-parliamentary struggle work only in their district, they scatterred their resources, isolating and discouraging some of their most militant members. This process was repeated within the MCM left's own internal organisation, which never developed any sustained consistency and coherence. In refusing to define itself as an open caucus it made it more difficult to define the content of that urban socialism which the 1975 executive report had raised. To the extent that such theoretical definition offers a vision of a new society and some ideas in working towards that goal, its absence hampers the efforts of those engaged in such struggles, as indeed it did for the MCM left. The documents it produced remained undeveloped or inconsistent in parts and sometimes substituted analysis for militant praxis.

In refusing to organise on a common basis and work out a common political position, the MCM left held back not only its own development, but that of the party as well. The left maintained its propensity to libertarian ideas in reaction to the social democrats within the MCM and to the Marxist-Leninists outside it, but it never articulated these ideas into a body of self-consciously held ideas. To some extent this reflected the lack of theoretical sophistication which was a hallmark of the MCM left's youthful constituency. To some extent it was a reflection of the newness of these ideas applied to the urban question and the relative unfamiliarity of the libertarian tradition among the left throughout western society. Nonetheless, the MCM left, despite its shortcomings, did put its energies into grass-roots mobilising, but the fundamental ambiguities in the party as a whole only led to a cycle of frustrations. On the one hand, the MCM left's own weaknesses made the building of a base seem even more arduous a task than it is. On the other hand, the left felt that it was doing all the work, and making little headway very slowly, while the party as a whole, which it had done much to maintain, was recouping its efforts for electoralist purposes.

The debate within the party became in some respects increasingly bitter and falsified, as its inability and refusal to thrash out significant theoretical divergences forced the debate onto the terrain of personalities and regulations. The 1976 congress was originally postponed by the party's general council for three months in order to permit the party to accumulate sufficient experience in housing struggles so as to provide food for reflection at the congress. The consciously reformist wing of the party succeeded in reversing that decision by attacking it as undemocratic and unconstitutional, and made it quite clear that they intended to wrest control of the party executive at the upcoming congress. The left fought back and organised, and succeeded in preventing the reformists from taking control of the party, but their victory proved pyrrhic indeed. Their candidate for president won out, but he was far from representing the most articulate and advanced positions that the left had already worked out. This situation, in which the left ostensibly 'controlled' the party but was unable to advance its ideas and carry through their practical implications, resulted from their lack of theoretical and organisational unity and their reluctance to work at bringing it about. Their proposals calling for the establishment of neighbourhood councils and street committees were passed, but with little understanding of their implications. Moreover, a considerable number of delegates had already walked out of the congress when two city councillors, who had been obliged to resign from the party when they ran in the provincial elections, were refused admission to the party.

At the 1975 congress the parliamentary caucus presented an extraordinary motion to the party which stipulated that any councillor who presented him or herself as a candidate in provincial or federal elections or held an executive post in another party had to resign his or her MCM membership. The motion passed unanimously and one councillor was forced to resign his membership in consequence. Two other MCM councillors also had to resign when they ran in the 1976 provincial elections. When their bid for office in the provincial legislature failed they applied for readmission to the party. As the original motion contained no provisions for such an eventuality, the 1976 congress passed a resolution allowing for this possibility subject to approval by two thirds of the delegates to both the district committee's general assembly and the annual party congress. Since the 1976 congress occurred in two stages with a month's interval between the two, this resolution made it possible to reintegrate these councillors at that congress. The general assembly of the district committee did accept these councillors back after the first session of the congress, but in their petition to the congress to confirm their decision the district committee's delegates made no reference to the principles at stake in the issue, expressed no regret at what had happened and justified their request solely on the grounds of district committee autonomy. Their request just failed to get the required majority and the majority of the district committee's delegates, along with a number of others, stormed out, labelling the decision undemocratic and symptomatic of the dogmatic and centralizing tendencies of an intransigent left.

In fact the decision was anything but undemocratic, but the lines of the debate showed how distorted certain positions became in the absence of a radical perspective and the willingness to work one out. It was not insignificant that the two councillors had been among the leading spokesmen of the reformist and electoralist wing of the party and received their support from the district committees which shared their views. In the face of an ostensibly radical programme and executive, district committee autonomy became, for those members of the party, a justification for reformist practice and a means to avoid political confrontation. The left, frustrated perhaps even more by the unwillingness to debate than the reformist practice itself, tried to circumvent this barrier by invoking party rules in order to ensure that the congress' decisions were respected and carried out. The old adage, however, proved more correct: you can bring a horse to water but you can't make him drink. Recourse to rules and regulations could prevent the worst from happening, but it could not oblige people to undertake radical struggles if they were not open to doing so.

The party spent considerable energy just trying to keep going. Throughout 1977 the executive tried to reconcile irreconcilable opposites, but the more conservative and careerist members of the reformist wing left anyway, only to surface a year later in the form of the Municipal Action Group, a rag-bag of politicians of the old-fashioned type running from former Civic Party hacks to up and coming young urbanists, whose sole claim to distinction will surely be its capacity to flush out every political opportunist in the city as they scramble for the spoils of municipal office. At the same time the left felt more discouraged and isolated. Fewer energies seemed to be going into radically articulated, extra-parliamentary struggles, while those that did seemed to find little echo at the executive level of most district committees or of the party. The left's own capacity for theoretical definition diminished, as some poured their energies into MCM activities and others, partly in reaction, drifted somewhat into a marxist-leninist perspective. Still others continued their attempts to give the urban socialist project a libertarian definition. At heart, though, the problem of the MCM left was also the problem of the party: the continuous papering over of fundamental contradictions which sapped people's energies and made it difficult to develop even a clear perspective on them.

Attempts to resolve those contradictions, albeit partially, even within the framework of the party's political education committee ran up against the same impasse. Activists from various districts met to discuss the strategic implications of the party's overall project, in so far as they conceived of it, and ways to implement them. It had become clear from the MCM's own experience that there were reformist and radical ways to approach both parliamentary and extra-parliamentary struggles and that the real differences only emerged when the discussion got around to the nitty-gritty details of political mobilisation. What do you say at a press conference or knocking on someone's door? How do you distil a radical analysis into a press communiqué or a conversation in an apartment building? What steps do you take in order to form a street committee and keep it going? Such questions, however, rarely got addressed, given the fundamental disagreements within the party about its overall political project; and since those disagreements were never adequately resolved, questions of strategy, many of which emerged out of a revolutionary libertarian perspective, were not properly assessed.

The political education committee itself concluded that it was impossible to ask it to run workshops on issues that the party had not politically resolved: did the MCM have a socialist programme or not? What was meant by socialism? How was it related to the urban question? What difference did it make to organising strategies? What did it mean by a commitment to popular power? How was that to be expressed? There are others, yet the declaration of principles submitted to the 1977 congress by the executive via the party's general council left the definition of the party's overall political project as vague as ever. Its adoption seemed to strengthen the MCM outwardly, but it weakened it internally, as the contradictions facing those members on the left persisted and intensified. How was it possible to keep pouring energies into mobilising people towards a political party with which one felt growing and fundamental disagreement? The effective base of the MCM, measured by the number of its autonomous, active members, was stagnant even as it met to adopt its administrative programme for the 1978 elections.

Of course the problems encountered by the MCM in building up a base were not only the outcome of the left's own shortcomings, nor only the consequence of the party's unresolved ambiguities, which themselves account for much of the left's weakness. They were also the very real problems of working out in practice the implications of that urban socialist project whose roots, especially in North America, are not yet well-established. At the same time, these problems reflected the ideological hold which capital has continued to exert over most people's everyday lives. Without a radical commitment on the part of the MCM, however, these problems will never get solved; they will only be reproduced within the party.

The surprising feature about the MCM, despite its tortured and contradictory history and rather limited political base, is the number of struggles in which it has participated and of radical elements it has included in its platform. To name but a few of its proposals: the creation of neighbourhood councils with extensive political and economic powers, the gradual implementation of free and expanded public transport, local control of land development, strict enforcement of a revamped housing code, and many others. The struggles in which it has participated include the collective negotiation of leases in a number of parts of town, protest against many demolitions, a campaign for free public transport for the elderly, civil disobedience against a transpo increase, support for striking city employees, demands for recreational use of open spaces. The question facing the MCM is: will it be willing and able to use the 1978 elections in order to develop the base it so sorely lacks? Will it be able to make clear that the electoral contest is not one between the MCM and Drapeau, but between the people and the prevailing system of power? Will it dare state so publicly? Will it work towards creating a popular unity between dockworkers, municipal employees, teachers, postal workers, gay rights activists, women's groups, cyclists, unemployed youth and old folk around joint radical demands? The general council of the MCM adopted an electoral strategy affirming that its goal was the construction of a popular movement that would exercise power and control over the development of urban life. However, the fine print of the document, and the MCM's own history of adopting resolutions which remained on paper, suggest that this commitment will not carry over into practice. Can the MCM overcome its own contradictions? Can the MCM left help resolve them and press the organisation further?

The Québec left, the current political context and the MCM

THE WEAKNESS of the MCM, and of the MCM left in particular, cannot be understood without reference to the Québec left as a whole. Its extra-parliamentary wing is dominated by the different Marxist-Leninist groups, all eager to build the true communist party and all marked by a doctrinal and organisational fanaticism which keeps them miles apart from the MCM, which they regard as bourgeois and reformist. The Marxist-Leninist left in Québec, however, suffers from exactly those oppressive features which mark its counterparts elsewhere, not to mention the traditional communist parties it aspires to supplant. Its lack of humility is boundless, but the arrogance of their cadres becomes virtually unsufferable when they begin to recount to you glories of Stalin's achievements. Their dogmatism can only compete with their historical illiteracy, while their internal organisation reproduces some of the worst forms of bourgeois oppression. One major Marxist-Leninist organisation has been known to pressure its members who live together in a heterosexual relationship into marrying, presumably on the grounds that conjugal stability makes for political reliability. So much for the principal contradiction and its ability to deal with sexism. Yet their structure, their organisational tightness, their relative numbers impress people, offering them security, or the illusion of it, in a world dominated by capital.

Some members of the MCM left have not escaped the pull exercised by the Marxist-Leninist left, as the MCM flounders in its contradictions and the libertarian left experiences difficulty in developing its own position. The Marxist-Leninist left at least offers a clearly-defined position, even if it dismisses all the ambiguity of social life in order to do so. Their current stranglehold over the radical left political culture in Québec, however, means that alternatives must define themselves against the Marxist-Leninist perspective. Although such a perspective does not itself tend to produce libertarian socialist thinking, the need to define oneself in opposition to that dominant left culture may very well lead in that direction.

Other elements of the radical left, such as the Trotskyist groupings, do not represent any significant departure from the Marxist-Leninist mold, despite a political line which appears in some respects more open. They too call for the construction of a party, only a workers' party founded by the trade union movement. Their reply to charges that such a party would most likely be reformist consists of the assertion that at least it would be the workers' own reformism. Some of their members were active in setting up the municipal project that led to the MCM, but withdrew when the Montréal council of the CSN refused to found the party on the basis of majority trade-union representation. Their base within the CSN lies in part with the maintenance employees union of the Montréal Transport Commission and their attitude has made it difficult for the MCM to establish direct contact at the base between their two organisations. The executive of the union, influenced by same of its Trotskyist leaders, has regarded the MCM as incorrigible because it is not a workers' party organised on a trade union basis, and consequently has been reluctant to develop solid links between their memberships, although it has welcomed MCM support for the strikes it has conducted against the Montréal Urban Community Transit Commission.

This attitude of some militant trade unionists has not helped the MCM left; on the contrary, it has contributed to its weakness and isolation. This abstentionist position has also characterized most of the independent left in Montréal, which consists principally of academics, students, and community activists of one kind or another. Their attitude to the MCM, even after the left succeeded in defeating the right's attempts to take over the party and getting its proposals on neighbourhood councils and grass-roots mobilisation passed at the 1976 congress, remained one of waiting for the MCM left to produce its revolutionary credentials. Their attitude was in part the result of the MCM left's failure to reach out to them, an action which its own lack of theoretical and organisational definition rendered highly problematic. Nonetheless, the significance of what the left within the MCM had managed to do on its own—after all, it's not every day that the left maintains such a predominant position within reformist parties—went virtually unnoticed, reflecting in some measure the Montréal left's rather dull political instincts for nuance, for the openings at a given moment or for the stakes at issue in a particular context.

Both the political and institutional stakes surrounding the MCM are high, viewed within the perspective of the historical conjuncture. Behind the reformist wing of the MCM stands the Parti Québécois which dominates the parliamentary wing of the social-democratic left in Québec. It is not simply a question of certain influential members of the Montréal region of the PQ being active within the MCM, trying to prevent it from outflanking the PQ on its left. It is also a question of the organisational resources they can draw on in a situation such as currently prevails in the MCM, where the absence of a large and active base and the fuzziness of its political stance makes it very vulnerable to the Parti Québécois. Given the ethnic composition of Montréal and the PQ's own timetable for the referendum on independence, it cannot afford to take over the MCM directly; but given the weakness and isolation of the MCM left, it does not have to. All it has to do is swim along with the current of reformist molasses which prevails beyond the MCM. The politics of the PQ are very much the politics of the technocracy which dominates it, for whom class and nationalism conveniently fuse in a political project oriented towards managing capital through control of the state apparatus. In that sense too the political weight of the PQ within the MCM is greater than the presence of its actual members, for the technocratic cast which the progressive péquistes give to urban politics is shared by other members of the MCM's reformist wing.

The behaviour of the PQ in office at the provincial level has been typical of the reformist politics of the managers of the fiscal crisis—austerity budgets; structural reforms such as amendments to the labour code which cost little and give to the workers as much as they take away; promises of administrative decentralisation and urban fiscal reform that mask the process of fiscal centralisation afoot in such measures as Bill 82, which used the debt incurred by the Montréal Olympics as a pretext to clamp down on future capital spending by the city. In attempting to manage the fiscal crisis, however, the PQ is caught in its own contradictions. Its indépendentiste project will require a massive campaign of popular mobilisation. Yet the pressures exerted by the fiscal crisis of the state have led it to refrain from any steps in that direction, while the pressures of parliamentary politics have considerably diluted the few reforms it has attempted. In its handling of municipal reform, for example, the PQ has been wary of provoking the conservative, local elites who still represent a considerable political force in Québec. This approach reflects their concern to rock the institutional boat as little as possible before the referendum debate and to neutralise potential points of opposition to the régime with a skill that has not been seen since the days of Duplessis, whose reputation, quite appropriately, the PQ is trying to dust off. Not for nothing did some members of the top leadership in the PQ try to persuade the MCM in the 1974 municipal elections to form a broad coalition of opposition to Drapeau around the mayoralty candidacy of one of Drapeau's former councillors. At the same time, the professionalisation of urban politics to which the PQ's project of urban reform leads—higher salaries for municipal councillors, state funding of municipal parties—reinforces its technocratic allies in the municipal reform movements. The structural and fiscal measures the PQ has undertaken, however, have introduced strains in that coalition. Even the reformist members of the MCM had trouble seeing the difference between the PQ and its predecessor when the former refused to halt construction on the Namur metro station or to set up an inquiry into the alleged collusion between the Montréal Urban Community administration and the private development corporation on whose behalf the station was planned.

The problem for the PQ at the Montréal level is to prevent these contradictions from bursting apart. Institutionally Montréal represents a very important political prize. Its capture by a political party committed to class politics would not only pierce the current hegemony of the PQ as issues were formulated outside its technocratic consensus. It would also explode some of capital's contradictions as demands were raised which would only exacerbate the fiscal crisis of the state that the PQ is so anxious to manage. The political importance of Montréal, and with it the MCM, extends beyond its institutional position as a basis for the left and for the emergence of a radical, popular movement. What is at stake is the very nature of the left and the radical movement which could emerge. Urban struggles imply a redefinition of the revolutionary project in terms of the libertarian tradition of revolution from below. The MCM holds out in a very limited, partial and fumbling way the possibility of carrying out that implication in practice. The question is: what are the possibilities, for the MCM and the libertarian left, given a left political culture that is dominated by the two poles of social-democracy and Marxist-Leninism, given the conjunctural importance of the political institution at stake, and given the internal contradictions and lack of an effective base, large, popular and organised, with which the MCM enters the fray?

The Future of the MCM

IT WOULD BE too unrealistic to expect a massive infusion of energy into the MCM on the part of the independent left in Montréal before the forthcoming elections. The MCM left will therefore have to develop a strategy on its own, based on a more long-term perspective which keeps radical options open. Such a strategy requires a critical participation in the MCM throughout the electoral period in order to see that its radical elements get articulated and to hold the MCM as much as possible to its commitment to the politics of mobilisation. The possibility of pushing the MCM into some forms of direct action and using the elections in order to initiate popular power and build up a radical base, however limited, exists. Participation along these lines would neither compromise the MCM left's politics nor absorb their energies in a futile manner. At the same time such a stance would not preclude the clarification of the left's own views and of the MCM's contradictions which must inevitably ensue.

The contradictions which rend the MCM must soon be confronted if the revolutionary project shared by some of its members is ever to get off the ground. The left within the MCM, however, is not ready for such a confrontation at the present moment, while the context of the elections makes a principled debate about the overall project virtually impossible. The best that can be hoped for is that the elections do not turn out to be a total disaster: neither a total victory, which would suck energies into municipal administration, nor a total defeat, that would wipe even the radical bases within the MCM off the political map. Besides, the MCM does represent a progressive change compared to the Drapeau régime, while the MCM's programme, viewed in the very short term, offers considerable room for manoeuver, especially considering the composition of the party. The attempt by an MCM administration to implement even some of its proposals would incur a certain amount of class conflict. On the other hand, should it jettison all its more radical proposals, especially those relating to the encouragement of a popular movement, the debate that would ensue in the party would at least clarify the air and possibly produce a redrawing of lines which would give the left a more solid base. Whatever the frustrations of the MCM left towards the party's reformist wing and the PQ presence that hovers around it, it is very short-sighted politics indeed that would provoke a confrontation in the MCM prior to the 1978 elections merely to prevent social democracy from occupying another institutional post.

History has already proved that social democracy is perfectly capable of defeating itself and the PQ has so far shown itself to be no exception to this rule. A revolutionary movement, however, has to emerge from a positive space; and the principled stand which the left within the MCM has to come up with cannot emerge from a politics that is antagonistic to the current of popular struggle and discontent that is going on in the city, however ambiguous be the form that it has taken so far. Part of that discontent has been reflected in the MCM's capture until now of the anti-Drapeau sentiment, which shows up electorally in a large protest vote. There is, as well, within the MCM a wealth of experience in the conduct of urban struggles, in the organisation of direct action and in the confrontation of the contradictions of the libertarian socialist perspective that must not be lost. That experience and, more important, the people who embody it can provide the core of a revolutionary libertarian movement that could emerge from recent urban struggles in Montréal. How many people willing to join much a movement, within and without the MCM, will remain unknown until its revolutionary project is elaborated and submitted for debate within and outside the MCM as soon after the elections as possible.

Hopefully the analysis and perspective presented in these pages will help to formulate this debate. The left, once it has reached a consensus around this analysis and perspective, should openly constitute itself as a libertarian socialist tendency within the MCM which should function as a network of collectives. This network would have to undertake a considerable amount of homework both for its own benefit and in order to prepare for the future transformation of the MCM. Our objective should be nothing short of the transformation of the MCM into a libertarian socialist movement, a popular movement of autonomous district associations pressing by means of direct action on a whole set of urban contradictions. This transformation must include a substantial revamping of the existing programme, the systematic introduction of libertarian principles and practice at all levels of the movement, the elaboration and implementation of a wide range of educational and parallel institutions which would offer the people of Montréal an alternative to the prevailing capitalist ideology and organisation of social life. This broad wedge into the dominant social order requires all the imagination and courage that mobilised our sisters and brothers in the revolutionary libertarian movements of the past. Either the MCM will be so transformed, or it will degenerate into a traditional political party and be abandoned. This is the challenge facing the MCM left; it is also their priority.

CHAPTER SEVEN

THE IMPOSSIBLE REVOLUTION AND ITS HISTORICAL NECESSITY

Urban politics as metaphor and practice

THE SIGNIFICANCE of urban struggles lies in the revolutionary challenge they present to the citizens of contemporary cities. This challenge appears at once as social vision and social reality; at stake is nothing less than the future of our civilisation. This statement is a rather large claim, but it reflects the historical truth that the development of urban life has not occurred independently of the transformations in class relations and modes of production that mark the course of civilisation.

There is one approach to the urban question that tends to associate the city with civilisation itself, by which is meant all those social constructs which humanity has created over time to transcend the state of brute existence. The references are not only to the rule of law, the flowering of the arts, the rise of scientific inquiry, but also to the extension of commerce understood as both the exchange of goods and the intercourse between cultures, the growing cosmopolitanism of social life as diversity becomes a prize and tolerance a virtue. The associations are the Greek polis and Roman communitas, the medieval towns and bourgs, the city-states of the Italian Renaissance, the great metropoles of the late nineteenth and early twentieth centuries; yet their contributions to human culture have always been fashioned on the basis of class privilege. Athenian democracy reposed on a slave economy and Roman citizenship, on the domination of empire. The medieval towns, with their episcopal character, guarded the inheritance of classical antiquity, but the new bourgs which spearheaded the revival of commerce developed a system of law and custom which sanctioned the prerogatives of the rising bourgeoisie which dominated them. The city air which made a person free depended on the exploitation of the countryside and the restrictive practices of the guilds. The cultural renaissance of the Italian city-states was supported by the financial aristocracy which ruled them, while the tremendous vitality of urban life at the turn of this century fed off the expansion of capitalism in its imperialist phase.[1]

1914 marked an historical watershed in so many ways, signalling that the choice facing humankind was truly one between socialism and barbarism. The task of socialists was henceforth made even more explicit: not only the overthrow of the bourgeoisie but the preservation of civilisation, as the bourgeoisie jettisoned the liberal values associated with its rise in order to preserve its class rule. The full and horrendous implications of their moral and political abdication have not yet reached their end. Today they lie submerged beneath the homogenised processes of everyday life that capital seeks to impose on its global village. Yet there is protest in that global village, which feeds off capitalism's contradictions and whose implications are more sanguine and revolutionary. Embedded in that protest lies a revolutionary project in which the overthrow of class rule is synonymous with the preservation of civilisation. This project, because it is oriented to the transformation of social relations rooted in contemporary capitalism, holds out the promise of realising the progressive and civilising features historically associated with urban life, in a society free of class privilege and political domination. It is the promise of libertarian socialism that urban struggles have put on the historical agenda.

To some such a project is utopian, negated by the very image of the city in its historical or modern form. After all, was life any more or any less problematic for people trying to make their way through the interstices of social life in the great Hellenized cities of the eastern Roman Empire than it was for those who wound their way, centuries later, through the arcades of Walter Benajmin's Paris?[2] Is there not something about the ambiguity of life itself, combined with the complexity of social interaction, that lends to all attempts at a planned society, however rational, a utopian aspect, suggesting an opposition between life and society, the former as unchanging as the latter is changing? The city, in such a world view, portrays this opposition, but it is the static image of social life that ultimately prevails, as has been argued à propos of Joyce's "portrayal of the modern city and the modern social world as an instance of the universal history of peoples and nations, at a deeper level always and everywhere the same".[3] Yet Stephen Daedalus also said in Ulysees: "History is a nightmare from which I am trying to awake."[4] No statement could be more revolutionary or more utopian, reminding us that it is only the utopian impulse that prevents history from becoming a never-ending nightmare, reminding us too that to abandon that impulse is to abandon the dialectic inherent in the metaphorical as well as the material history of the city.

That dialectical unfolding of social reality can best be seen in the current reassessment of the role of cities in the transition to capitalism. On the one hand the freedom of movement so essential to the expansion of commerce placed the towns in an antagonistic relationship to the feudal power which dominated the countryside. On the other hand the corporate monopoly which towns enjoyed turned them into bastions of conservatism, for despite the preparatory role of merchant capital in the rise of capitalism, the economy of the towns was very much integrated into the feudal setting. It was the rise of capitalist production relations in the countryside that marked the real break with feudalism, and with its urban corporate monopolies; and yet it was the autonomy of the towns which, paradoxically, made the transition from feudalism to capitalism possible in western Europe. Only later, with the expanded reproduction of capital, did factory cities emerge, thus suggesting that "towns, in spite of their role as *cultural* pace-makers, reflected the conditions of rural accumulation as much as contributed to it." This new understanding of the relationship between town and country demands a reevaluation of "the dualistic tendency to separate urban progress and rural backwardness" which has deep roots in English literature, "with its ambiguous shifting between idealization of rural innocence, the lost Arcadia, and urban disdain for 'rural idiocy'."[5] The ambiguity was not exclusively English; one has only to look at the poems of Rimbaud and the novels of Flaubert.[6] This ambiguity of the city as image reflected the reality of its relationship to the wider society, a relationship fundamentally dialectical, in which " 'urbanization' and 'ruralization' are opposite sides of the same process of the capitalist division of labour".[7] This division, like their opposition, can only be overcome with the abolition of capitalism itself, a revolutionary project whose historical necessity is matched only by its 'utopian' character.

It is of course to capital's advantage to dismiss such projects as unrealistic, not so much in the face of the specifically capitalist organisation of social life as in the face of life itself. Its efforts in this respect are highly mystifying, given the historical record of revolutionary insurrection and the material possibilities of contemporary society. The static image of the city only contributes to this mystification, suggesting that the limits of capitalism are the universal constraints of social life and obliterating its very own dialectical history. This is not to suggest that there are not very real limits to social organisation and to life itself, the most fundamental one being death; yet it is typical of capitalism as a repressive civilisation that it seizes on these very real limits and turns them into instruments of further domination. The stasis of capitalist urbanity mirrors the social control which underlies the city, as the image itself conveys death, the stillness of passivity, the abandonment of the dialectic, the surrender of the revolutionary will in the desire to escape from the nightmare of history:

> In a repressive civilisation, death itself becomes an instrument of repression. Whether death is feared as constant threat, or glorified as supreme sacrifice, or accepted as fate, the education for consent to death introduces an element of surrender into life from the beginning—surrender and submission. It stifles 'utopian' efforts. The powers that be have a deep affinity to death; death is a token of unfreedom, of defeat. Theology and philosophy today compete with each other in celebrating death as an existential category: perverting a biological fact into an ontological essence, they bestow transcendental blessing on the guilt of mankind which they help to perpetuate—they betray the promise of utopia. In contrast, a philosophy that does not work as the handmaiden of repression responds to the fact of death with the Great Refusal—the refusal of Orpheus the liberator. Death can become a token of freedom. The necessity of death does not refute the possibility of final liberation. Like the other necessities, it can be made rational—painless. Men can die without anxiety if they know that what they love is protected from misery and oblivion. After a fulfilled life, they may take it upon themselves to die—at a moment of their own choosing. But even the ultimate advent of freedom cannot redeem those who died in pain. It is the remembrance of them, and the accumulated guilt of mankind against its victims, that darken the prospect of a civilisation without repression."[8]

If the revolutionary, libertarian project is utopian, it is precisely because it is life-affirming, because it refuses to comply with the subversion of death into an instrument of greater repression. Hence its insistence on initiative and autonomy; hence its recognition that revolution is ultimately a question of individual responsibility which no analysis of objective conditions can resolve or explain; hence too its understanding that revolution is an action jointly undertaken by men and women to create a political community which respects those principles. Revolution occurs in opposition to class rule, but goes beyond its overthrow, just as socialism is only partly the abolition of capitalism. What comes in its wake, if it is truly liberating, can only be the creative product of free human beings directly exercising their political capacities and thereby affirming their integrity as actors shaping their own history, as opposed to passing through life, the creatures of a mode of production. Only such an outcome can truly hold out the possibility of an escape from the nightmare of history. In this respect, the libertarian revolutionary tradition connects back not only to the Paris Commune and the utopian uprisings of the four-century period marking the rise of capitalism, but also to those fundamental political virtues bequeathed to us by the class-based urban cultures of prevous times—the *philia* of ancient Greece, the *humanitas* of Rome, both fundamentally political categories which presumed the existence of individuals capable of discussing the world with their fellows and hence transforming it.[9]

These notions are pre-Marxist categories of political thought, but no less important for that. There is a tendency to dismiss these ideas as ethical abstractions of little relevance in the face of the realities of class power or to jettison them in favour of a more 'scientific' mode of analysis that explains revolution, and the failure of revolution, in the same terms of objective conditions used to explain the transformations in modes of production. What such an approach overlooks is that revolution is ultimately a subjective experience that comes out of a desire to change oneself and the world, and a readiness to assume a responsibility towards it. Without such a stance revolution itself is impossible, as the libertarian tradition never ceases to remind us. The choice ultimately is not that of capital but the proletariat, which is what Marx meant when he asserted that the proletariat is revolutionary or it is nothing. Ten years ago such a stance was prevalent throughout the societies of advanced capitalism. Today it leads almost an underground existence as traditional conceptions have reasserted themselves in new guises, "revolutionary" maoists on one side, nouveaux philosophes on the other, divorcing once again the personal from the political, rendering social life devoid of its utopian promise, and therefore of revolutionary politics as well.

Revolutionary politics in the here and now

THE PARADIGM of social control which permeates the capitalist organisation of urban life sows everywhere a fear of disorder, equating the disruption of everyday routine with social chaos and thereby hinting at the disaster that awaits us should we dare to attempt a revolutionary transformation of the social order. The hint becomes amplified when the utopianism of the Russian revolutionary movement is contrasted with the sordid reality depicted in the novels of Isaac Babel and the historical evaluation of contemporary thinkers who see in the utopianism of the revolution the seeds of its totalitarian dénouement. A rereading of the Russian experience has suggested that it was anything but utopian and that its totalitarian development was linked to the statist conception of the Leninist programme. What is surprising about the contemporary appearance of the former, rather traditional approach is that this is the second time such an assessment has been put forward, but this time it is advanced by those very people who, ten years earlier, had been debunking it by their praxis. That praxis understood full well the power of disruption, the importance of making a dent in the social monolith so as to release revolutionary energy, enable people to act instead of be acted upon, its link with revolution defined as collective creation towards unknown paths but away from the known undesirable. The renunciation of this praxis testifies to the staying power of the capitalist project, as it yokes our death instincts, with their tendency to repetition and rest, to complicity in a social order that values routine and distorts the most elemental relations of everyday life.

Yet the prevailing mood reflects something more than the feeling that the revolution is not imminent, more too than the recognition that immediacy was an important ingredient in new left political culture. It reflects too the fact that so many young people were radicalized in the sixties by burning moral issues that offered no room for ambiguity and concerned themselves first and foremost with the fate of people living far from the heart of the capitalist empire. When those issues were resolved people were still left with the muck at home; and the upsurge of revolutionary feeling unleashed by the confrontation of those issues, of which the Viet Nam War was the most central, now had to focus on the long, hard slog of daily life under capital, Gunter Grass' local anaesthetic.[10] Today many people wander about like the two characters at the end of "l'Education Sentimentale", looking back on the sixties with an air of nostalgia, as a time when life seemed real, and yet considering them too as part illusion, in contrast to the contemporary reality of jobs, kids, spouses, doing the laundary, washing the dishes, and making something of oneself. Hence the retreat into personal fulfillment as almost a substitute for politics, or into politics as a substitute for personal fulfillment, in a world whose dominant powers have a vested interest in keeping the two apart.

Their separation only confirms the traditional attitudes to politics—at worst manipulation, at best a commitment to liberalism and progressive causes. If the experience of the sixties taught us anything, however, it was that we had to go beyond these conceptions to define politics as counter-culture. Indeed, it was the contribution of the struggles of the sixties to turn everyday life into politics and revive the libertarian tradition to which this project was linked. As the historical record has shown, the most revolutionary politics are those that refuse to play by the official rules, that refuse to let capital or the state get a foot in the door, that subvert the processes of everyday life into points of opposition to the dominant forces. Such a revolutionary stance, which rejects the dichotomy between the personal and the political just as it rejects all the other dichotomies of capitalist society, is intensely life-affirming, fiercely defiant, highly dialectical and insistent on rethinking everything. It is dangerous for capital precisely because those who embrace it believe that city air should make a person free and are prepared to work towards that goal.

This commitment to revolutionary politics implies ultimately a willingness to confront one's own death and let it go, for in the revolutionary, libertarian tradition no one can make another free; freedom can only emerge through the process of struggle undertaken by people who desire to be free and therefore dare to think the unthinkable. Behind the suppression of desire, and the desire to be free, lies not only the fear of change, but also the fear of death, the ultimate mystification upon which capitalist politics plays, fusing it into our institutional and psychic structures such that we spend our time worried about losing lovers, property, elections and life itself, forgetting all the while that only under capitalism could we dare to make the preposterous assumption that it is possible to own them in the first place. Against this mystification stands the tradition of libertarian socialism, calling us to direct our energies to the truly important questions of love and revolution, to reaffirm our commitment, as did the characters in the film *Jonas, Who Will Be 25 In The Year 2000*, to the dialectic of time and history, which "is not the rapid forward movement we imagined and demanded in the sixties, but a progress that is hardly visible day-to-day amid the simpler and more immediate cyclical patterns of everyday life."[12] It is the task of revolutionaries to make that progress more visible; to unite, as did the characters in that film, everyday life with politics, revolution with freedom, the sounds of whales with the dialectics of political economy; and to assert, as did the inhabitants of Charenton and the sansculottes of Paris years ago, that we want our revolution now.

NOTES

(1.) Merrington, *op. cit.*; M. Freitag, "De la ville-société à la ville-milieu" in *Sociologie et Sociétés*, vol. 3, nu. 1, May 1977; H. Pirenne, *Economic and Social History of Medieval Europe*, N.Y., n.d.; Anderson, *op. cit.*; EZOP-Québec, *Une Ville à Vendre*, Cahier 1, Québec, 1972.
(2.) H. Arendt, "Walter Benjamin, 1892-1940" in Arendt, *Men in Dark Times*, London, 1970, p. 172-5.
(3.) S. Hampshire, "Joyce and Vico: The Middle Way" in *The New York Review of Books*, vol. xx, no. 16, Oct. 18, 1973, p. 12.
(4.) J. Joyce, *Ulysses*, London, 1966, p. 42.
(5.) Merrington, *op. cit.*; Anderson, *op. cit.*; Pirenne, *op. cit.*
(6.) A. Rimbaud, *Illuminations and Other Prose Poems*, (tr. L. Varese), N.Y., 1957; G. Flaubert, *L'Education sentimentale; histoire d'un jeune homme*, Paris, 1964; R. Williams, *The French Revolution of 1870-1871*, London, 1969, p. 81-2.
(7.) Merrington, *op. cit.*
(8.) H. Marcuse, *Eros and Civilization*, London, 1969, p. 188.
(9.) Arendt, "On Lessing" in *op. cit.*; also H. Arendt, *On Revolution*, N.Y., 1965; H. Arendt, *On Violence*, N.Y., 1970.
(10.) G. Grass, *Local Anaesthetic*, N.Y., 1970.
(11.) Flaubert, *op. cit.*
(12.) R. Kazis, "Berger-Tanner and the 'New Narcissism' ", in *Socialist Revolution*, 35, Sept-Oct. 1977, p. 151; A. Tanner (director), A. Tanner, J. Berger (screenplay), *Jonah Who Will Be 25 in the Year 2000*.

BIBLIOGRAPHY

Alternative Technology and the Politics of Technical Change, David Dickson (Fontana)
Anarchism: Theory and Practice, Daniel Guerin (Monthly Review Press)
The Anarchist Collectives: Workers' Self-Management in Spain 1936-39, Sam Dolgoff (Black Rose Books)
Appropriate Technology, R.J. Cogydon (Rodale Press)
The Bolsheviks and Workers' Control 1917-21, Maurice Brinton (Black Rose Books)
Bureaucracy and Revolution in Eastern Europe, Chris Harman (Pluto)
Capitalism in Crisis and Everyday Life, Michel Bosquet (Harvester Press)
Collectives in the Spanish Revolution, Gaston Leval (Freedom Press)
The Communards of Paris, 1871, Stewart Edwards, ed. (Thames & Hudson)
Communitas, Paul & Percival Goodman (Vintage)
Critical Theory of Society, Albrecht Wellmar (Seabury Press)
Critique of Domination, Trent Schroyer (Beacon Press)
Direct Action and Liberal Democracy, April Carter (Harper & Row)
The Dispossessed, Ursula K. LeGuin (Avon)
Durruti: The People Armed, Abel Paz (Black Rose Books)
Essays on Marx's Theory of Value, I.I.Rubin (Black Rose Books)
The Explosion: Marxism & The French Upheaval, Henri Lefebvre (Monthly Review Press)
Fields, Factories and Workshops, Peter Kropotkin (Allen & Unwin)
Hidden Injuries of Class, Richard Sennet & Jonathan Cobb (Vintage)
Hungary 1956, Bill Lomax (Allison & Busby)
Kronstadt Uprising, Ida Mett (Black Rose Books)
Lenin as Philosopher, Anton Pannekoek (Merlin)
Marx, Freud and the Critique of Everyday Life, Bruce Brown (Monthly Review Press)
The Mirror of Production, Jean Broudrillard (Telos Press)
The Occupation of the Factories: Italy 1920, Paolo Spriano (Pluto)
The Origins of Modern Leftism, Richard Gombin (Penguin)
People or Personnel, Paul Goodman (Vintage)
Post-Scarcity Anarchism, Murray Bookchin (Black Rose Books)
Proletarian Order, Gwyn A.Williams (Pluto)
Radical Technology, Boyle & Harper (Random)
Red Years/Black Years 1911-1937 Spain, Robert W.Kerns (ISHI)
Rosa Luxemburg, Peter Nettl (Oxford)
Self-Governing Socialism, Volumes 1 & 2, Horvat, Markovic, Supek (IASP)
The Socialist State, David Lane (Allen & Unwin)
A Worker in a Worker's State, Miklos Haraszti (Pelican)
Soviets At Saclay? Jacques Pesquet (Stage 1)
The Spanish Anarchists 1868-1936, Murray Bookchin (Harper & Row)
The State, Franz Oppenheimer (Black Rose Books)
The State in Capitalist Society, Ralph Miliband (Fontana)
Tenants Take Over, Colin Ward (Architecture Press)
Towards A new Marxism, Picone & Grahl (Telos Press)
The Uses of Disorder, Richard Sennet (Vintage)
What is to be undone, Michael Albert (Porter Sargent)
Workers' Control, Hunnius et al (Vintage)
The Working Class Majority, Andrew Levison (Penguin)

PORTUGAL :
The Impossible Revolution?
by Phil Mailer

"...(This book) is a weighty (work) dedicated to a militant exposition of the impact of popular power in a country which,... is 'drifting towards state capitalism'. ..."

Sunday Times of London

...In a vigorous book that is part blow-by-blow account, part vivid eye-witness reporting and part unashamedly polemical analysis, (the author) stresses what he sees as the revolution's most important feature — ordinary people spontaneously taking power for themselves. He presents a wealth of fascinating detail about workers' committees and peasants' cooperatives which is welcome antidote to the tiresome journalistic assumptions of the time that without a tank, a bomb or a dispossessed British businessman what happened in Portugal wasn't worth talking about."

New Society

"This is the best book so far on the Portugese revolution. ..."

Radical America

Shipyard and building workers, women in the northern textile mills, agricultural labourers taking over the farms, fishermen and bank employees all taking a hand in the making of history. The declarations of people in bitter struggle in their concern for fundamentals. Interviews, arguments, leaflets, and discussion. Laughter and tears, longing and frustration.

At the same time a serious attempt to analyse the economic and cultural background of modern Portugal, and to depict an overall pattern — the challenge and limitations of self-management and the recuperation of "popular power" by the various political "cupulas". Written as a new historiography, it is a significant, exciting and disturbing book.

"...Above all this whole book is alive. I am sure it will become a best-seller, perhaps the standard account of the first two years of the Portuguese revolution."

Maurice Brinton.

400 pages, illustrated/Hardcover $12.95/Paperback $5.95

ISBN: 0-919618-34-0/ISBN: 0-919618-33-2

BLACK ROSE BOOKS No. F 32

THE CITY AND RADICAL SOCIAL CHANGE

edited by
Dimitrios
Roussopoulos

What is the role of the city in determining the evolution of society as a whole? What perspective do people who fight to improve public transportation, housing, public health and related issues have? What are the results of the community-organising movement in cities like Montréal? How have the concepts of participatory democracy, decentralisation, and the creation of neighbourhood councils evolved?

With a focus on Montréal, the book examines through a collection of essays the dynamics of the community-organising movement and its impact on urban politics. The contributors follow the emergence of various municipal political parties including the Front d'Action Politique and the Montréal Citizens Movement (MCM). The major controversies surrounding the MCM are included, after it became the official opposition political party to the Drapeau dominated City Council. The internal developments of the MCM are analyzed, its strategies, its tactics, its overall impact on neighbourhoods as well as the evolution of its programme. Most of the articles are drawn from the journal *OUR GENERATION*. Additional material on the MCM is drawn from various documents and published reports. An evaluation of the MCM and the municipal elections during the fall of 1978 is included.

280 pages Hardcover $16.95/Paperback $5.95
ISBN: 0-919618-83-9/ISBN: 0-919618-82-0

Publication Date: December

Contains: Canadian Shared Cataloguing in Publication Data

BLACK ROSE BOOKS No. H44

THE POLITICS OF OBEDIENCE:

The Discourse of Voluntary Servitude

by Etienne de la Boetie

This classic work of political reflection seeks the answer to the question of why people submit to the tyranny of governments. La Boétie laid the groundwork for the concept of civil disobedience with his proposal that people could cut the bonds of habit and corruption that keep them obedient and complacent, and resolve to serve their masters no more. The *Discourse of Voluntary Servitude* has exerted an important influence on the tradition of pacifism and civil disobedience from Thoreau and Ralph Waldo Emerson, to Tolstoy, to Gandhi.

Etienne de la Boétie was a sixteenth century political philosopher and a close friend of Montaigne.

"(La Boétie's) analysis of tyranny and his insight into its psychological foundations ought to be one of the central documents in the library of anyone concerned with human liberty. It is ironic that the works of Machiavelli, advisor to rulers, should enjoy widespread currency, while the libertarian La Boétie is muted. Hopefully, publication of his 1550 *Discourse*, with its superb introduction by Murray Rothbard, will right the imbalance."

— Stanley Milgram
author of *Obedience to Authority*

88 pages / Hardcover $10.95 / Paperback $2.95
ISBN: 0-919618-58-8 / ISBN: 0-919618-57-X

Contains: Canadian Shared Cataloguing in Publication Data

BLACK ROSE BOOKS No. E 20

The Case for PARTICIPATORY DEMOCRACY
EDITED BY C. GEORGE BENELLO AND DIMITRIOS ROUSSOPOULOS

George Woodcock, Rosabeth Moss Kanter, Murray Bookchin, Christian Bay, Colin Ward, Martin Oppenheimer, Staughton Lynd, William Appelman Williams and others in this symposium have learned from their experience that participatory democracy works. They probe the historical roots of participatory democracy in Western culture, analyze its application to the problems of modern society, and explore the possible forms that it might take on every level of society from the work place to the community to the national level.

"The book is, by all odds, the most encompassing one so far in revealing the practical actual subversions that the New Left wishes to visit upon us."
— Karl Hess, The Washington Post

019 / 386 pages / SBN 670-20595-8
Hardcover $6.75

ESSAYS ON SOCIALIST HUMANISM, in honour of the Centenary of Bertrand Russell
EDITED BY KEN COATES

Contributors include Jean Paul Sartre, Vladimir Dedijer, Noam Chomsky, Lelio Basso, Mihailo Markovic and many others.

"How important... that the publishers should have brought out a volume to honour the Centenary of Bertrand Russell's birth and to explore the relationship between Russell's liberalism, libertarianism and pacifism and recent trends in the socialist movement. Great riches of social and political philosophy are to be found here, and that is not surprising... A very rewarding volume... and a whole range of writers combine a well-knit series of essays."
— Times Literary Supplement

021 / 220 pages / SBN 85124 047x
Hardcover $10.00

Printed by
the workers of
Editions Marquis, Montmagny, Que.
for
Black Rose Books Ltd.

THE IRRATIONAL IN POLITICS

by Maurice Brinton

The book gives examples of irrational behaviour — at the level of politics — of classes, groups and individuals. It proceeds to reject certain facile 'interpretations' put forward to explain these phenomena. It probes the various ways in which the soil (the individual psyche) has been rendered fertile (receptive) for an authoritarian, hierarchical and class-dominated culture. It looks at the family as the locus of reproduction of the dominant ideology, and at sexual repression as an important determinant of social conditioning, resulting in the mass production of individuals perpetually craving authority and leadership and forever afraid of walking on their own or of thinking for themselves. Some of the problems of the developing sexual revolution are then discussed. The book concludes by exploring a new dimension in the failure of the Russian Revolution. Throughout, the aim is to help people, acquire additional insight into their own psychic structure. The fundamental desires and aspirations of the ordinary individual, so long distorted and repressed, are in deep harmony with an objective such as the libertarian reconstruction of society.

76 pages | Hardcover $10.95 | Paperback $2.45
ISBN: 0-919618-24-3 / ISBN: 0-919618-75-8

Contains: Canadian Shared Cataloguing in Publication Data

BLACK ROSE BOOKS No. E 16